Library of Congress Catalog Card Number: 2005929599
ISBN: 0-97596012-1

About Prophet Muhammad

Ahmad H. Sakr, Ph.D.

Email: ahmadsakr@yahoo.com
Website: www.ahmadsakr.com

Published by:

Foundation for Islamic Knowledge
P.O. Box 665
Lombard, Illinois 60148 (USA)
Telephone: (630) 495-4817
FAX: (630) 627-8894
Tax I.D #36-377-4566

NOTE: Your generous contributions to this **Foundation** will enable us to publish more valuable literature and to render more services to all. The **Foundation** has a tax-exempt status with the IRS. Your donations are tax-deductible.

About Prophet Muhammad

Section (4)   Prophet's Supplications

Section (5)   Different Topics

Section (6)   Prophet In Madina

Section (7) Pieces Of Wisdom

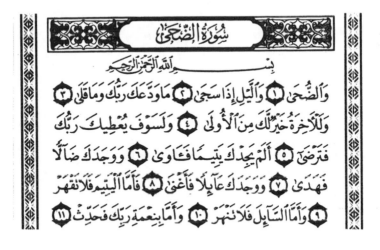

Ad-Dhuha: The Glorious Morning Light

By the Glorious Morning Light, and by the Night when it is still, the Guardian Lord has not forsaken you, nor is He displeased. And verily the Hereafter will be better for you than the present. And soon will the Guardian-Lord give you (that wherewith) you shall be well-pleased. Did he not find you an orphan and give you shelter (and care)? And He found you wandering, and He gave you guidance. And He found you in need, and made you independent. Therefore, treat not the orphan with harshness, nor repulse him who asks; but the Bounty of your Lord rehearse and proclaim. (93:111)

الله
جلّ جلاله

God's Majesty Exalted

This book is dedicated to Allah Ta'ala (Almighty) for all the favors He has bestowed upon me in creating and bringing me to this world. His Love, His Mercy, His Compassion, His Forgiveness, His Graciousness, His Kindness and His Bountifulness are above any humble person like me, to be able to thank Him enough and to praise Him.

O Allah ! I am humbly dedicating this work **to You.**

O Allah ! Accept my humble work and help me disseminate the information to those who need it.

O Allah ! Make this humble work worthy **of You.**

O Allah ! Forgive my shortcomings.

O Allah ! Help me   live as a Muslim and   die as a Mu'min (Believer).

O Allah ! Let me be summoned on the Day of Judgment with Prophet Muhammad (pbuh), with the other Prophets, the martyrs and all the noble believers. Ameen.

Acknowledgements كلمة الشكر

- The author wishes to thank all those friends who helped him in making this book and the previous books available to the readers. Special thanks go to Dr. Yusuf Kamaluddin (Yao-Keng) Chang and his wife, Audrey, for their tremendous help and moral support during the last few years. Thanks and appreciation go to the Vakil families (Abu Bakr, Usman, Farouq, Ishaq, Iqbal, and Akhtar) for their support to the author and the Foundation. May Allah (swt) bless them and bless their late parents (Umar and Amina). Thanks and Appreciation go to Dr. and Mrs. Ahmed K. Noor for taking care of the Newsletter: **Perspectives** for a number of years and from their own personal expenses.

- Moreover, the author wishes to thank all the respected brothers and sisters who have helped previously and are still helping. Among the many are Mr. Asad Khan and his wife, Sister Azma Khan; Dr. and Mrs. Mohammed Shafi; Mr. & Mrs. Javed Habib; Mr. & Mrs. Abdul Wahab; Mr. & Mrs. Saghir Aslam; Dr. & Mrs. Nadim Daouk; Mr. Refat M. Abo Elela; Dr. & Mrs. Zeyd A. Merenkov; Dr. and Mrs. Daudur Rahman; Mr. and Mrs. Shakeel Syed; Dr. and Mrs. Maqbool Ahmad; Mr. Zia Khan and his wife Tina Khan; Dr. and Mrs. Syed A. Zahir; Dr. and Mrs. Muhammad K. Zaman; Dr. and Mrs. Mostapha Arafa; Dr. & Mrs. Samir Arafeh; Dr. M. Munir Chaudry and his family; Late Dr. F.R. Khan and his respected wife Sister Farhat Khan, may Allah (swt) bless his soul, and many more.

- Thanks and appreciation to Dr. Dani Doueiri for translating some chapters from Arabic to English, as well as typing the Arabic texts on the computer. May Allah bless him and reward him and his family. Ameen.

- Special thanks and appreciation go to Sister Fawzia Akalal; Sister Sajeda Sultani and her family; Sister Houyda Najjar Mertaban and her family; Brother Mohammed Bilal Khan; and Brother Waseem Najmi and his wife Yasmeen; for their kind help in many areas. Also our thanks and appreciations are extended to Sister Azizah Abdul Rahman of Singapore, on behalf of her late parents Aminah Bint Ahmad and Abdul Rahman bin Mohamed. May Allah (swt) be pleased with her and her late parents. Ameen.

- Special thanks and appreciation go to Sister Shadia Hassan and her children for their help, advice, and contributions for the love of Allah (swt). Our prayers of Maghfirah for her late husband Mr. Samir Hassan and her late father Mr. Ahmad Ali. May Allah (swt) bless their souls and make their final stay in Paradise. Ameen. We are thankful and grateful to Mr. Muhammad El-Bdeiwi and his family for their generosity in helping this Foundation for Da'wah purposes. Our thanks also go to Mr. & Mrs. Abu Ramy Assaf, as well as to Dr. Yusuf K. Deshmukh and his family. Our thanks and appreciations go to Mr. Ammar Charani and his brother Samer Charani of MEF for their help. May Allah (swt) bless them all.

- Thanks and appreciations go to Mr. Khaled Obagi for his support to the Foundation on behalf of his late father and mother Aref Obagi and Nabila Al-Beik. Our thanks and appreciations also go to Mr. Ahmad Al-Khatib for his support to the Foundation on behalf of his mother Soraya, and his late father Adel Baheej Al-Khatib. Thanks and appreciation also goes to Dr. Osama Haikal on behalf of his late father, Mr. Omar Haikal. May Allah (swt) be pleased with them and may Allah (swt) keep their relatives in Paradise. Ameen. Our thanks and affections go to Brother Fathy Haggag and his family for their tremendous support to the author for all the years in California. It is only Allah (swt) Who will reward them. Our special thanks also go to my brother, Samir and his family for his excellent management and maintenance of this Foundation.

- Thanks and appreciations go also to Dr. Muhammad Waleed Khalife and his family for their support to this Foundation. May Allah (swt) bless them and reward them.

- Last but not least, my thanks, appreciation and love are to my wife, Zuhar Barhumi Sakr and our loving children: Sara and her husband Mohammad Nasser and their children Nada, Abdul Rahman, Ibrahim, Jenna, Hannah, Amber and Sabrina; to Hussein and his wife Dania and daughters Ayah and Dana; to Jihad and his wife Nasrin and son Hamza; to Basil and his wife La Reina and daughters Amina and Randa. *We pray to Allah (swt) to open the hearts of other friends to invest with Allah (swt).*

Has not the time arrived for the Believers that their hearts humbly should engage in remembrance of Allah. Qur'an (42:16)

Special Prayers · دُعَاءُ افتِتَاحِي

- The author prays to Allah (swt) to bless Prophet Muhammad and the family of Prophet Muhammad (pbuh), in as much as He blessed Prophet Ibrahim and the family of Prophet Ibrahim (pbuh). The author also prays to Allah (swt) to bless the Khulafaa' Rashidoon (Rightly guided) and the Sahaba (Companions) of the Prophet (pbuh) as well as the Tabi`oon (Followers) and the Followers of the Followers till the Day of Judgment.

- The author prays to Allah (swt) to reward all the `Ulama', who carried the Message of Allah (swt) and His Prophet (pbuh), and who transmitted it to the new generations.

- The author prays to Allah (swt) to reward his parents: his late father Al-Hajj Hussain Mustafa Sakr and his late mother Al-Hajjah Sara Ramadan Sakr for their sacrifices on their twelve children in general and to this author in specific. The author prays to Allah (swt) to reward the late brother of the author, Mr. Muhammad H. Sakr, for helping the author get his academic education, and his late brothers Mahmood H. Sakr, and Mustafa H. Sakr for taking care of the author's responsibilities overseas.

- Special prayers go to the Shaikh of the author who taught him Islam, and trained him from childhood to practice its teachings: Shaikh Muhammad `Umar Da`ooq. May Allah (swt) be pleased with him.

- A special Du`aa' goes to Al-Shaheed Shaikh Hassan Khalid, the late Grand Mufti of Lebanon, who also had a great impact on the author's knowledge of Islam. May Allah (swt) bless his soul and make him stay in Paradise.

---

1. swt: Subhanahu Wa Ta`ala (Glory be to Allah, and He is The High).
2. pbuh: Peace Be Upon Him (The Prophet).

x

- Special prayers and Du`aa' go to the many teachers, scholars and `Ulamaa' who were directly tutoring this author at the time of his youth. Through the efforts of Shaikh Muhammad `Umar Da'ooq, the following is a partial list of the teachers who taught this author: Dr. Mustafa Siba`ee; Shaikh Muhammad M. Al-Sawwaf; Dr. Muhammad Al-Zo`by; Shaikh Muhammad `Itani; Shaikh Muhammad M. Da`ooq; Shaikh Al-Fudail Al-Wartalani; Shaikh Muhammad `Abdel Kareem Al-Khattabi; Shaikh Malik Bennabi; Shaikh Faheem Abu`Ubeyh; Shaikh Muhammad Al-Shaal; Dr. Sa`eed Ramadan; Atty. `Abdel Hakeem `Abideen; Dr. Tawfic Houri; Shaikh Abu Salih Itani; Shaikh Hashim Daftardar Al-Madani; and the late Shaikh Abdul Badee` Sakr. May Allah (swt) bless them and reward them all.

- Our thanks and appreciation go to Dr. M. Faseehuddin and all his family members for their contribution to this Foundation. A special thanks and appreciation go to Sister Dr. Sayeeda Sultana for donating on behalf of her mother Mrs. Sultany Begum. May Allah (swt) reward Dr. Sultana, and may Allah (swt) bless her mother Sultany Begum. Moreover, we do thank Mr. and Mrs. Haitham Bundakji for their generosity to this Foundation at the time of needs. Ameen. A special thanks and appreciation go to Mr. Talat Radwan for helping this Foundation on behalf of his late father Mr. Mahmoud Radwan. May Allah (swt) bless them and be pleased with them both. Moreover, we do thank Dr. M.F. Shoukfeh, M.D. and his family for their generous help to this Foundation. Thanks and appreciation go to brother Ali Alnajjar and his family and the family of his sister for their help. May Allah bless them all.

- A final prayer is to the readers who took their precious time in reading this humble **Book of Prophet Muhammad (pbuh)**. May Allah (swt) bless them all. Allahumma Ameen.

Supplication دُعَاء

O Allah ! I seek refuge **in You** from anxiety and grief; I seek refuge **in You** from incapacity and laziness; and I seek refuge **in You** from the overcoming burden of debts and the overpowering of people.

O Allah ! I seek refuge **in You** from poverty except **to You,** from humiliation except **for You,** and from fear except **from You.**

O Allah ! I seek refuge **in You** from stating a false testimony, or committing immorality, or provoking **You**; and I seek refuge **in You** from the malice of the enemies, and from enigmatic disease, and from the despair of hope.

O Allah ! I seek refuge **in You** from the wicked people, from the worries of the livelihood, and from the ill-nature such as having a bad attitude.

O Allah ! **You are** the Mercy of the mercies, and **You are** the Lord of the Universe.

O Allah!
and Allahumma Ameen.

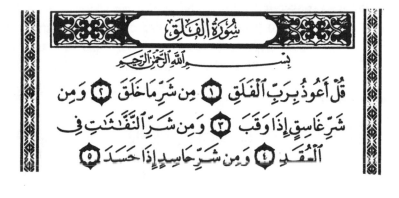

Al-Falaq: The Dawn

Say: I seek refuge with the Lord of the Dawn, from the mischief of created things; from the mischief of Darkness as it overspreads; from the mischief of those who blow on knots; and from the mischief of the envious one as he practices envy. (113:1-5)

It is not easy to write about Prophet Muhammad (pbuh). He was selected by Allah (swt) to be the best person, the best prophet, and the best messenger. Allah chose him, and He trained him to be the best in the history of mankind. We cannot understand Qur'an and Hadith unless we study his Sirah. One has to study the life history of the Prophet (pbuh) with a good number of Muslim scholars who love him, and appreciate what he contributed to the success of mankind.

One has to study the following topics so as to appreciate the personality of the Prophet (pbuh) and the Message that he received from Allah (swt) through Angel Jibril. Each and every subject is a course by itself: Lineage ... From Childhood to Youth ... From Marriage to Prophethood... From Revelation to Umar's Conversion... From Boycott to the Year of Sorrows... From Persecution to Migration to Africa... From Israa' and Mi'raaj to the Covenant of Al-`Aqabah... Emigration to Yathrib (Madinah)... Madinah Period and the Establishing of a Mosque and a Solid Community ... Battles from the Enemies against Islam and the Prophet... Treaties that the Prophet Signed with Christians, Jews, Pagans, Tribes and Leaders from outside Arabian Peninsula... Liberation of Makkah From Idols and From Paganism... Delegation of Abu Bakr to lead the Hajj with Muslims... Hajj Al-Widaa' (Farewell Pilgrimage) ... Last Revelation ... Death of the Prophet ... His Successors... etc.

It is not enough to study the personality of Prophet Muhammad (pbuh), people have to try to mimic the qualities of the Prophet in their private and public life. By following his personality character, they will definitely be able to establish a society on solid foundation. One has to recognize that Allah (swt)

2

as a role model to follow and to apply in their daily life. Allah (swt) says in Surah Al-Ahzab (The Clans) the following:

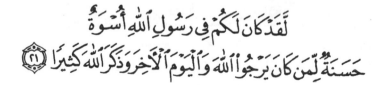

You have indeed in the Apostle of God a beautiful pattern (of conduct) for any one whose hope is in God and the Final Day, and who engages much in the praise of God. (33:21)

In this Book, certain topics about Prophet Muhammad (pbuh) were selected with the hope that the readers will be able to benefit from them. One should say that something is better than nothing. To make it easy, the topics were classified into different sections so that it will be easy to read and realize the significance of these topics. It will not be enough for the reader to read only one chapter or one topic. One has to read the whole book, and then to associate himself with a group of Muslim Scholars on a daily basis so as to benefit from their knowledge and wisdom.

We pray to Allah (swt) to accept our humble contribution about Prophet Muhammad (pbuh), as well as to forgive us for our shortcomings. Ameen.

3

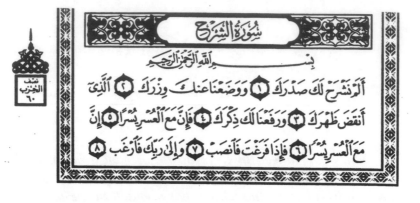

Al-Inshirah: The Expansion

Have We not expanded your breast? And removed from you your burden, to which did gall your back? And raised high the esteem (in which) you are held? So, verily, with every difficulty, there is relief: Verily, with every difficulty there is relief. Therefore, when you are free (from your immediate task), still labor hard, and to your Lord turn (all) your attention. (94:1-8)

I. Introduction

The topic of this chapter is about the occasion of the birth of Prophet Muhammad (pbuh). Allah says about Muhammad (pbuh) in the Qur'an the following in Surah Al-Ahzab (The Confederates)

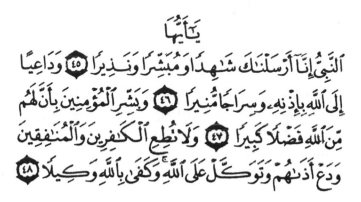

O Prophet! Truly We have sent you as a witness, a bearer of glad tidings, and a warner, and as one who invites to God's (Grace) by His leave, and as a Lamp spreading Light. Then give the glad tidings to the believers, that they shall have from God a very great bounty. And obey not (the behests) of the unbelievers and the hypocrites, and heed not their annoyances but put your trust in God. For enough is God as a disposer of affairs. (33:45-48)

It should be mentioned here that Prophet Muhammad (pbuh) himself did not celebrate his own birthday. His companions never celebrated his birthday, and none celebrated their own birthdays. To celebrate the Prophet's birthday might be considered a Bid'ah

5

(innovation) in Islam. Hence, such type of an activity would be wrong to be done.

There is another group of Muslim 'Ulamaa' who permit Muslims to commemorate the Sirah of the Prophet, rather to celebrate the Day of his birth. Muslims are encouraged to remember, to study and to reflect upon the life history of the Prophet. In so doing, they will be able to imitate his personality and emulate his character in their private and public life.

This occasion does remind us that some Muslims of today do celebrate their own birthdays with special parties. Some of which are religious, and many are devoid of the spirit of Islam. Let these Muslims remember that one year of their personal lives is over, and they are one step closer to their death, graves, and meeting Allah..

II. Reflections

Let us remember that when we meet to remember our beloved Prophet (pbuh), we are to remember his personality character, and the teachings he brought to us all. Hence, let me remind you of the following about him and his message:

A. Allah sent Muhammad (pbuh) as a mercy to all the creatures of the universe including: mankind, jinns, angels, animals, plants and other creatures that we don't know about. In this respect, Allah says in the Qur'an in Surah Al-Anbiyaa' (The Prophets):

We sent you not, but as a mercy for all creatures.
(21:107)

B. Allah (swt) sent Muhammad (pbuh) as Messenger to all people
    of the world to give them glad tidings and to warn them too. In
    this respect Allah says in the Qur'an in Surah Saba' (Sheba):

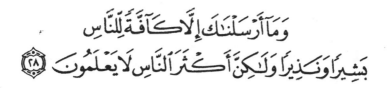

We have not sent you but as a universal Messenger
to mankind, giving them glad tidings, and warning them
(against sin), but most men understand not. (34:28)

C. Allah (swt) sent Prophet Muhammad (pbuh) as an excellent
    example to be followed. The Qur'an states the following:

We have indeed in the Apostle of God a beautiful
pattern (of conduct) for any one whose hope is in God
and the final day, and who engages much in the praise
of God. (33:21)

7

D. Allah (swt) sent Muhammad (pbuh) to be followed, and to be obeyed. In this regard, the Qur'an states the following:

$$\text{﴿٦﴾ مَّا أَفَاءَ اللَّهُ عَلَىٰ رَسُولِهِ مِنْ أَهْلِ الْقُرَىٰ فَلِلَّهِ وَلِلرَّسُولِ وَلِذِي الْقُرْبَىٰ وَالْيَتَامَىٰ وَالْمَسَاكِينِ وَابْنِ السَّبِيلِ كَيْ لَا يَكُونَ دُولَةً بَيْنَ الْأَغْنِيَاءِ مِنكُمْ وَمَا آتَاكُمُ الرَّسُولُ فَخُذُوهُ وَمَا نَهَاكُمْ عَنْهُ فَانتَهُوا وَاتَّقُوا اللَّهَ إِنَّ اللَّهَ شَدِيدُ الْعِقَابِ ﴿٧﴾}$$

So take what the Apostle assigns to you, and deny yourselves that which he withholds from you. And fear God; for God is strict in punishment. (59:7)

E. Muhammad (pbuh) was sent to be the last and the final Prophet to mankind. In this respect, Allah (swt) says about Muhammad (pbuh):

$$\text{﴿٣٩﴾ مَّا كَانَ مُحَمَّدٌ أَبَا أَحَدٍ مِّن رِّجَالِكُمْ وَلَٰكِن رَّسُولَ اللَّهِ وَخَاتَمَ النَّبِيِّينَ وَكَانَ اللَّهُ بِكُلِّ شَيْءٍ عَلِيمًا ﴿٤٠﴾}$$

Muhammad is not the father of any of your men, but (he is) the Apostle of God, and the seal of the Prophets: And God has full knowledge of all things. (33:40)

F. His finality brought with him the Qur'an as the last and complete Book from Allah to all mankind. The Qur'an is the

8

summation, purification and culmination of all the previous messages that God sent through His prophets. For whoever is interested to find out the original divine revealed Bible unto Jesus, is to find it in the Qur'an. Moreover, whoever is interested to find out the original divine revealed Torah unto Moses, is to find it in the Qur'an.

III. Recommendations

A. While you are commemorating the Sirah of the Prophet Muhammad (pbuh), please read his life history; discuss it among yourselves, and among your family members. Remember Allah (swt) with Zikr, gratitude, thanks and appreciation for all the favor He has done for us, by sending His beloved Prophet and His final Messenger Muhammad (pbuh). Remember Prophet Muhammad (pbuh) and make your Salat for him as we have been instructed by Allah (swt) in the Qur'an:

$$\text{إِنَّ ٱللَّهَ وَمَلَـٰٓئِكَتَهُ يُصَلُّونَ عَلَى ٱلنَّبِيِّ ۚ يَـٰٓأَيُّهَا ٱلَّذِينَ ءَامَنُوا۟ صَلُّوا۟ عَلَيْهِ وَسَلِّمُوا۟ تَسْلِيمًا}$$

God and His Angels send blessings on the Prophet:
O you that believe! Send your blessings on him, and
salute him with all respect. (33:56)

B. It is good to remember that the name of Prophet Muhammad (pbuh) as the Messenger of Allah (swt) was annexed to the name of Allah (swt) through the proclamation of the creed of Islam. This creed is the first pillar of Islam. We say it during Salat, we say it during Azan, and we say it everyday on many occasions. This creed is:

There is no one worthy of worship except God (Allah) and Muhammad is the Messenger of Allah.

The other form of the creed is:

أشهدُ أن لا إله إلا الله وأشهد أن محمداً عبدُهُ ورسولهُ.

I bear witness, that there is no one worthy of worship except God (Allah), and I bear witness that Muhammad is the Messenger of Allah.

Let us pray that Allah (swt) and His Prophet Muhammad (pbuh) be pleased with us. Let us ask Allah (swt) guidance, and let us ask Him forgiveness. Ameen.

Allah is the Greatest!

ولادة رَسُول الإنسَانيّة

Chapter (3) Birth Of The Messenger Of Mankind

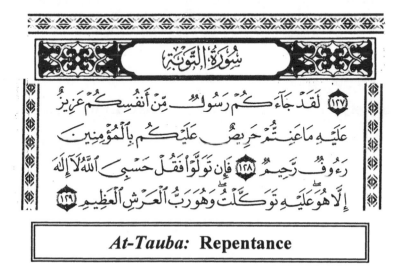

سُورَةُ التَّوبَةِ

لَقَدْ جَاءَكُمْ رَسُولٌ مِّنْ أَنفُسِكُمْ عَزِيزٌ ﴿١٢٧﴾ عَلَيْهِ مَا عَنِتُّمْ حَرِيصٌ عَلَيْكُم بِالْمُؤْمِنِينَ رَءُوفٌ رَّحِيمٌ ﴿١٢٨﴾ فَإِن تَوَلَّوْا فَقُلْ حَسْبِيَ اللَّهُ لَا إِلَٰهَ إِلَّا هُوَ عَلَيْهِ تَوَكَّلْتُ وَهُوَ رَبُّ الْعَرْشِ الْعَظِيمِ ﴿١٢٩﴾

At-Tauba: Repentance

Now has come unto you a Messenger from among yourselves: it grieves him that you should suffer, ardently anxious is he over you: to the Believers is he most kind and merciful. But if they turn away, "Allah sufficed me: There is no god but He, on Him is my trust, He the Lord of the Throne Supreme. (9:128-129)

I. Introduction

This chapter is going to be about the "Birth of Prophet Muhammad" – birth of the Messenger to Mankind. Allah (swt) says in Qur'an in Surah Al-Ahzab (The Clans) about Muhammad:

يَٰٓأَيُّهَا
ٱلنَّبِيُّ إِنَّآ أَرْسَلْنَٰكَ شَٰهِدًا وَمُبَشِّرًا وَنَذِيرًا ۝ وَدَاعِيًا
إِلَى ٱللَّهِ بِإِذْنِهِۦ وَسِرَاجًا مُّنِيرًا ۝ وَبَشِّرِ ٱلْمُؤْمِنِينَ بِأَنَّ لَهُم
مِّنَ ٱللَّهِ فَضْلًا كَبِيرًا ۝ وَلَا تُطِعِ ٱلْكَٰفِرِينَ وَٱلْمُنَٰفِقِينَ
وَدَعْ أَذَىٰهُمْ وَتَوَكَّلْ عَلَى ٱللَّهِ وَكَفَىٰ بِٱللَّهِ وَكِيلًا ۝

O Prophet! Truly We have sent you as a Witness, a Bearer of Glad Tidings, and a Warner and as one who invites to Allah's (Grace) by His leave and as a (Siraj Muneer) Lamp Spreading Light. Then give the glad tidings to the Believers that they shall have from Allah a very great Bounty. And obey not the (behest) of the Unbelievers and the Hypocrites, and disregard their insolence but put your trust in Allah. For enough is Allah as a Disposer of affairs. (33:45-48)

Muslims all over the world commemorate the month of Rabi' Awwal as the month of the birth of Prophet Muhammad (pbuh). They do commemorate the Sirah of the beloved Messenger of Allah to mankind on the 12th of Rabi'Awwal.

12

The Sirah is commemorated but not to be celebrated. We do not celebrate the birthday of the Prophet but we do commemorate His Sirah. When we commemorate the Sirah, we are to be reminded of the teachings of the Prophet, his lifestyle, the code of ethics he laid down for us, his attitude, his behavior, and his character. When Muslims commemorate the Sirah of the Prophet, they study his life history in order to adopt, imitate and emulate his personality. In this respect Allah (swt) says in Surah Al-Ahzab (The Clans):

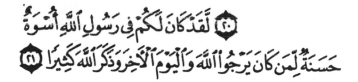

You have indeed the Messenger of Allah an excellent exempler for him who hopes in Allah and the final Day and who remembers Allah Much. (33:21)

II. Reflections

A. Allah (swt) sent Muhammad (pbuh) as a Mercy to all mankind. He was sent for every human being and for the non-human being too, that is, the Jinn and others. In this respect Allah (swt) says in the Qur'an in Surah Al-Anbiyaa' (The Prophets):

۝ وَمَاۤ أَرْسَلْنَٰكَ إِلَّا رَحْمَةً لِّلْعَٰلَمِينَ ۝

"We sent you not, but as a Mercy for all creatures."
(21:107)

B.   The name of the Prophet Muhammad (pbuh) is associated
with the name of Allah (Swt). The Kalimah (Kalimat of Al-
Tawheed) or the proclamation of faith is:

أشهدُ أن لا إله إلا الله واشهد أن محمداً عبدُهُ ورسولهُ.

To be a Muslim, one has to believe in this Kalimah. The
Kalimah is to be pronounced vocally in the following fashion:

In the Adhan, call for prayer, one says:

أَشْهَدُ أَنْ لاَ إِلَهَ إِلاَّ اَللَّهَ ، وَأَشْهَدُ أَنَّ مُحَمَّـداً رَسُوْلُ

اَللَّـــــهِ

The pillars of Islam are five, one of which is the belief in the
creed of Islam. In this respect the Prophet (pbuh) says:

عَنْ ابْنِ عُمَرَ رَضِيَ اللَّهُ عَنْهُمَا ، أَنَّهُ قَالَ : قَـــالَ

رَسُوْلُ اللَّهِ صَلَّى اللَّهُ عَلَيْهِ وَسَلَّمَ :

" بُنِيَ الإِسْلاَمُ عَلَى خَمْسٍ ، شَهَادَةُ أَنْ لاَ إِلَهَ إِلاَّ اللَّـــهُ ،

وَأَنَّ مُحَمَّداً عَبْدُهُ وَرَسُوْلُهُ ، وَآقَامِ الصَّلاَةِ ، وَإِيْتَـــــاءِ

الزَّكَاةِ ، وَالْحَجِّ ، وَصَوْمِ رَمَضَانَ • "   متفق عليه

14

Narrated by Ibn Umar saying that the Messenger of Allah said:

> *"Islam is built on five (pillars): bearing witness that there is no one worthy to be worshipped except Allah; and that Muhammad is His servant and Messenger; performing the regular prayers, paying Zakat, performing Pilgrimage and fasting the month of Ramadan."* Agreed

Whoever believes in Allah (swt) has to believe in Muhammad (pbuh), as a Prophet, as a Messenger and as a final prophet of Allah (swt) to mankind. Allah informed us that Muhammad (pbuh) was the last and the final Prophet of Allah to mankind. The Qur'an states in Surah Al-Ahzab (The Clans), the following:

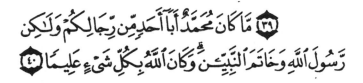

> *Muhammad is not the father of any of your men, but (he is) the Apostle of God, and the Seal of the prophets: And God has full knowledge of all things."* (33:40)

III. Allah's Declaration

A. Let us listen to what Allah says about Muhammad in the Qur'an. Allah (swt) asked Muhammad (pbuh) to declare his mission to people that he was the Messenger of Allah. Allah then, asked us to believe in Him and His Messenger. In Surah Al-A'raf (The Heights) Allah says:

قُلْ

يَـٰٓأَيُّهَا ٱلنَّاسُ إِنِّى رَسُولُ ٱللَّهِ إِلَيْكُمْ جَمِيعًا ٱلَّذِى لَهُۥ مُلْكُ ٱلسَّمَـٰوَٰتِ وَٱلْأَرْضِ لَآ إِلَـٰهَ إِلَّا هُوَ يُحْىِۦ وَيُمِيتُ فَـَٔامِنُوا۟ بِٱللَّهِ وَرَسُولِهِ ٱلنَّبِىِّ ٱلْأُمِّىِّ ٱلَّذِى يُؤْمِنُ بِٱللَّهِ وَكَلِمَـٰتِهِۦ وَٱتَّبِعُوهُ لَعَلَّكُمْ تَهْتَدُونَ ﴿١٥٨﴾

Say: O men! I am sent unto you all, as the Apostle of God, to Whom belong the dominion of the heavens and the earth: There is no god but He: It is He that give both life and death. So believe in God and His Apostle, the unlettered Prophet, who believe in God and His Words: Follow him that (so) you may be guided. (7:158)

B. Let us also hear what Allah (swt) said in the Qur'an to all of us as human beings regarding Prophet Muhammad (pbuh) Surah Al-Nisaa' (The Women):

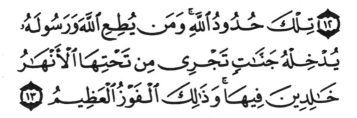

﴿١٣﴾ تِلْكَ حُدُودُ ٱللَّهِ وَمَن يُطِعِ ٱللَّهَ وَرَسُولَهُۥ يُدْخِلْهُ جَنَّـٰتٍ تَجْرِى مِن تَحْتِهَا ٱلْأَنْهَـٰرُ خَـٰلِدِينَ فِيهَا وَذَٰلِكَ ٱلْفَوْزُ ٱلْعَظِيمُ ﴿١٣﴾

Those are limits set by God: those who obey Allah
and His Apostle will be admitted to Gardens with rivers
flowing beneath; to abide therein (forever) and that will
be the Supreme achievement. (4:13)

C. Let us listen to Allah (swt) informing us to pronounce our
prayers and our greetings to Prophet Muhammad (pbuh). In
Surah Al-Ahzab (The Clan), Allah (swt) says:

إِنَّ ٱللَّهَ وَمَلَٰٓئِكَتَهُۥ يُصَلُّونَ عَلَى ٱلنَّبِىِّ يَٰٓأَيُّهَا ٱلَّذِينَ ٥٥

ءَامَنُوا۟ صَلُّوا۟ عَلَيْهِ وَسَلِّمُوا۟ تَسْلِيمًا ٥٦

God and His Angeles send blessings on the Prophet:
O you that believe! Send your blessings on him, and
salute him with all respect. (33:56)

IV. Recommendations

A. Prophet Muhammad (pbuh) encouraged Muslims to say
greetings and Du`aa unto Him. He said:

عَنْ عَبْدِ اللَّهِ بْنِ عَمْرِو بْنِ العَاصِ رَضِيَ اللَّهُ عَنْهُمَا –

أَنَّهُ سَمِعَ رَسُولَ اللَّهِ صَلَّى اللَّهُ عَلَيْهِ وَسَلَّمَ يَقُولُ :

" مَنْ صَلَّى عَلَيَّ صَلَاةً صَلَّى اللَّهُ عَلَيْهِ بِهَا عَشْراً " .

Narrated by Abdullah Ibn Amr Bin Al-`Ass that he heard the
Prophet saying: *Whoever says one prayer unto me, Allah will say*
His Blessings on him ten times."   Muslim

17

B. Muslims say their prayers five times a day; and in every Tashahhud they say Al-Tahiyyat which includes the following:

(السَّلَامُ عَلَيْكَ أَيُّهَا النَّبِيُّ وَرَحْمَةُ اللَّهِ وَبَرَكَاتُه)

O Prophet: The Peace, the Mercy and the Blessings of Allah are upon you."

The same Tashahhud also includes acknowledgement to Muhammad (pbuh) and the belief in him after believing in Allah. We say daily:

أَشْهَدُ أَنْ لَا إِلَهَ إِلَّا اللَّهَ ، وَأَشْهَدُ أَنَّ مُحَمَّدًا عَبْـــــدُهُ وَرَسُـــــولُهُ

I bear witness there is no god to be worshipped except God (Allah), and I bear witness that Muhammad is His servant and His Messenger.

In the daily prayer, Muslims say As-Salat Al-Ibrahimiyah (The prayer of Prophet Ibrahim):

" أَللَّهُمَّ صَلِّ عَلَى مُحَمَّدٍ وَعَلَى آلِ مُحَمَّدٍ،كَمَا صَلَّيْتَ عَلَى إِبْرَاهِيمَ وَعَلَى آلِ إِبْرَاهِيمَ ، وَبَارِكِ اللَّهُمَّ عَلَى مُحَمَّـــد وَعَلَى آلِ مُحَمَّدٍ ، كَمَا بَارَكْتَ عَلَى إِبْرَاهِيمَ وَعَلَــــى آلِ إِبْرَاهِـــيمَ • "

18

*"O Allah! Bestow your Blessings (prayers) on Muhammad
and the family of Muhammad as You made Your Blessings onto
Ibrahim and the family of Ibrahim. O Allah! Bless Muhammad and
the family of Muhammad as you blessed Ibrahim and the family of
Ibrahim."*

V. Prophet's Recommendations

A. Let us listen to Prophet Muhammad (pbuh) saying to us
about our prayers unto him:

عن أوس بن أوس رضي الله عنه ، قال : قال رسول
الله صلى الله عليه وسلم : " إنَّ مِنْ أفْضل أيَّامكُمْ
يوْمُ الجُمعَة فأكْثِرُوا عَليَّ مِنَ الصَّلاةِ فيهِ ، فإنَّ صلاتَكم
مَعْرُوضَةٌ عَليَّ . " قَالُوا يَارَسُولَ اللّهِ ، وكَيْفَ تُعْـرَضُ
صَلاتُنَا عَلَيْكَ وَقَدْ أرِمْتَ . قَالَ يَقُولُ بَلِيْتَ . قَـــالَ:
إنَّ اللّهَ حَرَّمَ عَلَى الأرْضِ أجْسَادَ الأنْبِيَاءِ . "

رواه أبو داود

Narrated by Aws Ibn Aws that the Prophet said:

*The best day is Friday, increase your prayers unto
Me because your prayers will be brought to Me.*

The companions asked Muhammad (pbuh); How could this
happen when you will be dead: He replied by saying: *"Allah
forbade the earth to eat up the flesh of the Prophets."* *Reported by
Abu Dawood*

19

B. Let us hear the Prophet saying to us that we should be
generous and not miser in saying our prayers unto Him.

عن علي رضي الله عنه قال : قال رسول اللـــــه

صلى الله عليه وسلم :

" البَخِيْلُ مَنْ إِذَا ذُكِرْتُ عِنْدَهُ وَلَمْ يُصَلِّ عَلَيَّ . "

Narrated by Ali (May Allah be pleased with him) saying that
the Messenger of Allah (pbuh) said:

*The real miser (stingy) is that person who when my name is
mentioned to him, does not say prayer unto me.*

C. Let us hear Him also asking us to say prayers unto Him:

عن أبي هريرة رضي الله عنه ، قال : قال رسـول

الله صلى الله عليه وسلم :

" لاتجعلُوا قَبْرِيْ عِيْداً،وَصَلُّوا عَلَيَّ،فَإِنَّ صلاتكم تبلغنيَّ

حيث كنتم . "   رواه أبو داود .

Narrated by Abu Hurairah that the Messenger of Allah
said: "*Don't make grave a place of festivity, and say your
prayers unto Me. Your prayers will reach Me from wherever
you are.*"

20

VI. Final Remarks

Let me remind you about your greeting and salutation to the Prophet. Muhammad (pbuh) said in this respect:

عن أبي هريرة رضي الله عنه ، ان رسول اللـــه

صلى الله عليه وسلم قال :

" مَامِنْ أَحَدٍ يُسَلِّمُ عَلَيَّ إِلاَّ رَدَّ اللهُ عَلَيَّ رُوحِي حَـــتى

أَرِدَّ عَلَيْهِ السَّـــلاَمُ . "

رواه أبو داود

Narrated by Abu Hurairah saying that the Messenger of Allah said: *"Whenever anyone says a greeting of Salam unto me, Allah brings back my soul to my body so as to answer his Salam."* Reported by Abu Dawud

Finally, let us, dear Muslims, listen to the advice of Prophet Muhammad (pbuh), the Messenger of Allah, advising us how to say our Salat unto Him:

عن ابي محمد كعب بن عجرة رضي الله عنه قال :

خَرَجَ عَلَيْنَا النَّبِيُّ صَلَّى اللهُ عَلَيْهِ وَسَلَّمَ ، فَقُلْنَـــا :

يَارَسُولَ اللهِ ، قَدْ عَلِمْنَا كَيْفَ نُسَلِّمُ عَلَيْكَ ، فَكَيْـــفَ

نُصَلِّي عَلَيْكَ ؟ قَالَ : " قُولُوا : اللَّـهُمَّ صَلِّ عَلَى مُحَمَّـــد

وَعَلَى آلِ مُحَمَّدٍ ، كَمَا صَلَّيْتَ عَلَى آلِ إِبْرَاهِيمَ إِنَّكَ حَمِيْدٌ

مَجِيْدٌ . اللَّـهُمَّ بَارِكْ عَلَى مُحَمَّدٍ وَعَلَى آلِ مُحَمَّدٍ كَمَـــا

بَارَكْتَ عَلَى آلِ إِبْرَاهِيمَ إِنَّكَ حَمِيْدٌ مَجِيْدٌ . "

متفق عليـــه

21

Narrated by Abi Muhammad Ka'ab Ibn 'Ajrah saying that the Messenger of Allah came to us and we said to him:

O Messenger of Allah! We know how to say Salam unto you, but how can we say our prayers unto you?" He said:

"Say O Allah! Make your blessings unto Muhammad and unto the family of Muhammad, as You made your blessings unto Ibrahim and the family of Ibrahim. You are praised and exalted. O Allah! Bless Muhammad and the family of Muhammad as You blessed Ibrahim and the family of Ibrahim. You are praised and exalted." Agreed Upon

Let us make sure that we teach our children the love for Allah and the love for Muhammad (pbuh). While it is very important to teach our children the love of Allah (swt) and His Prophet Muhammad (pbuh), we have to practice what we teach them in private and in public life. Then the children will mimic their parents and all will live in peace and harmony. They will be rewarded Paradise in the Day of Judgment. Let us ask Allah Almighty forgiveness. Ameen.

God has the Power over everything

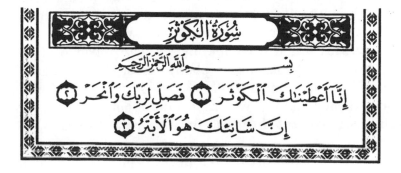

محمد ﷺ فى القرآن

Chapter (4)   **Muhammad In The Qur'an**

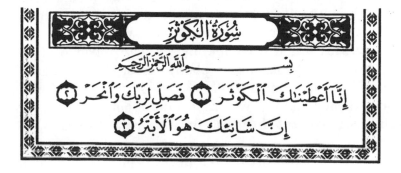

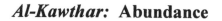

Al-Kawthar: **Abundance**

To you have We granted the Abundance. Therefore to your Lord turn in Prayer and Sacrifice. For he who hates you, He will be cut off (From Future Hope.) (108:1-3)

23

I.   Introduction

To write about Prophet Muhammad (pbuh) one has to go directly to the Holy Qur'an. The only way to appreciate this approach is when one admits that the Qur'an is the word of God and that this Book was revealed unto Muhammad (pbuh). Through this approach one will be able to see what Allah Almighty had revealed unto Muhammad (pbuh) about Muhammad (pbuh) himself. The revelation from God has to inform Muhammad (pbuh) about himself as well as to inform him about mankind and their needs in order to live peacefully as human beings.

In the Qur'an we see that Prophet Ibrahim (May Allah's peace be upon him) reconstructed the Ka'bah with his son Isma'il and prayed to Allah to accept his supplication. In this regard, Allah says in the Qur'an on behalf of Ibrahim (May Allah's peace be upon him):

رَبَّنَا وَٱبۡعَثۡ فِيهِمۡ رَسُولٗا مِّنۡهُمۡ يَتۡلُواْ عَلَيۡهِمۡ ءَايَٰتِكَ وَيُعَلِّمُهُمُ ٱلۡكِتَٰبَ وَٱلۡحِكۡمَةَ وَيُزَكِّيهِمۡۚ إِنَّكَ أَنتَ ٱلۡعَزِيزُ ٱلۡحَكِيمُ (٢ : ١٢٩)

Our Lord! Send amongst them an apostle of their own, who shall rehearse Your Signs to them and instruct them in scripture and wisdom, and sanctify them: for You are the Exalted in Might, the Wise." (2:129)

II.   Qur'an about Muhammad

1. We have been told in the Qur'an that Jesus, the Messiah, and the son of Mary the virgin, informed his people that a Prophet by the name of Ahmad (Muhammad) (pbuh)

would come after him to complete his mission to mankind. In this respect we see in the Qur'an in Surah Al-Saff (Battle Array) the following verse:

وَإِذْ قَالَ عِيسَى ٱبْنُ مَرْيَمَ يَـٰبَنِىٓ إِسْرَٰٓءِيلَ إِنِّى رَسُولُ ٱللَّهِ إِلَيْكُم مُّصَدِّقًا لِّمَا بَيْنَ يَدَىَّ مِنَ ٱلتَّوْرَىٰةِ وَمُبَشِّرًۢا بِرَسُولٍ يَأْتِى مِنۢ بَعْدِى ٱسْمُهُۥٓ أَحْمَدُ

And remember Jesus, the Son of Mary, said: 'O children of Israel! I am the Apostle of God (sent) to you, confirming the Law (which came) before me, and giving glad tidings of an Apostle to come after me, whose name shall be Ahmad. (61:6)

2.   The prayer of Prophet Ibrahim (May Allah's peace be upon him) has been accepted and Allah sent Muhammad (pbuh) as a Prophet and Messenger from within the children of Prophet Isma'il (May Allah's peace be upon him). In this regard Allah says in the Qur'an in Surah Al-Jumu`ah (Friday Assembly) the following:

هُوَ ٱلَّذِى بَعَثَ فِى ٱلْأُمِّيِّـۧنَ رَسُولًا مِّنْهُمْ يَتْلُواْ عَلَيْهِمْ ءَايَـٰتِهِۦ وَيُزَكِّيهِمْ وَيُعَلِّمُهُمُ ٱلْكِتَـٰبَ وَٱلْحِكْمَةَ وَإِن كَانُواْ مِن قَبْلُ لَفِى ضَلَـٰلٍ مُّبِينٍ

It is He who has sent amongst the unlettered an Apostle from among themselves, to rehearse to them His signs, to sanctify them, and to instruct them in Scripture and Wisdom,-although they had been, before, in manifest error: (62:2)

25

3. The previous verse informs us that Muhammad (pbuh) was sent from among the people. This means that he is a human being selected to deliver the Message of the Merciful God. The following verse reassures the choice of Muhammad (pbuh) as a human being to receive the revelation of God to be delivered to mankind. Allah says in Surah Kahf (Cave):

قُلْ إِنَّمَا أَنَا بَشَرٌ مِّثْلُكُمْ يُوحَىٰ إِلَيَّ أَنَّمَا إِلَٰهُكُمْ إِلَٰهٌ وَاحِدٌ فَمَن كَانَ يَرْجُواْ لِقَآءَ رَبِّهِ فَلْيَعْمَلْ عَمَلًا صَالِحًا وَلَا يُشْرِكْ بِعِبَادَةِ رَبِّهِ أَحَدًا ﴿١١٠﴾

Say: I am but a man like yourselves, (but) the inspiration has come to me, that Your God is One God: whoever expects to meet his Lord, let him work righteousness, and in the worship of his Lord, admit no one as partner. (18:110)

4. Allah reconfirmed the appointment of Muhammad (pbuh) as a prophet and a Messenger over and over again. The Qur'an is full of these verses. The following verse in Surah Al-Nisaa' (The Women) is one of them:

وَأَرْسَلْنَاكَ لِلنَّاسِ رَسُولًا وَكَفَىٰ بِاللَّهِ شَهِيدًا ﴿٧٩﴾

And We have sent you as an Apostle to instruct mankind. (4:79)

5. The purpose of sending Prophet Muhammad (pbuh) to mankind was a mercy, and in this regard one sees in the Qur'an the following verse in Surah Al-Anbiyaa' (The Prophets):

26

وَمَآأَرْسَلْنَاكَ إِلَّا رَحْمَةً لِّلْعَالَمِينَ

We sent you not, but as a Mercy for all creatures.
(21:107)

We also see that Allah sent Muhammad (pbuh) as a universal Messenger to all mankind and in this regard Allah says in Surah Saba' the following:

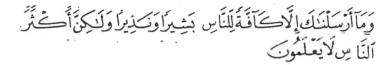

We have not sent you but as a Universal Messenger to mankind, giving them glad tidings, and warning them against sin, but most men understand not. (34:28)

6. Allah, by sending Muhammad (pbuh) as a Messenger, showed us a beautiful example to be followed, a model to be imitated, and a symbol of respect and admiration to be followed. In this respect Allah says in the Qur'an in Surah Al-Ahzab, (The Confederators):

لَّقَدْ كَانَ لَكُمْ فِي رَسُولِ اللَّهِ أُسْوَةٌ حَسَنَةٌ لِّمَن كَانَ يَرْجُواْ اللَّهَ وَالْيَوْمَ الْآخِرَ وَذَكَرَ اللَّهَ كَثِيرًا

You have indeed in the Apostle of God a beautiful pattern of Conduct for anyone whose hope is in God and the Final Day, and who engages much in the praise of God. (33:21)

7. Muhammad (pbuh) was sent as a witness for Allah to mankind. He will be a witness for people or a witness against them, depending upon man's acceptance of the message of Allah or his rejection. In this regard Allah says in Surah Al-Baqarah (The Cow) the following:

وَكَذَٰلِكَ جَعَلْنَٰكُمْ أُمَّةً وَسَطًا لِّتَكُونُوا۟ شُهَدَآءَ عَلَى ٱلنَّاسِ وَيَكُونَ ٱلرَّسُولُ عَلَيْكُمْ شَهِيدًا (١٤٣ : ٢)

Thus have We made of you an Ummat justly balanced, that you might be witnesses over the nations, and the Apostle a witness over yourselves. (2:143)

8. When Muhammad (pbuh) was sent as a mercy, as a witness, and as a Messenger to mankind, he was sent not to be a warden and/or a disposer of their affairs. In this regard Allah says in the Qur'an in Surah Al-Nisaa' (The Women) the following:

وَمَن تَوَلَّىٰ فَمَآ أَرْسَلْنَٰكَ عَلَيْهِمْ حَفِيظًا

We have not sent you to watch over them. (4:80)

However, in Surah Al-Israa' (Night Travel), Allah says the following:

وَمَآ أَرْسَلْنَٰكَ عَلَيْهِم وَكِيلًا ﴿٥٤﴾

We have not sent you to be a disposer of their affairs for them. (17:54)

28

On the other hand, Muhammad (pbuh) was sent as a Messenger to give glad tidings as well as to warn people about their sins. Allah says in the Qur'an in this regard in Surah Al-Israa' (Night Travel) the following:

$$ وَبِٱلْحَقِّ أَنزَلْنَٰهُ وَبِٱلْحَقِّ نَزَلَ وَمَآ أَرْسَلْنَٰكَ إِلَّا مُبَشِّرًا وَنَذِيرًا ﴿١٠٥﴾ $$

...and We sent you but to give glad tidings and to warn the sinners. (17:105)

III. Mission of the Prophet

The following verse in the Qur'an in Surah Al-Ahzab (The Confederates) summarizes the mission of the Prophet Muhammad (pbuh).

$$ يَٰٓأَيُّهَا ٱلنَّبِيُّ إِنَّآ أَرْسَلْنَٰكَ شَٰهِدًا وَمُبَشِّرًا وَنَذِيرًا ﴿٤٥﴾ وَدَاعِيًا إِلَى ٱللَّهِ بِإِذْنِهِۦ وَسِرَاجًا مُّنِيرًا ﴿٤٦﴾ وَبَشِّرِ ٱلْمُؤْمِنِينَ بِأَنَّ لَهُم مِّنَ ٱللَّهِ فَضْلًا كَبِيرًا ﴿٤٧﴾ وَلَا تُطِعِ ٱلْكَٰفِرِينَ وَٱلْمُنَٰفِقِينَ وَدَعْ أَذَىٰهُمْ وَتَوَكَّلْ عَلَى ٱللَّهِ وَكَفَىٰ بِٱللَّهِ وَكِيلًا $$
(٣٣ : ٤٥ - ٤٨)

O Prophet! Truly we have sent you as a witness, a bearer of glad tidings, and a warner, and as one who invites to God's grace by His leave, and as a lamp spreading light. Then give the glad tidings to the believers that they shall have from God a very great bounty. And obey not the behests of the unbelievers and the hypocrites, and heed not their annoyances, but put your trust in God. For enough is God as a Disposer of Affairs. (33:45-48)

29

We have also been told in the Qur'an that Muhammad (pbuh) was a mortal Messenger like any other Messenger. After all, he was a man chosen by God to deliver His message. In this regard Allah says in Surah Al-Imran (The Family of Imran), the following:

$$\text{وَمَا مُحَمَّدٌ إِلَّا رَسُولٌ قَدْ خَلَتْ مِن قَبْلِهِ الرُّسُلُ}$$

Muhammad is no more than an Apostle: many were the Apostle that passed away before him. *(3:144)*

$$\text{إِنَّكَ مَيِّتٌ وَإِنَّهُم مَّيِّتُونَ}$$

Truly you will die (one day), and truly they (too) will die (one day). (39:30)

IV. Final Remarks

Finally, we are told that Muhammad (pbuh) was sent as a last prophet to mankind. He was the last and the seal of prophets and he was to complete the series of messages to mankind. In Surah Al-Ahzab (The Confederates), Allah says the following:

$$\text{مَّا كَانَ مُحَمَّدٌ أَبَا أَحَدٍ مِّن رِّجَالِكُمْ وَلَٰكِن رَّسُولَ اللَّهِ وَخَاتَمَ النَّبِيِّنَ}$$
$$\text{وَكَانَ اللَّهُ بِكُلِّ شَيْءٍ عَلِيمًا}$$
(٣٣ : ٤٠)

Muhammad is not the father of any of your men, but he is the Apostle of God, and the Seal of the Prophets: and God has full of knowledge of all things. (33:40)

30

In sending Prophet Muhammad (pbuh), Allah has completed His favor upon mankind, perfected His religion to mankind and chosen Islam as a way of life to mankind to abide by and to live accordingly. In this respect Allah says in the Qur'an in Surah Al-Maa-idah (Table Spread) the following:

اَلْيَوْمَ أَكْمَلْتُ لَكُمْ دِينَكُمْ وَأَتْمَمْتُ عَلَيْكُمْ نِعْمَتِي وَرَضِيتُ لَكُمُ الإِسْلَامَ دِينًا

This day have I perfected your religion for you, completed My favor upon you, and have chosen for you Islam as your religion... (5:3)

Through this type of approach, in attempting to present a picture of the Prophet Muhammad (pbuh) according to the Qur'an, it is hoped that an interest is generated in the believers of the Prophet Muhammad (pbuh) to read more about him in the Qur'an and in the Hadith. Moreover, Muslims should read about the Sirah of the Prophet (pbuh) from the time he was born till the time he died and went back to Allah (swt). Reading is not enough but studying with different Muslims scholars is necessary. One has to add here that one has to associate himself with scholars on a daily basis so as to practice what he learned. May Allah bless us all and accept our humble prayers. Ameen.

There is No Deity except Allah,
And Muhammad is the
Messenger Of Allah.

Chapter (5) **Family Tree Of Prophet Muhammad**

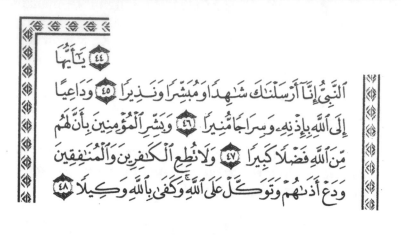

Al-Ahzab: The Confederates

O Prophet! Truly We have sent you as a Witness, a Bearer of Glad Tidings, and a Warner and as one who invites to Allah's (Grace) by His leave and as a (Siraj Muneer) Lamp Spreading Light. Then give the glad tidings to the Believers, that they shall have from Allah a very great Bounty. And obey not the (behest) of the Unbelievers and the Hypocrites, and disregards their insolence but put your trust in Allah. For enough is Allah as a Disposer of affairs. (33:45-48)

I. Introduction

Allah says about Prophet Muhammad in Surah Al-Tawbah (Repentance) the following:

$$لَقَدْ جَآءَكُمْ رَسُولٌ مِّنْ أَنفُسِكُمْ ۝ عَزِيزٌ عَلَيْهِ مَا عَنِتُّمْ حَرِيصٌ عَلَيْكُم بِالْمُؤْمِنِينَ رَءُوفٌ رَّحِيمٌ ۝$$

Now has come unto you a Messenger from amongst yourselves: it grieves him that you should suffer, ardently anxious is he over you: to the Believers is he most kind and merciful. (9:128)

It was felt necessary to present the family tree of Prophet Muhammad. The lineage of the Prophet of Islam goes to Prophets Isma'il and Ibrahim. It was a known fact that Prophet Ibrahim took his wife Hajar and their son Isma'il from Palestine to Makkah. They settled there. Prophet Ibrahim rebuilt the Ka'bah with his son Isma'il. He prayed to Allah to bless mankind through the offspring of Isma'il. That prayer (Du`aa') was heard and recorded by Allah. His Du`aa' was answered after 2,800 years. Prophet Muhammad was sent as a Mercy to all the creatures of the worlds.

Muhammad was born as an orphan. His father died when his mother, Aminah, was seven months pregnant. His midwife's name was Al-Shifa' (the healer). His nursing mother was Haleemah Al-Sa'diyah. His baby-sitter's name was Barakah Umm Ayman. His grandfather, Abdul-Muttalib took care of him. His grandfather died when Muhammad was five (5) years old. Therefore, his uncle Abu-

33

Talib took care of him. However, his mother died when Muhammad was seven (7) years old. Hence, his Aunt, the wife of Abu-Talib took care of him. Her name was Fatimah Bint Asad, and she was the mother of Ali Ibn Abi Talib.

II. Lineage

From the chart, one can realize that the lineage of Prophet Muhammad goes from Abdullah, Abdul Muttalib, Hashim Abd Manaf, Qusay, Hakeem, Murrah, Ka'b, Lu'ay, Ghalib, Quraish, Ismai'il and finally to Ibrahim.

His lineage from his mother, Aminah, goes also to Isma'il and Ibrahim through a similar route. It is not a coincident but the decision of Allah that the lineage of both the father and the mother go back to prophets Isma'il and Ibrahim. See next page a chart of the Family Tree of Prophet Muhammad.

III. Final Remarks

Family Lineage is very important biologically and socially. Every person should be able to trace his linage for a good number of generations. Without a Family Tree, one will be an insignificant person on this planet. In animal zoos, each animal does have a lineage that has been recorded by those who maintain the zoo.

Allah did answer the prayer of Prophet Ibrahim after purifying the genes and the DNA's of his offspring till Muhammad came. Allah brought Muhammad as the best human being on this planet. His genes were pure, and he was considered as a role model to all humanity at large.

FAMILY TREE OF PROPHET MUHAMMAD

FATHER'S SIDE	MOTHER'S SIDE
Ibrahim	Ibrahim
Isma'il	Isma'il
Adnan	Adnan
Ma'add	Ma'add
Nadhar	Nadhar
Mudar	Mudar
Ilyas	Ilyas
Mudrikah	Mudrikah
Khuzaymah	Khuzaymah
Kinanah	Kinanah
Al-Nadar	Al-Nadar
Malik	Malik
Fihr	Fihr
Ghalib	Ghalib
Lu'ayy	Lu'ayy
Ka'ab	
Murrah	
Hakeem	Hakeem
Qusayy	Zahra
Abd Manaf	Abd Manaf
Hashim	
Abdul Muttalib	Wahab

Abdullah	Aminah

MUHAMMAD

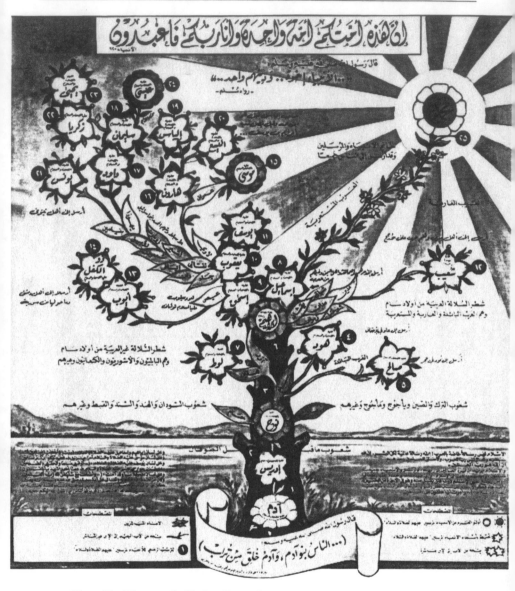

**Family Tree of all the Prophets from the Day of Adam
until the Day of Prophet Muhammad (peace be upon them)**

محمد رسول السلام

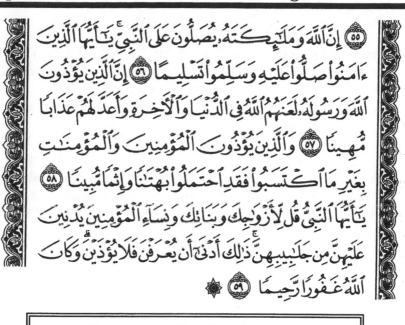

Al-Ahzab: The Confederates

Lo! Allah and His angels send blessings on the Prophet. O you who believe! Send your blessings on him and salute him with all respect. Those who annoy Allah and His Messenger, Allah has cursed them in this world and in the Hereafter, and has prepared for them a humiliating Punishment. And those who annoy believing men and women undeservedly, bear (on themselves) a calumny and a glaring sin. O Prophet! Tell your wives and daughters, and the believing women, that they should cast their outer garments over their persons (when out of doors): That is most convenient, that they should be known (as such) and not molested. And Allah is Oft-Forgiving, Most Merciful. (33:56-59)

36

I. Introduction

The subject of my talk is "Muhammad The Messenger of Peace." The word PEACE HAS BEEN MENTIONED IN THE Qur'an about 138 in 39 different forms and in 47 different Surahs. The subject is very important in every person's life. Each and every one wants to live in peace and harmony. Many were seeking peace through wrong channels and were unable to find it.

As you are aware, the religion of Islam is the religion of peace, and Muslims are those who try to live in peace in all aspects of life. One of Allah's Attributes is that He is THE PEACE. Prophet Muhammad (pbuh) came with the Message of Peace, I.E. the Message of Islam.

II. Message of Peace

I will try to summarize the highlights of the Message of Peace that Prophet Muhammad came with:

1. Allah (swt) invites people to live in peace and harmony. He who accepts the invitation will be guided by Allah (swt). The Qur'an states in Surah Yunus the following:

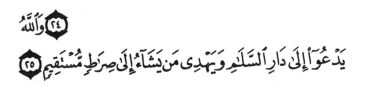

"And God does call to the Home of Peace: He does guide whom He pleases to a Way that is straight." (10:25)

37

2. Believers are invited to enter into peace. The Qur'an states in
    Surah Al-Baqarah (The Cow) the following:

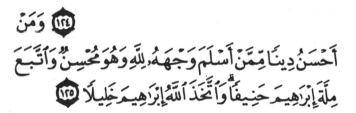

> *"O you who believe! enter into Islam whole-*
> *heartedly; and follow not the footsteps of the Evil One;*
> *for he is to you an avowed enemy."* *(2:208)*

3. The peace that Prophet Muhammad (pbuh) invited us to is
    the one which is for every aspect of our life such as:

a. Peace with the Creator: He Who establishes peace with the
    Creator will receive blessings. Allah says in the Qur'an in
    Surah Al-Nisaa (The Women) the following:

> *Who can be better in religion than one who submits*
> *his whole self to Allah, and does good..."* *(4:125)*

b. Peace within the self: He who follows Islam will be guided and will live in peace and harmony. He will not have a split personality or to be mentally disturbed. Allah says in Surah Al-Ma'idah (The Table Spread) the following:

وَقَالَتِ ٱلۡيَهُودُ وَٱلنَّصَرَىٰ نَحۡنُ أَبۡنَٰٓؤُاْ ٱللَّهِ وَأَحِبَّٰٓؤُهُۥ قُلۡ فَلِمَ يُعَذِّبُكُم بِذُنُوبِكُم بَلۡ أَنتُم بَشَرٌ مِّمَّنۡ خَلَقَ يَغۡفِرُ لِمَن يَشَآءُ وَيُعَذِّبُ مَن يَشَآءُ وَلِلَّهِ مُلۡكُ ٱلسَّمَٰوَٰتِ وَٱلۡأَرۡضِ وَمَا بَيۡنَهُمَا وَإِلَيۡهِ ٱلۡمَصِيرُ ۝

"Wherewith Allah guides all who seek His good pleasure to ways of peace and safety, and leads them out of darkness by His Will, unto the light, --guides them to a Path that is straight." (5:18)

c. The other types of peace that Prophet (pbuh) brought through Islam is Peace with spouses, Peace between parents and children, Peace with the extended families, Peace with neighbors, Peace with the society, Peace with other societies, Peace with other creatures, Peace with other Prophets, and Peace with the Environment.

The Message of Peace that our beloved Prophet (pbuh) brought is also a Message of Peace beyond this life. Peace in the Grave and Peace in Paradise. We are informed by the Prophet (pbuh) that the life in the grave is a life of peace and happiness or a life of penalty and distress. The grave is a place in Paradise or a ditch in hell.

As far as the Peace in Paradise is concerned, we are told that the residence of the believers in Paradise is called the House of Peace (Dar Assalam). Allah (swt) says in Surah Al-An'am (The Cattles):

"For them will be a Home of Peace in the presence of their Lord: He will be their Friend, because they practiced (righteousness)." (6:127)

For those who are to live in Paradise, will be welcomed with Peace. Allah (swt) informs us in Surah Al-Zumar (The Crowds) the following:

وَسِيقَ ٱلَّذِينَ ٱتَّقَوْا۟ رَبَّهُمْ إِلَى ٱلْجَنَّةِ زُمَرًا حَتَّىٰٓ إِذَا جَآءُوهَا وَفُتِحَتْ أَبْوَٰبُهَا وَقَالَ لَهُمْ خَزَنَتُهَا سَلَٰمٌ عَلَيْكُمْ طِبْتُمْ فَٱدْخُلُوهَا خَٰلِدِينَ

And those who feared their Lord will be led to the Garden in groups until behold, they arrive there; it gates will be opened; and its Keepers will say: "Peace be upon you! Well have you done! You enter here to dwell therein. (39:73)

Those who are to live in Paradise are to be greeted daily with the greeting of Peace. The Qur'an states in Surah Ibrahim the following:

40

وَأُدۡخِلَ ٱلَّذِينَ ءَامَنُواْ وَعَمِلُواْ ٱلصَّـٰلِحَـٰتِ جَنَّـٰتٍ ٢٢
تَجۡرِى مِن تَحۡتِهَا ٱلۡأَنۡهَـٰرُ خَـٰلِدِينَ فِيهَا بِإِذۡنِ رَبِّهِمۡ تَحِيَّتُهُمۡ
فِيهَا سَلَـٰمٌ ٢٣

"...to dwell therein for aye with the leave of their
Lord. Their greeting therein will be." Peace!" (14:23)

The Message of Prophet Muhammad (pbuh) was the Message
of Peace with Justice. It has its universal standards that emitted
from the source of Peace, namely Allah (swt). Peace can only be
established if all the segments of life, death, hereafter and universe
are taken into consideration. It should be stated here that creatures
in the whole universe submitted themselves willingly to the Will of
Allah and are living in Peace, Concord and Harmony. The Qur'an
states the following in Surah Al'Imran (The Family of Imran).

أَفَغَيۡرَ دِينِ ٱللَّهِ يَبۡغُونَ وَلَهُۥٓ أَسۡلَمَ مَن فِى ٱلسَّمَـٰوَٰتِ
وَٱلۡأَرۡضِ طَوۡعًا وَكَرۡهًا وَإِلَيۡهِ يُرۡجَعُونَ ٨٣

Do they seek for other than the Religion of Allah?-
while all creatures in the heavens and on earth have,
willing or unwilling, bowed to His will (accepted Islam).
And to Him shall they all be brought back. (3:83)

There are hundreds of millions of people in the world who are
searching for Peace and Tranquility. They will never attain Peace
till they accept the Religion of Peace namely Islam. Therefore, it is

the responsibility of the Muslims who have already accepted Islam to bring peace. It is also their responsibility to establish peace in every society they dwell in.

III. Final Remark

We hope and pray that we will try our best to live in peace so that we earn the pleasure and the Blessings of Allah (swt). We hope we are among those whom Allah has already accepted and is pleased with. Allah (swt) says in the Qur'an in Surah Al-Baiyah (The Clear Evidence) the following:

$$جَزَآؤُهُمْ عِندَ رَبِّهِمْ جَنَّـٰتُ عَدْنٍ تَجْرِى مِن تَحْتِهَا ٱلْأَنْهَـٰرُ خَـٰلِدِينَ فِيهَآ أَبَدًا ۚ رَّضِىَ ٱللَّهُ عَنْهُمْ وَرَضُوا۟ عَنْهُ ۚ ذَٰلِكَ لِمَنْ خَشِىَ رَبَّهُۥ ۝$$

"...God will be pleased with them, and they with Him: All this for such as fear their Lord and Cherisher." (98:8)

Let us ask Allah for His Guidance, His Mercy, and His Forgiveness. Ameen.

That is indeed a Qur'an most honorable,
In a Book well-guarded...
[Qur'an, 56:77-78]

صفات الرسول (ص)

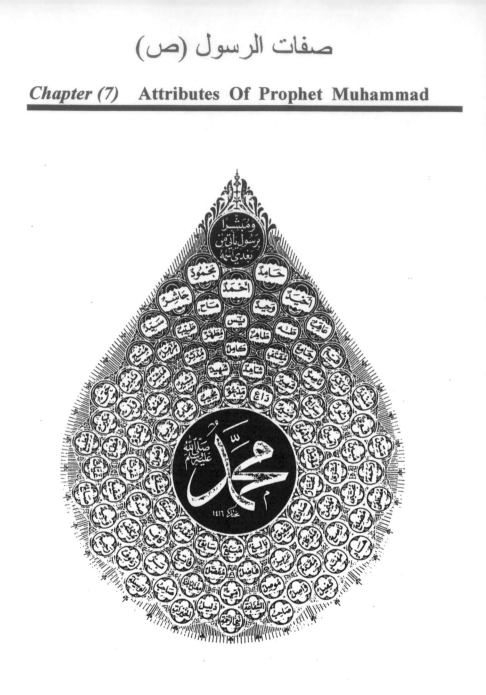

Attributes Of Prophet Muhammad

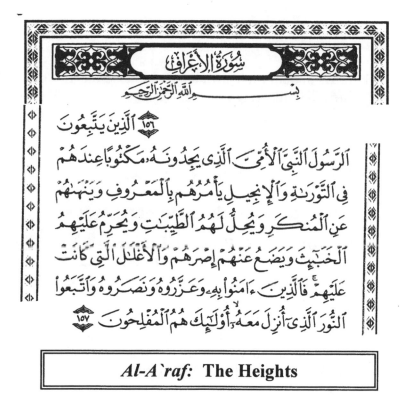

Al-A`raf: The Heights

Those who follow the Messenger, the unlettered Prophet, whom they find mentioned in their own (Scriptures), in the Taurat and the Gospel; for he commands them what is just and forbids them what is evil; he allows them as lawful what is good (and pure) and prohibits them from what is bad (and impure); He releases them from their heavy burdens and from the yokes that are upon them. So it is those who believe in him, honor him, help him, and follow the Light which is sent down with him, it is they who will prosper. (7:157)

I. Introduction

Allah says about Prophet Muhammad in Surah Al-Ahzab (The Confederates) the following:

يَٰٓأَيُّهَا ٤٤

ٱلنَّبِيُّ إِنَّآ أَرْسَلْنَٰكَ شَٰهِدًا وَمُبَشِّرًا وَنَذِيرًا ٤٥ وَدَاعِيًا

إِلَى ٱللَّهِ بِإِذْنِهِۦ وَسِرَاجًا مُّنِيرًا ٤٦

O Prophet! Truly We have sent you as a Witness, a Bearer of Glad Tidings, and a Warner, and as one who invites to Allah's (grace) by His leave, and as a lamp spreading light. (33:45-46)

Prophet Muhammad was chosen by Allah to deliver the Message of Islam to all creatures. He was honored by Allah in making him the Final Prophet and the Final Messenger. His name is annexed with the Name of Allah in many aspects of life and especially with the Pledge of Allegiance and Obedience, i.e., La Ilaha Illa Allah, and Muhammad is Rasullullah. In the Qur'an, Allah gave Prophet Muhammad many adjectives, attributes and qualities. Some of them are mirror images of Allah's Attributes. However, Allah's Beautiful Names are recognized as The Most ---, etc. while Prophet Muhammad is recognized as a..., a...., and a...

If one goes through the Qur'an, he will find numerous adjectives and attributes given by Allah to Prophet Muhammad. Each and every quality reflects his personality, his entity and his innate beauty and mercy to all living creatures.

44

II. Attributes

The only way to recognize Prophet Muhammad is to study the Qur'an and find out how Allah addressed him with all the beautiful names, attributes and adjectives.

A. Kind and Merciful

1. In one place in the Qur'an in Surah Al-Tawbah (Repentance) Allah says in the following Surah:

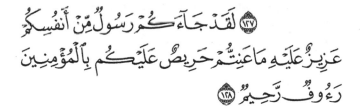

Now has come unto you a Messenger from amongst yourselves: it grieves him that you should suffer, ardently anxious is he over you: to the Believers is he most kind and merciful. (9:128)

2. Also, Allah says about Prophet Muhammad the following in Surah Al-Anbiyaa' (The Prophets):

وَمَآ أَرْسَلْنَـٰكَ إِلَّا رَحْمَةً لِّلْعَـٰلَمِينَ ۝

We sent you not, but as a Mercy for all creatures. (21:107)

B. Best Example

However, in Surah Al-Ahzab (The Confederates) Allah explained to the Muslims that the Prophet Muhammad was the best example for them to follow. The Qur'an states the following:

اللَّهَ حَسَنَةٌ ۝ لَّقَدْ كَانَ لَكُمْ فِي رَسُولِ اللَّهِ أُسْوَةٌ حَسَنَةٌ

لِمَن كَانَ يَرْجُوا اللَّهَ وَالْيَوْمَ الْآخِرَ وَذَكَرَ اللَّهَ كَثِيرًا ۝

You have indeed in the Messenger of Allah an excellent example. For him who hopes in Allah and the Final Day, and who remember Allah much. (33:21)

C. Last Messenger

This chapter is not designed to explain the details about the personality of the Prophet, and all the degrees of honors that he received from Allah. However, it should be stated here that Muhammad is the Last Prophet and the Last Messenger from Allah to all the creatures of the universe. In Surah Al-Ahzab (The Coalition) the Qur'an states the following:

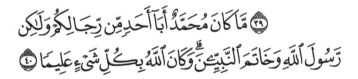

مَّا كَانَ مُحَمَّدٌ أَبَآ أَحَدٍ مِّن رِّجَالِكُمْ وَلَٰكِن

رَّسُولَ اللَّهِ وَخَاتَمَ النَّبِيِّنَ وَكَانَ اللَّهُ بِكُلِّ شَيْءٍ عَلِيمًا ۝

Muhammad is not the father of any of your men, but (he is) the Messenger of Allah, and the Seal of the

46

Prophets. And Allah has full knowledge of all things.
(33:40)

Different authors have selected different numbers of attributes about the prophet. The least number is fifty (50) and the most is 201. The author of this book is presenting the least number so as to be on the conservative side. The author requests the readers to go through these attributes and then try to imitate the Prophet in his private and public life.

NAMES OF PROPHET MUHAMMAD

Transliteration	Arabic	English
Ahmad	احمد	Commendable, Praise-worthy
Ameer	أمير	Commander
Ameen	أمين	Trustworthy
Basheer	بشير	Bringer of Good News
Jawwad	جواد	Generous
Hamid	حامد	Praising
Habibullah	حبيب الله	Beloved of God
Khatim	خاتم	Last, Seal
Khaleel	خليل	Friend
Daa'ee	داع	Inviter
Siraj	سراج	Lamp
Sayyid	سيد	Chief, Leader
Shafee	شافي	Healing
Shaheed	شاهد	Witness
Shaheer	شهير	Famous
Sadiq	صادق	Truthful
Safiy-Allah	صفى الله	The pure one of God
Tayyib	طيب	Good
'Adil	عادل	Just
'Aqib	عاقب	End, Goal
Abdullah	عبدالله	Servant of God

47

NAMES OF PROPHET MUHAMMAD (Continued)

Transliteration	Arabic	English
Fatih	ناتح	Opener, Conqueror
Qasim	قاسم	Distributor
Qareeb	قريب	Near, Close
Ma'moon	مأمون	Trusted
Mubashshir	مبشر	Spreader of Good News
Mubeen	مبين	Evident
Mateen	متين	Firm
Mujtaba	مجتبى	Selected
Muharram	محرم	Sacred
Muhammad	محمد	Praiseworthy, Commendable
Mahmood	محمود	Praiseworthy
Mad'oo	مدعو	Called
Mudhakkir	مذكر	Reminder
Murtada	مرتضى	Agreeable
Mashhood	مشهود	Attested, Proven
Musaddiq	مصدق	One who attests to the truth
Mustafa	مصطفى	Chosen
Mutahhar	مطهر	Purifier
Mutee'	مطيع	Obedient
Ma'loom	معلوم	Known
Muqtasid	مقتصد	Intelligent
Mukarram	مكرم	Honoured
Munajjee	منج	Rescuer
Mansoor	منصور	Victorious
Muneer	منير	Radiant
Mahdee	مهدى	Guided
Nahee	ناهى	Prohibitor
Nadheer	نذير	Warner
Hadee	هادى	Guide

48

III. Final Remarks

Prophet Muhammad was chosen by Allah to be the last Prophet and last Messenger. Allah molded him and shaped him to be the best example to be followed. Muslims try their best to mimic his personality, his character, his manners and his behavior in life. By so doing they will live in peace and harmony. Muslims try to study the life history of the Prophet as a child, as a youth, as a businessman, as a husband, as a father, as a grand father, as a prophet, as a statesman, and as a leader to humanity at large. The more Muslims study the attributes of the prophet, the more they will live peacefully among themselves and among the non-Muslims. Therefore, every one should go and study the Attributes of the Prophet. Ameen.

Moreover, to mimic and to practice some of the qualities of the Prophet, one has to associate himself with a series of scholars on a daily basis. One will be able to benefit from their different qualities that are complimentary to one another. Hence he would be able to practice them at a young age. Youth should be the ones who should look for the Muslim scholars to associate with them as soon as possible. The scholars should <u>Not</u> run after the youth from house to house, rather the youth should run after the scholars and be with them as much as possible. May Allah bless us all. Ameen

When you went to your garden, you should have said: There is no
power but with Allah... Qur'an (18:39)

49

Chapter (8)   What The Prophet Said About Himself

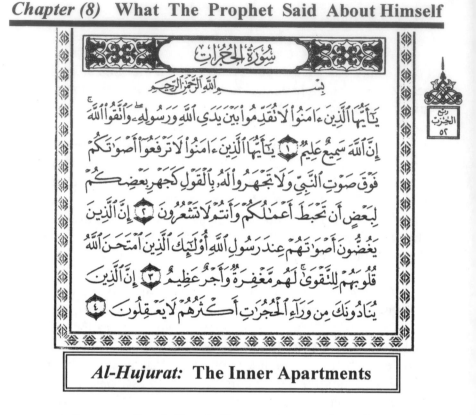

سُورَةُ الحُجُرَاتِ

بِسْمِ اللَّهِ الرَّحْمَنِ الرَّحِيمِ

يَـٰٓأَيُّهَا ٱلَّذِينَ ءَامَنُوا۟ لَا تُقَدِّمُوا۟ بَيْنَ يَدَيِ ٱللَّهِ وَرَسُولِهِۦ وَٱتَّقُوا۟ ٱللَّهَ إِنَّ ٱللَّهَ سَمِيعٌ عَلِيمٌ ۝ يَـٰٓأَيُّهَا ٱلَّذِينَ ءَامَنُوا۟ لَا تَرْفَعُوٓا۟ أَصْوَٰتَكُمْ فَوْقَ صَوْتِ ٱلنَّبِيِّ وَلَا تَجْهَرُوا۟ لَهُۥ بِٱلْقَوْلِ كَجَهْرِ بَعْضِكُمْ لِبَعْضٍ أَن تَحْبَطَ أَعْمَٰلُكُمْ وَأَنتُمْ لَا تَشْعُرُونَ ۝ إِنَّ ٱلَّذِينَ يَغُضُّونَ أَصْوَٰتَهُمْ عِندَ رَسُولِ ٱللَّهِ أُو۟لَـٰٓئِكَ ٱلَّذِينَ ٱمْتَحَنَ ٱللَّهُ قُلُوبَهُمْ لِلتَّقْوَىٰ لَهُم مَّغْفِرَةٌ وَأَجْرٌ عَظِيمٌ ۝ إِنَّ ٱلَّذِينَ يُنَادُونَكَ مِن وَرَآءِ ٱلْحُجُرَٰتِ أَكْثَرُهُمْ لَا يَعْقِلُونَ ۝

Al-Hujurat: The Inner Apartments

O you who believe! Put not yourselves forward before Allah and His Messenger; but fear Allah: for Allah is He Who hears and knows all things. O you who believe! Raise not your voices above the voice of the Prophet, nor speak aloud to him in talk, as you may speak aloud to one another, lest your deeds become vain and you perceive not. Those that lower their voice in the presence of Allah's Messenger, their hearts has Allah tested for piety: for them is forgiveness and a great Reward. Those who shout to you from without The Inner Apartments-most of them lack understanding. (49:1-4)

The following is a partial list of information about Prophet Muhammad (pbuh), and what He said about himself:

I. Hadith No (1)

A. Arabic Text

اِنّي فِيمَا لَم يُوحَى اِليَّ كَأَحَدِكُم.

(الطبراني)

B. English Translation

"I am just like [any] one of you [in the matters] that were not revealed to me [by God]" (Reported by at-Tabarani)

II. Hadith No (2)

A. Arabic Text

عَنْ أبي هُرَيْرَةَ أنَّ رَسُولَ اللّهِ صَلَّى اللّهُ عَلَيْهِ وَسَلَّمَ قالَ فُضِّلتُ عَلَى الأنْبِيَاء بِسِتّ: أعْطِيتُ جَوَامِعَ الكَلِمِ وَنُصِرْتُ بالرُّعْبِ وَأحِلَّتْ لِيَ الغَنَائِمُ وَجُعِلَتْ لِيَ الأرْضُ طَهُورًا وَمَسْجِدًا وَأرْسِلتُ إلى الخَلْقِ كَافَّة وَخُتِمَ بِيَ النَّبِيُّونَ.

(مسلم)

B. English Translation

Abu Huraira narrated: *"the Messenger of Allah (pbuh) said: 'I have been given superiority over the other prophets in six respects: I have been given words which are concise but comprehensive in meaning; I have been helped by terror (in the hearts of enemies);*

51

spoils have been made lawful to me; the earth has been made for me clean and a place of worship; I have been sent to all mankind; and the line of prophets is sealed with me. (Reported by Muslim)

III. Hadith No (3)

A. Arabic Text

أَدَّبَنِي رَبِّي فَأَحسَنَ تَأديِبِي.
(العسكري وابن السمعاني)

B. English Translation

"My Lord has cultivated my manners so [indeed] He excelled in my formation." (al-Askari & Ibn as-Sam'ani)

IV. Hadith No (4)

A. Arabic Text

عَنْ أَبِي هُرَيْرَةَ رَضِيَ اللَّهُ عَنْهُ عَنِ النَّبِيِّ صَلَّى اللَّهُ عَلَيْهِ وَسَلَّمَ قَالَ مَا بَعَثَ اللَّهُ نَبِيًّا إلا رَعَى الْغَنَمَ فقالَ أَصْحَابُهُ وَأَنتَ فَقالَ نَعَمْ كُنْتُ أَرْعَاهَا عَلَى قَرَارِيطَ لأَهْلِ مَكَّةَ.
(رواه البخاري)

B. English Translation

Abu Hurayrah (may Allah be pleased with him) narrated that *the Prophet (pbuh) said: "Whenever Allah sent a prophet, he made*

*him herd sheep (and goats)" His companions said: "And you?"
[the Prophet] said: "Yes, I used to herd them with pennies for the
inhabitants of Makkah."* (Reported by al-Bukhari)

V. Hadith No (5)

A. Arabic Text

أَنَا حَبِيبُ اللَّهِ وَلا فَخْرَ وَأَنَا حَامِلُ لِوَاءِ الْحَمْدِ يَوْمَ الْقِيَامَةِ وَلا
فَخْرَ وَأَنَا أَوَّلُ شَافِعٍ وَأَوَّلُ مُشَفَّعٍ يَوْمَ الْقِيَامَةِ وَلا فَخْرَ وَأَنَا أَوَّلُ مَنْ
يُحَرِّكُ حِلَقَ الْجَنَّةِ فَيَفْتَحُ اللَّهُ لِي فَيُدْخِلُنِيهَا وَمَعِي فُقَرَاءُ الْمُؤْمِنِينَ
وَلا فَخْرَ وَأَنَا أَكْرَمُ الْأَوَّلِينَ وَالْآخِرِينَ وَلا فَخْرَ.   (الترمذي)

B. English Translation

*I am the "beloved to Allah" and I am not arrogant about it. I [will
be] carrying the Banner of Praise on the Day of Judgment
whereby Adam will stand below it and those after him. I am not
arrogant about it. I am the first intercessor and first preemptor on
the Day of Judgment, and I am not arrogant about it. I am the first
who will move the rings of paradise over which Allah will open it
and make me enter it with the impoverished and the believers, and
I am not arrogant about it. And I am the most noble among those
[who are] first and those [who are] last towards Allah, and I am
not arrogant about it.* (Reported by at-Tirmidhi.)

There is no god but Allah, and Muhammad is the Messenger of Allah.

53

VI. Hadith No (6)

A. Arabic Text

عَنْ أَنَس قَالَ قَالَ النَّبِيُّ صَلَّى اللَّهُ عَلَيْهِ وَسَلَّمَ لا يُؤْمِنُ أَحَدُكُمْ حَتَّى أَكُونَ
أَحَبَّ إِلَيْهِ مِنْ وَالِدِهِ وَوَلَدِهِ وَالنَّاس أَجْمَعِين. (رواه البخاري)

B. English Translation

Anas narrated: *the Prophet (pbuh) said: "none of you will attain faith until I become more beloved to him than his own father, his children and all of humankind."* (Reported by al-Bukhari)

VII. Hadith No (7)

A. Arabic Text

عَنْ أَبِي هُرَيْرَةَ قَالَ قَالَ رَسُولُ اللَّهِ صَلَّى اللَّهُ عَلَيْهِ وَسَلَّمَ إِنَّمَا بُعِثْتُ لأُتَمِّمَ
صَالِحَ الأَخْلاق.
(أحمد)

B. English Translation

Abu Huraira narrated: *the Messenger of Allah (pbuh) said: "I was indeed sent to perfect (and complete) noble manners".* (Reported by Ahmad)

VIII. Hadith No (8)

A. Arabic Text

عَنْ أَبِي هُرَيْرَةَ قَالَ قِيلَ يَا رَسُولَ اللَّهِ ادْعُ عَلَى الْمُشْرِكِينَ قَالَ إِنِّي لَمْ أُبْعَثْ لَعَّانًا وَإِنَّمَا بُعِثْتُ رَحْمَةً.

(مسلم)

B. English Translation

Abu Huraira narrated: *"It was said O Messenger of Allah curse the unbelievers. He said: 'I was not sent as a cursor but instead I was sent as a mercy [to mankind].'"* (Reported by Muslim)

IX. Hadith No (9)

A. Arabic Text

سَعْدِ بْنِ هِشَامِ بْنِ عَامِرٍ قَالَ أَتَيْتُ عَائِشَةَ فَقُلْتُ يَا أُمَّ الْمُؤْمِنِينَ أَخْبِرِينِي بِخُلُقِ رَسُولِ اللَّهِ صَلَّى اللَّهُ عَلَيْهِ وَسَلَّمَ قَالَتْ كَانَ خُلُقُهُ الْقُرْآنَ.

(أحمد)

B. English Translation

Sa`ad Ibn Hisham bin Aamir narrated: *"I came to `Aisha and I said: 'O mother of the believers, tell me about the character of the Messenger of Allah (pbuh)', she said: 'his character (mannerism) was the Qur'an.'"* (Reported by Ahmad)

55

X. Hadith No (10)

A. Arabic Text

عَنْ أَبِي سَعِيدٍ الخُدْرِيِّ رَضِيَ اللَّهُ عَنْهُ قَالَ كَانَ النَّبِيُّ صَلَّى اللَّهُ عَلَيْهِ وَسَلَّمَ
أَشَدَّ حَيَاءً مِنَ العَذْرَاءِ فِي خِدْرِهَا حَدَّثَنِي مُحَمَّدُ بْنُ بَشَّارٍ حَدَّثَنَا يَحْيَى وَابْنُ
مَهْدِيٍّ قَالا حَدَّثَنَا شُعْبَةُ مِثْلَهُ وَإِذَا كَرِهَ شَيْئًا عُرِفَ فِي وَجْهِهِ.
(متفق عليه)

B. English Translation

Abu Saeed al-Khudry (may Allah be pleased with him) said:
*"The Messenger of Allah (pbuh) was more modest than the Virgin
(i.e. Maryam, mother of Jesus) [when she was] in her private
quarter; and when he saw something that he disliked we knew it
from his face.* (Agreed upon)

XI. Hadith No (11)

A. Arabic Text

قَالَ أَنَسٌ كَانَ رَسُولُ اللَّهِ صَلَّى اللَّهُ عَلَيْهِ وَسَلَّمَ مِنْ أَحْسَنِ النَّاسِ خُلُقًا.
(متفق عليه)

B. English Translation

Anas may Allah be please with him said: *"the Messenger of
Allah (pbuh) was the best mannered person from among the
people."* (Agree Upon)

XII. Hadith No (12)

A. Arabic Text

عَنْ أَنَسٍ رَضِيَ اللَّهُ عَنْهُ قَالَ مَا مَسِسْتُ حَرِيرًا وَلا دِيبَاجًا أَلْيَنَ مِنْ كَفِّ
النَّبِيِّ صَلَّى اللَّهُ عَلَيْهِ وَسَلَّمَ وَلا شَمِمْتُ رِيحًا قَطُّ أَوْ عَرْقًا قَطُّ أَطْيَبَ مِنْ رِيح
أَوْ عَرْقِ النَّبِيِّ صَلَّى اللَّهُ عَلَيْهِ وَسَلَّمَ ولقد خَدَمْتُ النَّبِيَّ صَلَّى اللَّهُ عَلَيْهِ وَسَلَّمَ
عَشْرَ سِنِينَ فَمَا قَالَ لِي أُفٍّ قَطُّ وَمَا قَالَ لِشَيْءٍ صَنَعْتُهُ لِمَ صَنَعْتَهُ وَلا لِشَيْءٍ
تَرَكْتُهُ لِمَ تَرَكْتَهُ.
(متفق عليه)

B. English Translation

Anas may Allah be pleased with him said: *"I have never touched a brocade (from silk) or silk which is softer than the palm of the Messenger of Allah (pbuh), and I have never smelled a scent or sweat more pleasant than the scent of the Messenger of Allah (pbuh); I had attended to the Messenger of Allah (pbuh) for ten years and he never expressed [the slightest sign of] discontent, and never told me about something I did: 'why did you do this?' nor [did he tell me regarding] anything I didn't do: "why didn't you do it?'"* (Agreed upon)

XIII. Hadith No (13)

A. Arabic Text

عَنْ عَائِشَةَ رَحِمَهَا اللَّهُ قَالَتْ كَانَ كَلامُ رَسُولِ اللَّهِ صَلَّى اللَّهُ عَلَيْهِ وَسَلَّمَ
كَلامًا فَصْلا يَفْهَمُهُ كُلُّ مَنْ سَمِعَهُ.
(أبو داوود)

B. English Translation

`Aisha (may Allah be pleased with her) said: *The words (or speech) of the Messenger of Allah (pbuh) was comprehensible (unambiguous), whoever listens to it does understand it.*
(Reported by Abou Dawood)

XIV.   Hadith No (14)

A. Arabic Text

قَالَ أَنَسٌ كَانَ رَسُولُ اللَّهِ صَلَّى اللَّهُ عَلَيْهِ وَسَلَّمَ مِنْ أَحْسَنِ النَّاسِ خُلُقًا فَأَرْسَلَنِي يَوْمًا لِحَاجَةٍ فَقُلْتُ وَاللَّهِ لا أَذْهَبُ وَفِي نَفْسِي أَنْ أَذْهَبَ لِمَا أَمَرَنِي بِهِ نَبِيُّ اللَّهِ صَلَّى اللَّهُ عَلَيْهِ وَسَلَّمَ فَخَرَجْتُ حَتَّى أَمُرَّ عَلَى صِبْيَانٍ وَهُمْ يَلْعَبُونَ فِي السُّوقِ فَإِذَا رَسُولُ اللَّهِ صَلَّى اللَّهُ عَلَيْهِ وَسَلَّمَ قَدْ قَبَضَ بِقَفَايَ مِنْ وَرَائِي قَالَ فَنَظَرْتُ إِلَيْهِ وَهُوَ يَضْحَكُ فَقَالَ يَا أُنَيْسُ أَذَهَبْتَ حَيْثُ أَمَرْتُكَ قَالَ قُلْتُ نَعَمْ أَنَا أَذْهَبُ يَا رَسُولَ اللَّهِ قَالَ أَنَسٌ وَاللَّهِ لَقَدْ خَدَمْتُهُ تِسْعَ سِنِينَ مَا عَلِمْتُهُ قَالَ لِشَيْءٍ صَنَعْتُهُ لِمَ فَعَلْتَ كَذَا وَكَذَا أَوْ لِشَيْءٍ تَرَكْتُهُ هَلا فَعَلْتَ كَذَا وَكَذَا.
(مسلم)

B. English Translation

Anas may Allah be pleased with him said: *"Allah's Messenger (pbuh) had the best disposition amongst people. He sent me on an errand one day, and I said: 'By Allah, I would not go'. I had, however, this idea in my mind that I would do as Allah's Prophet (pbuh) had commanded me to do. I went out until I happened to come across children who had been playing in the marketplace. In the meanwhile, Allah's Messenger (pbuh) came there and he caught me by the back of my neck from behind me. As I looked*

*towards him I found him smiling and he said: 'O Unais, did you go
where I commanded you to go?' I said: 'Allah's Messenger, yes, I
am going'. Anas further said: I served him for nine years but I
know not that he ever said to me about a thing which I had done
'why did you do this or that?', or about a thing I had left 'why
didn't you do this or that?'"* (Reported by Muslim)

XV. Hadith No (15)

A. Arabic Text

كَانَ رَسُولُ اللَّهِ صلَّى اللَّهُ عَلَيْهِ وَسَلَّمَ طَوِيلَ الصَّمْتِ قَلِيلَ الضَّحِكِ.

(أحمد)

B. English Translation

*"The Messenger of Allah (pbuh) used to [have] long
[moments] of silence and laughed a little.* (Reported by Ahmad)

XVI. Hadith No (16)

A. Arabic Text

عَنْ عَائِشَةَ رَضِيَ اللَّهُ عَنْهَا قَالَتْ مَا رَأَيْتُ النَّبِيَّ صلَّى اللَّهُ عَلَيْهِ وَسَلَّمَ
مُسْتَجْمِعًا قَطُّ ضَاحِكًا حَتَّى أَرَى مِنْهُ لَهَوَاتِهِ إِنَّمَا كَانَ يَتَبَسَّمُ.

(البخاري)

B. English Translation

'Aisha (may Allah be pleased with her) narrated: *"I never saw the Prophet (pbuh) laughing loudly enough to enable me to see his uvula, but instead he used to only smile.* (Reported by Bukhari)

XVII. Hadith No (17)

A. Arabic Text

عَنْ عَائِشَةَ قَالَتْ كَانَ النَّبِيُّ صلَّى اللَّهُ عَلَيْهِ وَسَلَّمَ يُحِبُّ التَّيَمُّنَ مَا اسْتَطَاعَ فِي شَأْنِهِ كُلِّهِ فِي طُهُورِهِ وَتَرَجُّلِهِ وَتَنَعُّلِهِ.
(متفق عليه)

B. English Translation

'Aisha (may Allah be pleased with her) narrated: *the Messenger of Allah (pbuh) used to like to start with the right hand side in all of his affairs: in cleaning himself, in getting off, and in wearing shoes.* (Agreed upon)

XVIII. Hadith No (18)

A. Arabic Text

عَنْ عَائِشَةَ زَوْجِ النَّبِيِّ صَلَّى اللَّهُ عَلَيْهِ وَسَلَّمَ أَنَّهَا قَالَتْ مَا خُيِّرَ رَسُولُ اللَّهِ صَلَّى اللَّهُ عَلَيْهِ وَسَلَّمَ بَيْنَ أَمْرَيْنِ إِلا أَخَذَ أَيْسَرَهُمَا مَا لَمْ يَكُنْ إِثْمًا فَإِنْ كَانَ إِثْمًا كَانَ أَبْعَدَ النَّاسِ مِنْهُ وَمَا انْتَقَمَ رَسُولُ اللَّهِ صَلَّى اللَّهُ عَلَيْهِ وَسَلَّمَ لِنَفْسِهِ إِلا أَنْ تُنْتَهَكَ حُرْمَةُ اللَّهِ عَزَّ وَجَلَّ.
(البخاري ومسلم)

60

B. English Translation

'Aisha, the wife of the Prophet (pbuh) narrated that: *"Whenever Allah's Apostle was given the choice of one of two matters, he would choose the easier of the two, as long as it was not sinful to do so, but if it was sinful to do so, he would be, amongst all people, the one who would stay the most distant from it. Allah's Apostle never took revenge (over anybody) for his own sake but (he did) only when Allah's Legal Bindings were violated in which case he would take revenge for Allah's Sake.* (Reported by Bukhari & Muslim)

XIX. Hadith No (19)

A. Arabic Text

عَنْ الْبَرَاءِ بْنِ عَازِبٍ قَالَ كَانَ رَسُولُ اللَّهِ صَلَّى اللَّهُ عَلَيْهِ وَسَلَّمَ إِذَا أَوَى إِلَى فِرَاشِهِ نَامَ عَلَى شِقِّهِ الْأَيْمَنِ ثُمَّ قَالَ اللَّهُمَّ أَسْلَمْتُ نَفْسِي إِلَيْكَ وَوَجَّهْتُ وَجْهِي إِلَيْكَ وَفَوَّضْتُ أَمْرِي إِلَيْكَ وَأَلْجَأْتُ ظَهْرِي إِلَيْكَ رَغْبَةً وَرَهْبَةً إِلَيْكَ لا مَلْجَأَ وَلا مَنْجَا مِنْكَ إِلا إِلَيْكَ آمَنْتُ بِكِتَابِكَ الَّذِي أَنْزَلْتَ وَبِنَبِيِّكَ الَّذِي أَرْسَلْتَ وَقَالَ رَسُولُ اللَّهِ صَلَّى اللَّهُ عَلَيْهِ وَسَلَّمَ مَنْ قَالَهُنَّ ثُمَّ مَاتَ تَحْتَ لَيْلَتِه مَاتَ عَلَى الْفِطْرَةِ.
(رواه البخاري)

B. English Translation

Al-Baraa' Ibn 'Aazib (may Allah be pleased with both of them) narrated: *"Whenever the Messenger of Allah went to bed, he used to lie on his right side and say: 'O Allah! I surrender my soul to You and I position my face towards You and I entrust [all] my affairs to You and depend upon You for Your Blessings both with hope and fear of You. There is no fleeing from You, and there is no place of protection and safety except with You O Allah! I believe in Your Book (i.e. the Qur'an) which You have revealed and in Your Prophet (Muhammad) whom You have sent. Then the Messenger of Allah (pbuh) said that whoever repeats this and dies on that very night, he will die with faith (i.e. or the religion of Islam).* (Reported by Bukhari)

XX.   Hadith No (20)

A. Arabic Text

عَنْ أَبِي هُرَيْرَةَ أَنَّ النَّبِيَّ صَلَّى اللَّهُ عَلَيْهِ وَسَلَّمَ كَانَ إِذَا أُتِيَ بِطَعَامٍ سَأَلَ عَنْهُ فَإِنْ قِيلَ هَدِيَّة أَكَلَ مِنْهَا وَإِنْ قِيلَ صَدَقَة لَمْ يَأْكُلْ مِنْهَا.

(مسلم)

B. English Translation

Abu Huraira may Allah be pleased with him reported: *"Whenever the Prophet of Allah (pbuh) was presented with food, he asked about it, if he was told that it was a gift, he ate out of it, and if he was told that it was a charity he did not eat out of it.* (Reported by Muslim)

XXI.   Hadith No (21)

A. Arabic Text

عَنْ أَبِي هُرَيْرَةَ قَالَ مَا عَابَ رَسُولُ اللَّهِ صَلَّى اللَّهُ عَلَيْهِ وَسَلَّمَ طَعَامًا قَطُّ كَانَ
إِذَا اشْتَهَى شَيْئًا أَكَلَهُ وَإِنْ كَرِهَهُ تَرَكَهُ.
(متفق عليه)

B. English Translation

Abu Huraira reported *that Allah's Messenger (pbuh) never found fault with food (served to him). If he liked anything, he ate it, and if he did not like it, he left it.* (Agreed upon)

XXII.   Hadith No (22)

A. Arabic Text

عَنْ كَعْبِ بْنِ مَالِكٍ أَنَّ رَسُولَ اللَّهِ صَلَّى اللَّهُ عَلَيْهِ وَسَلَّمَ كَانَ لا يَقْدَمُ مِنْ سَفَرٍ
إِلا نَهَارًا فِي الضُّحَى فَإِذَا قَدِمَ بَدَأَ بِالْمَسْجِدِ فَصَلَّى فِيهِ رَكْعَتَيْنِ ثُمَّ جَلَسَ فِيهِ.
(متفق عليه)

B. English Translation

Ka'b bin Malik reported: *The Prophet of Allah (pbuh) never came back from a journey except by day time in the forenoon, and when he arrived, he first went to the Mosque, prayed two rak'ahs in it and he sat down in it.* (Agreed upon)

XXIII. Hadith No (23)

A. Arabic Text

عَنْ عَلِيٍّ رَضِيَ اللَّهُ عَنْهُ قَالَ كُنَّا إِذَا احْمَرَّ الْبَأْسُ وَلَقِيَ الْقَوْمُ الْقَوْمَ اتَّقَيْنَا بِرَسُولِ اللَّهِ صَلَّى اللَّهُ عَلَيْهِ وَسَلَّمَ فَمَا يَكُونُ مِنَّا أَحَدٌ أَدْنَى مِنَ الْقَوْمِ مِنْهُ. (أحمد)

B. English Translation

Ali (may Allah be pleased with him) narrated: *when the battle became heated and the people (i.e., the fighters) faced the [other] people (i.e. the enemy), we sought protection from the Messenger of Allah (pbuh) and none of us was closer to the enemy [ranks] than him.* (Reported by Ahmad)

XXIV. Hadith No (24)

A. Arabic Text

كَانَ النَّبِيُّ صَلَّى اللَّهُ عَلَيْهِ وَسَلَّمَ إِذَا أَرَادَ أَنْ يَسْتَوْدِعَ الْجَيْشَ قَالَ أَسْتَوْدِعُ اللَّهَ دِينَكُمْ وَأَمَانَتَكُمْ وَخَوَاتِيمَ أَعْمَالِكُمْ. (أبو داوود)

B. English Translation

Abdullah al-Khutami may Allah be pleased with him narrated: *"When the Messenger of Allah (pbuh) wanted to say farewell to an army, he would say: 'I entrust Allah on your religion, what you are responsible for, and your final deeds'* (Reported by Abu Dawood)

XXV. Hadith No (25)

A. Arabic Text

عَنْ عَبْدِ اللَّهِ بْنِ عَمْرٍو أَنَّ رَسُولَ اللَّهِ صَلَّى اللَّهُ عَلَيْهِ وَسَلَّمَ خَرَجَ يَوْمَ بَدْرٍ
فِي ثَلاثِ مِائَةٍ وَخَمْسَةَ عَشَرَ فَقَالَ رَسُولُ اللَّهِ صَلَّى اللَّهُ عَلَيْهِ وَسَلَّمَ اللَّهُمَّ إِنَّهُمْ
حُفَاةٌ فَاحْمِلْهُمْ اللَّهُمَّ إِنَّهُمْ عُرَاةٌ فَاكْسُهُمْ اللَّهُمَّ إِنَّهُمْ جِيَاعٌ فَأَشْبِعْهُمْ فَفَتَحَ اللَّهُ لَهُ
يَوْمَ بَدْرٍ فَانْقَلَبُوا حِينَ انْقَلَبُوا وَمَا مِنْهُمْ رَجُلٌ إِلا وَقَدْ رَجَعَ بِجَمَلٍ أَوْ جَمَلَيْنِ
وَاكْتَسَوْا وَشَبِعُوا. (أبو داوود)

B. English Translation

Abdullah ibn Amr narrated: *"The Messenger of Allah (pbuh) went out on the Day of Badr along with three hundred and fifteen (men). The Messenger of Allah (pbuh) said: 'O Allah, they are on foot, provide mount for them; O Allah, they are naked, clothe them; O Allah, they are hungry, provide food for them.' Allah then bestowed victory on them on the Day of Badr. They returned when they were clothed. There was no man among them who didn't return with one or two camels; they were clothed and ate to their fill.* Reported by Abu Dawood.

XXVI. Hadith No (26)

A. Arabic Text

عَنْ ابْنِ عَبَّاسٍ رَضِيَ اللَّهُ عَنْهُمَا أَنَّ رَسُولَ اللَّهِ صَلَّى اللَّهُ عَلَيْهِ وَسَلَّمَ قَالَ
وَهُوَ فِي قُبَّةٍ يَوْمَ بَدْرٍ اللَّهُمَّ إِنِّي أَنْشُدُكَ عَهْدَكَ وَوَعْدَكَ اللَّهُمَّ إِنْ تَشَأْ لا نُعْبَدْ

بَعْدَ اليَوْمِ فَأَخَذَ أَبُو بَكْرٍ بِيَدِهِ فَقَالَ حَسْبُكَ يَا رَسُولَ اللَّهِ أَلْحَحْتَ عَلَى رَبِّكَ وَهُوَ
يَثِبُ فِي الدِّرْعِ فَخَرَجَ وَهُوَ يَقُولُ

﴿ سَيُهْزَمُ الجمع ويولون الدبر ﴾

(رواه البخاري)

B. English Translation

Ibn Abbas (may Allah be pleased with both of them) narrates: *"While in his tent on the day the Battle of Badr, the Prophet said, 'O Allah! I request You (to fulfill) Your promise and contract. O Allah! If You wish that the Believers be destroyed, You will never be worshipped henceforth.' On that, Abu Bakr held the Prophet by the hand and said: 'That is enough, O Allah's Apostle! You have appealed to your Lord too pressingly' The Prophet was wearing his armor and then went out reciting: 'Their multitude will be put to flight and they will show their backs.'* (54.45) (Reported by Bukhari)

XXVII. Hadith No (27)

A. Arabic Text

قَالَ حُذَيْفَةُ كَانَ رَسُولُ اللَّهِ صَلَّى اللَّهُ عَلَيْهِ وَسَلَّمَ إِذَا حَزَبَهُ أَمْرٌ صَلَّى.
(أحمد)

B. English Translation

Huthayfa narrated: *"the Messenger of Allah (pbuh) used to pray when a matter befell on him."* (Reported by Ahmad)

XXVIII.   Hadith No (28)

A. Arabic Text

كَانَ رَسُولُ اللَّهِ صلَّى اللَّهُ عَلَيْهِ وَسَلَّمَ إِذَا سَمِعَ المُؤَذِّنَ قَالَ مِثْلَ ما يَقُولُهُ.
(الطحاوي)

B. English Translation

Whenever the Messenger of Allah (pbuh) used to hear the caller of the prayer, he used to repeat [after him] the same words. (at-Tahawi)

XXIX.   Hadith No (29)

A. Arabic Text

كَانَ رَسُولُ اللَّهِ صلَّى اللَّهُ عَلَيْهِ وَسَلَّمَ يُعَلِّمُ مَنْ أَسْلَمَ يَقُولُ اللَّهُمَّ اغْفِرْ لِي
وَارْحَمْنِي وَاهْدِنِي وَارْزُقْنِي.
(مسلم)

B. English Translation

The Messenger of Allah (pbuh) used to teach the person who embraces Islam to say: *"O Allah forgive me, have mercy on me, guide me, and provide for me."* (Reported by Muslim)

67

XXX.   Hadith No (30)

A. Arabic Text

عَنْ أَنَسٍ قَالَ قَالَ رَسُولُ اللَّهِ صَلَّى اللَّهُ عَلَيْهِ وَسَلَّمَ حُبِّبَ إِلَيَّ النِّسَاءُ وَالطَّيبُ
وَجُعِلَتْ قُرَّةُ عَيْنِي فِي الصَّلَاةِ.
(النسائي)

B. English Translation

Anas narrated: *"the Messenger of Allah (pbuh) said: 'I was made to have likeness in women and pleasant smells; and prayer is the delight of my eye.'"* (Reported by an Nasa'i)

** Final Remarks

It is not easy for any person to talk about himself, otherwise people may misunderstand that person. They may say that he is bragging and boasting his ego. Here, it is contrary! The Prophet (pbuh) never bragged about himself. Anytime he had to say something about the privileges that Allah (swt) has blessed him with, he used to say them, and then he.said: "Wa Laa Fakhr", i.e. without bragging! And without being proud, but these qualities are blessings and gifts from Allah (swt).

And He (Allah) has power over all things. Qur'an (5:123)

68

Chapter (9) Privileges Of Prophet Muhammad

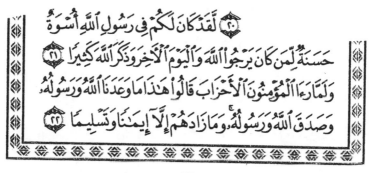

٤٢٠

Al-Ahzab: The Confederates

You have indeed in the Messenger of Allah an excellent exempler for him who hopes in Allah and the Final Day and who remember Allah much. When the believers saw the Confederates forces, they said: "This is what Allah and His Messenger told us what was true." And it only added to their faith and their zeal in obedience. (33:21-22)

I. Introduction

My subject today is about the Privileges of Prophet Muhammad (pbuh). Allah (swt) granted Prophet Muhammad (pbuh) many privileges over other prophets and over human beings. Let me first quote for you an Ayah from the Qur'an summarizing the mission of Prophet Muhammad (pbuh). In Surah Al-Ahzab (The Confederates), Allah says:

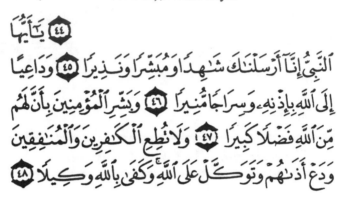

O Prophet! Truly We have sent you as a witness, a bearer of glad tidings, and a warner, and as one who invites to God's (Grace) by His leave, and as a Lamp spreading Light. Then give the glad tidings to the believers, that they shall have from God a very great bounty. And obey not (the behests) of the unbelievers and the hypocrites, and heed not their annoyances but put your trust in God. For enough is God as a disposer of affairs. (33:45-48)

II. Privileges

I will summarize some of the major privileges that were bestowed upon the Prophet (pbuh) from Allah (swt). Many of the privileges were granted to him over other human beings, and some were granted to him over other prophets too. Let me make it clear here that none of these privileges allowed Muhammad (pbuh) to be excused from performing his obligations to Allah (swt). None of them released him from fulfilling his daily, weekly, monthly, or yearly duties as any other Muslim. These privileges are indeed degrees of honor, respect and dignity from Allah (swt) to Prophet Muhammad (pbuh). The following are some of the many privileges that Prophet Muhammad (pbuh) was granted by Allah:

1. **Prophethood**: He was entrusted with prophethood. He was called Prophet of Allah or The Prophet. In Surah Al Anfal (Spoils of War), Allah says:

يَـٰٓأَيُّهَا ٱلنَّبِيُّ حَسْبُكَ ٱللَّهُ وَمَنِ ٱتَّبَعَكَ مِنَ ٱلْمُؤْمِنِينَ

"O Apostle! Sufficient unto you is Allah,--(unto you) and unto those who follow you among the Believers." (8:64)

2. **The Message**: He was entrusted with the Message and was called the Messenger of Allah. In Surah Al-Fath (The Victory), Allah says:

مُّحَمَّدٌ رَّسُولُ ٱللَّهِ وَٱلَّذِينَ مَعَهُۥٓ أَشِدَّآءُ عَلَى ٱلْكُفَّارِ رُحَمَآءُ بَيْنَهُمْ

71

"Muhammad is the Messenger of Allah ..." (48:29)

While in Surah Al-A`raf (The Heights), Allah informs us that Muhammad (pbuh) is the Messenger and the Prophet of Allah:

الَّذِينَ يَتَّبِعُونَ ١٥٦ الرَّسُولَ النَّبِيَّ الْأُمِّيَّ الَّذِي يَجِدُونَهُ مَكْتُوبًا عِندَهُمْ فِي التَّوْرَنةِ وَالْإِنجِيلِ يَأْمُرُهُم بِالْمَعْرُوفِ وَيَنْهَنْهُمْ عَنِ الْمُنكَرِ وَيُحِلُّ لَهُمُ الطَّيِّبَنتِ وَيُحَرِّمُ عَلَيْهِمُ الْخَبَنَثِثَ وَيَضَعُ عَنْهُمْ إِصْرَهُمْ وَالْأَغْلَلَ الَّتِي كَانَتْ عَلَيْهِمْ فَالَّذِينَ ءَامَنُوا بِهِ وَعَزَّرُوهُ وَنَصَرُوهُ وَاتَّبَعُوا النُّورَ الَّذِي أُنزِلَ مَعَهُ أُوْلَئِكَ هُمُ الْمُفْلِحُونَ ١٥٧

"Those who follow the Apostle (The Messenger), the unlettered Prophet, whom they find mentioned in their own (Scriptures), -- in the Law and the Gospel for he commands them what is just and forbids them what is evil; he allows them as lawful what is good (and pure)..." (7:157)

3. **Believing in Muhammad:** One Surah in the Qur'an is called Surah of Muhammad. It is Surah number 47. Allah demanded from us to believe in Muhammad (pbuh) and what was revealed to him by saying:

$$\textربٌ وَالَّذِينَ ١$$

(Arabic Quranic verse)

"But those who believe, and work deeds of righteousness, and believe in the revelation sent down to Muhammad – for it is the truth from their Lord, ..." (47:2)

4. **Annexing His Name with Allah:** The name of Muhammad (pbuh) was annexed with the Name of Allah in many aspects and in many places and situations:

a. To pronounce the Kalimah (The statement of creed or Tawhid), one has to utter the following:

$$\text{لا إله إلا الله محمد رسول الله}$$

"There is no deity except Allah, and Muhammad is the Messenger of Allah."

b. To become a Muslim, one has to pronounce the declaration statement of faith; namely:

$$\text{أَشهدُ أن لا إله إلا الله}$$

(I bear witness that there is no one worthy of worship except the only one God [Allah])

$$\text{وأشهد أن محمداً عبدُهُ ورسولهُ.}$$

(And I bear witness that Muhammad is the servant and the final prophet and messenger of Allah.)

73

"I bear witness that there is no deity except Allah, and I bear witness that Muhammad is the servant and the Messenger of Allah."

c. His name is to be pronounced with the Name of Allah while reciting the call to prayer (Adhan):

« الله أكبر الله أكبر ، الله أكبر الله أكبر . أشهد أن لا إله إلا الله ، أشهد أن
لا إله إلا الله ، أشهد أن محمداً رسول الله ، أشهد أن محمداً رسول الله . حي
على الصلاة ، حي على الصلاة . حي على الفلاح حي على الفــلاح ، الله أكبر
الله أكبر ، لا إله إلا الله »

*I bear witness that there is no deity except Allah" (twice)
"I bear witness that Muhammad is the Messenger of Allah"
(twice)*

d. The name of Muhammad (pbuh) is to be pronounced with the Name of Allah, while reciting the call for the starting of the prayer (Iqamah):

ثانياً : تثنية التكبير الأول والأخير وقــد قامت الصلاة ، وإفراد سائر
كلماتها فيكون عددها إحدى عشرة كلمة.وفي حديث عبد الله بن زيد المتقدم :
ثم تقول إذا أقمت : الله أكبر الله أكبر ،أشهد أن لا إله إلا الله ، أشهد أن
محمداً رسول الله ، حيّ على الصلاة حي على الفلاح ، قد قامت الصلاة قد
قامت الصلاة ، الله أكبر الله أكبر ، لا إله إلا الله .

e. Muhammad's name is to be mentioned with Allah's Name after an infant is delivered. One person, (preferably his father), is to recite the

    (1) Adhan in his right ear, and
    (2) Iqama in his left ear

f. Muhammad's name is to be pronounced with the Name of Allah when a Muslim is performing prayer. While kneeling on the floor, a Muslim is to say in the process of greeting:

أشهدُ أن لا إله إلا الله واشهد ان محمداً عبدُهُ ورسولهُ.

"I bear witness that there is no deity except Allah, and I bear witness that Muhammad is the servant and the Messenger of Allah."

5. **Blessings of Allah unto Muhammad:** Allah gave His blessings unto Muhammad (pbuh); and instructed the Angels to do the same. In Surah Al-Ahzab (The Confederates), Allah says:

إِنَّ ٱللَّهَ وَمَلَٰٓئِكَتَهُۥ يُصَلُّونَ عَلَى ٱلنَّبِيِّ يَٰٓأَيُّهَا ٱلَّذِينَ ءَامَنُوا۟ صَلُّوا۟ عَلَيْهِ وَسَلِّمُوا۟ تَسْلِيمًا

"Lo! Allah and his Angels shower blessings on the Prophet..." *(33:56)*

6. **Pronouncing His Name Before Lecturing:** A Muslim Imam or a speaker is to start his speeches with praises to Allah, and the greetings on the Prophet (pbuh).

Any Muslim speaker or Imam who starts his speeches or his khutbah without the pronunciation of these two statements, his speech is useless, he is not to be rewarded for his efforts, and his speech is refuted and rejected by Allah (swt).

7. **Greetings To Muhammad**: Muslims are to give greetings to Muhammad (pbuh) many fold.

   a. Allah instructed the believing Muslims to greet Muhammad (pbuh). They are to request Allah's Blessings and Mercy to be given to him. In Surah Al-Ahzab (The Confederates), Allah says:

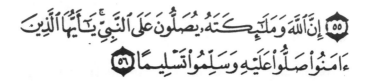

"Lo! Allah and His angels shower blessings on the Prophet. O ye who believe! Ask blessings on him and salute him with a worthy salutation..." (33:56)

   b. During prayer, and while kneeling, a Muslim is to recite the greetings (Al-Tahiyat). It goes as follows:

تشهد ابن مسعود في الصحة تشهد ابن عباس قال : كان النبي صلى الله عليه وسلم يعلمنا التشهد كما يعلمنا القرآن ، وكان يقول « التحيات المباركات ، الصلوات الطيبات لله ، السلام عليك أيها النبي ورحمة الله وبركاته ؛ السلام علينا وعلى عباد الله الصالحين ، أشهد أن لا إله إلا الله ، وأشهد أن محمداً عبده ورسوله » رواه الشافعي ومسلم وأبو داود والنسائي .

"The greetings are due to Allah; the prayers and the good things (are to Allah). Peace (of Allah) be upon you O Prophet, as well as the Mercy of Allah and His blessings."

76

c. During the five daily prayers, and while kneeling, a Muslim is to recite the (Salat Ibrahimiyah), i.e., the greetings. Includes the request of the Muslim to Allah to bless Prophet Muhammad (pbuh). It is stated as follows:

اَللّٰهُمَّ صَلِّ عَلَى مُحَمَّدٍ، وَعَلَى آلِ مُحَمَّدٍ، كَمَا صَلَّيْتَ عَلَى إِبْرَاهِيمَ [وَآلِ إِبْرَاهِيمَ]، إِنَّكَ حَمِيدٌ مَجِيدٌ، وَبَارِكْ عَلَى مُحَمَّدٍ، وَعَلَى آلِ مُحَمَّدٍ، كَمَا بَارَكْتَ عَلَى [إِبْرَاهِيمَ وَ] آلِ إِبْرَاهِيمَ، إِنَّكَ حَمِيدٌ مَجِيدٌ

d. Whoever gives greetings to the Prophet (pbuh), Muhammad (pbuh) himself will answer the greetings to that person. In one Hadith narrated by Abu-Hurairah that the Prophet (pbuh) said:

١٤١٠ ـ وعنه أن رسول اللّٰه ﷺ ، قال : « مَا مِنْ أَحَدٍ يُسَلِّمُ عَلَيَّ إِلَّا رَدَّ اللّٰهُ عَلَيَّ رُوحِي حَتَّى أَرُدَّ عَلَيْهِ السَّلَامَ » رواه أبو داود بإسنادٍ صحيح .

"When a person gives greetings to me, Allah will bring my soul back to me so that I will answer him."

e. Whoever gives greetings to the Prophet (pbuh) and ask the blessings of Allah for the Prophet (pbuh), Allah will give that person ten times blessings. In one Hadith narrated by Abdullah Ibn Amr Ibn Al-'Ass that the Prophet (pbuh) said:

١٤٠٥ ـ وعن عبد اللّٰه بن عمرو بن العاص ، رَضِيَ اللّٰهُ عنهما ، أنه سَمِعَ رسول اللّٰه ﷺ ، يقول : « مَنْ صَلَّى عَلَيَّ صَلَاةً ، صَلَّى اللّٰهُ عَلَيْهِ بِهَا عَشْراً » رواه مسلم .

"Whoever gives greetings to me, Allah (swt) will give him ten times greetings." Muslims

f. During Fridays, Muslims are to increase their salat and greetings onto the Prophet (pbuh). As such, Allah will reward them more than what they will receive during the week.

8. **Being Honored:** Prophet Muhammad (pbuh) informed us without bragging that he was honored over the other prophets. His being honored and preferred over the others is summarized in these two Hadiths.

a. In one Hadith, he says that he was honored with six characteristics over the other prophets:

١٣٦٠ –عن أبي هريرة رضي الله عنه أن رسول الله ﷺ قال : « فُضلتُ
على الأنبياء بست : أعطيت جوامع الكلم، ونصرت بالرعب، وأحلت لي
الغنائم، وجعلت لي الأرض طهوراً ومسجداً، وأرسلت إلى الخلق كافة، وختم
بي النبيون » (١) . رواه مسلم

"I was preferred over the other prophets with six (characteristics): I was given the best sayings; I was given victory over others due to their fear (from me); the bounties were made lawful for me; the earth was made for me clean and a place for prayer: I was sent to all the creatures; and (the door) of prophethood was closed with me."

b. In another Hadith it is reported by Tirmizi that the Prophet (pbuh) said:

78

أَنَا حَبِيبُ اللهِ وَلَا فَخْرَ . وَأَنَا حَامِلُ لِوَاءِ الْحَمْدِ يَوْمَ
الْقِيَامَةِ تَحْتَهُ آدَمُ فَمَنْ دُونَهُ وَلَا فَخْرَ . وَأَنَا أَوَّلُ شَافِعٍ وَأَوَّلُ مُشَفَّعٍ
يَوْمَ الْقِيَامَةِ وَلَا فَخْرَ . وَأَنَا أَوَّلُ مَنْ يُحَرِّكُ حَلَقَ الْجَنَّةِ فَيَفْتَحُ اللهُ لِي
فَيُدْخِلُنِيهَا وَمَعِي فُقَرَاءُ الْمُؤْمِنِينَ وَلَا فَخْرَ . وَأَنَا أَكْرَمُ الْأَوَّلِينَ
وَالْآخِرِينَ عَلَى اللهِ وَلَا فَخْرَ .   (الترمذي)

*"I am the loving (person) to Allah without bragging; I am
to carry the flag of thanks during the day of resurrection
while Adam is under it and the rest are behind without
being proud; I am the first to intercede and the first to
request forgiveness during the Day of Judgment, without
pride; I am the first to open the gulp (door) of paradise,
and Allah will make me to enter paradise while the poor of
the believers will be with me without pride; and I am the
most honorable person to Allah among the first and the last
without bragging."*   *Tirmizi*

9. **Isra' and Mi'raj:** During the occasion of Isra' and Mi'raj,
   Prophet Muhammad (pbuh) was bestowed with the following:

   a. He was taken from Ka'bah in Makkah to the Farthest
      Mosque in Jerusalem and brought back in one night. In
      Surah Al-Isra' Allah says:

79

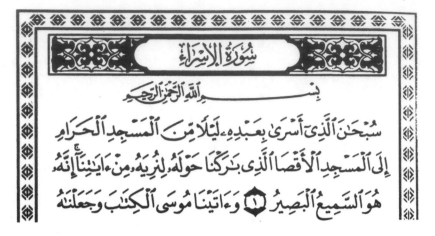

بِسْمِ اللهِ الرَّحْمَنِ الرَّحِيمِ

سُبْحَنَ ٱلَّذِىٓ أَسْرَىٰ بِعَبْدِهِۦ لَيْلًا مِّنَ ٱلْمَسْجِدِ ٱلْحَرَامِ
إِلَى ٱلْمَسْجِدِ ٱلْأَقْصَا ٱلَّذِى بَرَكْنَا حَوْلَهُۥ لِنُرِيَهُۥ مِنْ ءَايَتِنَآ إِنَّهُۥ
هُوَ ٱلسَّمِيعُ ٱلْبَصِيرُ ۝ وَءَاتَيْنَا مُوسَى ٱلْكِتَبَ وَجَعَلْنَهُ

"Glory to (God) Who did take His Servants for a journey by night from the Sacred Mosque to the Farthest Mosque, whose precincts We did Bless, in order that We might show him some of our signs: for He is the One Who hears and sees (All things)." (17:1)

b. He prayed as an Imam with all the prophets and Messengers of Allah inside Al-Masjid Al-Aqsa in Jerusalem.

c. He was taken to the upper heaven on that night and received special instructions from Allah. One may read Surah Al-Najm (The Star) for details (53:1-18).

d. While ascending to the upper heaven, he met many Prophets and Messengers and they showed him different scenes of Paradise and Hell etc.

10. **His Miracle From Allah:** While the miracles of the previous prophets ended with their death, the miracle of Muhammad

(pbuh) is still alive and will remain alive until the Day of Judgment. It is that of the Qur'an itself. Because the Qur'an is exactly the words of Allah, hence it is preserved by Allah Himself till eternity. Allah says the following in Surah Al-Hijr (The Rocky Tract):

$$ ﴿٨﴾ إِنَّا نَحْنُ نَزَّلْنَا ٱلذِّكْرَ وَإِنَّا لَهُۥ لَحَٰفِظُونَ ﴿٩﴾ $$

"We have without doubt, sent down the Message; and We will assuredly guard it (from corruption)." (15:9)

11. **His Nicknames:** Muhammad (pbuh) was given many names and adjectives, all of which reflect his personality, his character his nobility and his entity. Some of these names are: Ahmad, Muhammad Mustafa, Mahmoud, Nabi, Rasul, Sa'I, Bashir, Nathir, Sahfi, Rahim, Jawad, Siraj, Munir, Al-Amin, Khatam, Khalil, Shahid, Sadiq, Abdullah, and etc.

12. **The Last Prophet:** The lines of prophethood were closed with this advent. He was the last but the most important and the most influential prophet and Messenger to mankind. He is considered to be the summation, culmination and purification of all the messages and the Messengers. He is the final Messenger of Allah to all mankind and to other creatures too. Allah (swt) says in Surah Al-Ahzab (The Confederates) the following:

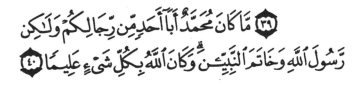

$$ ﴿٣٩﴾ مَّا كَانَ مُحَمَّدٌ أَبَآ أَحَدٍ مِّن رِّجَالِكُمْ وَلَٰكِن رَّسُولَ ٱللَّهِ وَخَاتَمَ ٱلنَّبِيِّـۧنَ وَكَانَ ٱللَّهُ بِكُلِّ شَىْءٍ عَلِيمًا ﴿٤٠﴾ $$

"Muhammad is not the father of any of your men, but (he is) the Apostle of Allah, and the Seal of the Prophets: and Allah has full knowledge of all things."
(33:40)

13. **Greetings During Du`aa':** Muslims are to make their salutation and greetings onto Prophet Muhammad (pbuh) at the beginning and at the end of their Du`aa'.

14. **Greeting During Ear Rings:** Muslims are to make their prayers to Allah onto the Prophet (pbuh), as well as their greetings to the Prophet (pbuh) whenever their ears ring.

15. **Prophecy of Previous Prophets:** The previous Prophets and Messengers prophesized the advent of Muhammad (pbuh), who will complete their missions and their messages.

III. Final Remarks

Finally, it would be a good idea to narrate a Hadith and an Ayah: Our Prophet (pbuh) says:

١٤١١ ـ وعن عليّ رضي اللَّهُ عنه ، قال : قال رسُولُ اللَّهِ ﷺ : « الْبَخِيلُ مَنْ ذُكِرْتُ عِنْدَهُ ، فَلَمْ يُصَلِّ عَلَيَّ » رواه الترمذي وقال : حديث حسن صحيح .

"The stingy person and the most stingy one is that person when my name is pronounced to him and does not make prayer and greeting onto me."

Allah says in Surah Al-Imran (The Family of Imran):

82

بِسْمِ ﴿٣١﴾ قُلْ أَطِيعُوا۟ ٱللَّهَ وَٱلرَّسُولَ فَإِن تَوَلَّوْا۟ فَإِنَّ ٱللَّهَ لَا يُحِبُّ

ٱلْكَـٰفِرِينَ ﴿٣٢﴾ ۝

"Say: 'Obey Allah and His Messenger". But if they turn back, Allah loves not those who reject Faith. (3:32)

Therefore, it is requested that the faithful believers in Allah (swt) should obey the Prophet (pbuh) in their private and public life. They should respect him, and request Allah to accept from them their deeds, actions and intentions. They should humbly request Allah (swt) to allow prophet Muhmmad (pbuh) to be a witness for them so that Allah (swt) will forgive them, and allow them to enter paradise without difficulty. All what it needs is to pray and to request. By praying the daily prayers and by requesting Allah (swt) after each prayer (Salat), to bless them with His Mercy and Forgiveness, Allah (swt) indeed will accept their request. We hope and pray that Muslims will try their best to be close to Allah (swt) daily. Ameen.

The Sacred Ka'bah In Makkah

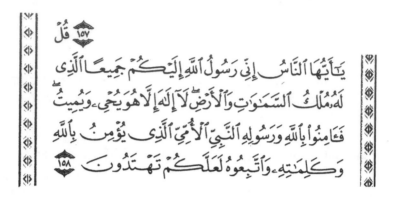

Al-A`raf: The Heights

O men! I am sent unto you all, as the Messenger of Allah, to Whom belongs the dominion of the heavens and the earth: there is no god but He: it is He that gives both life and death. So believe in Allah and His Messenger. The unlettered Prophet, who believes in Allah and His Words: follow him that (so) you may be guided. (7:158)

A. **ENCYCLOPEDIA BRITANNICA** *confirms:* " ..... a mass of detail in the early sources shows that he (Muhammad) was an honest and upright man who had gained the respect and loyalty of others who were like-wise honest and upright men." *(Vol. 12).*

B. *Lamartine, the renowned historian speaking on the essentials of human greatness wonders:* "If greatness of purpose, smallness of means and astounding results are the three criteria of human genius, who could dare to compare any great man in modern history with Muhammad? The most famous men created arms, laws and empires only. They founded, if anything at all, no more than material powers which often crumbled away before their eyes. This man moved not only armies, legislation, empires, peoples and dynasties, but millions of men in one-third of the then inhabited world; and more than that, he moved the altars, the gods, the religions, the ideas, the beliefs and soul...his forbearance in victory, his ambition, which was entirely devoted to one idea and in no manner striving for an empire; his endless prayers, his mystic conversations with God, his death and his triumph after death; all these attest not to an imposture but to a firm conviction which gave him the power to restore a dogma. This dogma was two-fold, the unity of God and the immateriality of God; the former telling what God is, the latter telling what God is not; the one overthrowing false gods with the sword, the other starting an idea with the words.

Philosopher, orator, apostle, legislator, warrior, conqueror of ideas, restorer of rational dogmas, of a cult without images, the founder of twenty terrestrial empires and one spiritual empire, that is MUHAMMAD. As regards all the standards by which Human Greatness may be measured, we may well ask, IS

THERE ANY MAN GREATER THAN HE?   *(Lamartine, Historoire de la Turquie, Paris, 8154, Vol II, pp. 276-277).*

C. **Mahatma Gandhi,** *speaking on the character of Muhammad (pbuh) says in* 'YOUNG INDIA'*:* "I wanted to know the best of one who holds today undisputed sway over the hearts of millions of mankind ... I became more than convinced that it was not the sword that won a place for Islam in those days in the scheme of life. It was the rigid simplicity, the utter self-effacement of the Prophet, the scrupulous regard for his pledges, his intense devotion to his friends and followers, his intrepidity, his fearlessness, his absolute trust in God and in his own mission. These and not the sword carried everything before them and surmounted every obstacle. When I closed the 2nd volume (of the Prophet's biography), I was sorry there was not more for me to read of the great life".

D. **Thomas Calyle** *in his 'Heroes and Heroworship', was simply amazed as to:* "How one man single handedly, could weld warring tribes and wandering Bedouins into a most powerful and civilized nation in less than two decades".

E. **Diwan   Chand Sharma** *wrote;* "Muhammad was the soul of kindness, and his influence was felt and never forgotten by those around him" (D.C. Sharma, The Prophet of the East', Calcutta, 1935, pp.12)

F. **Edward Gibbon and Simon Ockley** *speaking on the profession of* ISLAM *write:* " 'I BELIEVE IN ONE GOD, AND MAHOMET, AN APOSTLE OF GOD' is the simple and invariable profession of Islam. The intellectual image of the Deity has never been degraded by any visible idol; the honor of the Prophet has never transgressed the measure of human virtues; and his living precepts have restrained the gratitude of his disciples within the bounds of reason and religion". (*History of the Saracen Empires, London, 1870, p.54*)

G. *Speaking on the aspect of equality before God in Islam, the famous poetess of India,* **Sarojini Naidu** *says:* "It was the first religion that preached and practiced democracy; for, in the mosque, when the call for prayer sounded and worshippers are gathered together, the democracy of Islam is embodied five times a day when the peasant and king kneel side by side and proclaim:" "God Alone is Great"..."I have been struck over and over again by this indivisible unity of Islam that makes man instinctively a brother". (S. Naidu, Ideals of Islam, vide Speeches & Writings, Madras, 1918, p. 169).

H. *In the words of* **Prof. Hurgronje:** "The league of nations founded by the prophet of Islam put the principle of international unity and human brotherhood on such universal foundations as to show candle to other nations". *He continues:* The fact is that no nation of the world can show a parallel to what Islam has done towards the realization of the idea of the League of Nations".

I. **Michael H. Hart** *in his recently published book on ratings of men who contributed towards the benefit and upliftment of mankind writes:* "My choice of Muhammad to lead the list of the world's most influential persons may surprise some readers and may be questioned by others, but he was the only man in history who was supremely successful on both the religious and secular levels". Of humble origins, Muhammad founded and promulgated one of the world's great religions, and became an immensely effective political leader. Today, thirteen centuries after his death, his influence is still powerful and pervasive. *(M.H. Hart, 'The 100: A Ranking of the Most Influential Persons in History', New York, 1978, pp 3).*

J. *K. S. Ramakrishna Rao, an Indian Professor of Philosophy in his booklet, Muhammad, The Prophet of Islam, calls him the* "PERFECT MODEL FOR HUMAN LIFE". *Prof. Ramakrishna Rao explains his point by saying,* "The personality of Muhammad, it is most difficult to get into the whole truth of it. Only a glimpse of it I can catch. What a dramatic succession of picturesque scenes? There is Muhammad the Prophet. There is Muhammad, the Warrior; Muhammad, the Businessman; Muhammad, the Statesman; Muhammad, the Orator; Muhammad, the Reformer; Muhammad, the Refuge of Orphans; Muhammad, the Protector of Slaves; Muhammad, the Emancipator of Women; Muhammad, the Judge; Muhammad, the Saint. All in all these magnificent roles, in all these departments of human activities, he is alike a hero."

K. *Napoleon Bonaparte,* "I hope the time is not far off when I shall be able to unite all the wise and educated men of all the countries and establish a uniform regime based on the principles of the Qur'an, which alone are true and which alone can lead men to happiness."

L. *James A. Michener,* The Qur'an is probably the most often read book in the world, surely the most often memorized, and possibly the most often read book in the world, surely the most often memorized, and possibly the most influential in the daily life of the people who believe in it.

M. *George Bernard Shaw,* "I have always held the religion of Muhammad in high esteem because of its wonderful vitality. It is the only religion which appears to me to possess that assimilating capacity to the changing phase of existence which can make itself appeal to every age."

"Medieval ecclesiastics, either through ignorance or bigotry, painted Muhammadanism in the darkest colors. They were, in fact, trained to hate both the man Muhammad and his religion. To them, Muhammad was anti-Christ. I have studied him, the wonderful man, and in my opinion, far from being an anti-Christ, he must be called the savior of humanity." G.B. Shaw

N. *W. Montgomery,* "...Islam is certainly a strong contender for the supplying of the basic framework of the one religion of the future."

O. *DeLacy O' Leary,* "History makes it clear however, that the legend of fanatical Muslims sweeping through the world and forcing Islam at the point of a sword upon conquered races is one of the most fantastically absurd myths that historians have ever repeated."

P. *Annie Besant,* In her book: The Life and Teachings of Muhammad, Ms. Besant says "It is impossible for anyone who studies the life and character of the great Prophet of Arabia, who knows how he taught and how he lived, to feel anything but reverence for that mighty Prophet, one of the great messengers of the Supreme. And although in what I put to you I shall say many things which may be familiar to many, yet I myself feel whenever I re-read them, a new way of admiration, a new sense of reverence for that mighty Arabian teacher."

Q. *Geoffrey Parrinder,* a noted British author has observed: "No great religious leader has been so maligned as Prophet Mohammed. Attacked in the past as a heretic, an impostor, or a sensualist, it is still possible to find him referred to as "the false prophet." Certainly the Prophet's record was better than the head of the Church of England, Henry VIII."

R. *Maurice Bucaille,* "A totally objective examination of it (The Qur'an) in the light of modern knowledge, leads us to recognize the agreement between the two, as has been already noted on repeated occasions. It makes us deem it quite unthinkable for a man in Muhammad's time to have been the author of such statements on account of the state of knowledge in his day. Such considerations are part of what gives the Qur'anic Revelation its unique place, and forces the impartial scientist to admit his inability to provide an explanation which calls solely upon materialistic reasoning."

PS.

1. Maurice Bucaille, a noted French scientist who converted to Islam after studying the scientific miracles in the Qur'an.

2. Prophet Muhammad was born in Arabia in the year 570 C.E. (common era). He started his mission of preaching the religion of Truth, Islam (submission to One God) at the age of forty, and departed from this world at the age of sixty three.

مِن وَصَايَا الرَّسُول

Chapter (11)   Commandments Of The Messenger

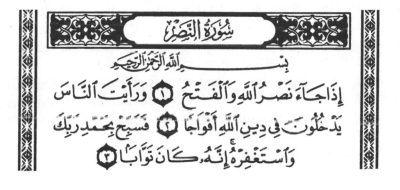

An-Nasr: The Help

When comes to help of Allah, and Victory, and you do see the people enter Allah's Religion in crowds, celebrate the praises of your Lord, and pray for His Forgiveness: for He is Oft-Returning (In forgiveness) (110:1-3)

I. Introduction

Prophet Muhammad (pbuh) gave during his life span a series of Advices and Commandments to many individuals, groups, tribes and leaders. His advices were for the benefits of all people of the world till the Day of Judgment. His Commandments were practical, easy to apply and easy to achieve. His recommendations were spread out to all human beings of the world. These revelations were inspirational and were applicable to daily life. They were meant to help people to live peacefully without being tough or arrogant. Those advices are to help humanity how to live in peace and harmony with others irrespective of color, nationality, ethnicity, gender, creed or religion.

People should try to read these Commandments of the Prophet (pbuh). By reading them, by understanding them, and by applying them in private and in public, a better society will be built on this planet earth. All what it takes, that Muslims should bring these Commandments of the Prophet (pbuh) in public, and inform the non-Muslims about them. If Muslims try to apply the meanings of these Commandments in their life wherever they are, then it would be easy for the non-Muslims to apply the meanings and the benefits of such Commandments. We hope that Muslims will take the initiative and try to deliver the Message of Allah (swt) as well as that of Prophet Muhammad (pbuh).

In this section the author tried to select some of the Commandments of the Prophet. They were translated to the English language while keeping the original Arabic Texts for those who know the Arabic language. We pray to Allah (swt) to give credits to all those who assume certain responsibilities in delivering the Message of Islam in theory and in action. We pray to Allah (swt) to accept our humble efforts, and to forgive our shortcomings. Ameen.

II. Qur'an On Commandments

● ... ذَٰلِكُمْ وَصَّىٰكُم بِهِۦ لَعَلَّكُمْ تَعْقِلُونَ ﴿١٥١﴾

... thus does He (God) command you, that you may learn wisdom. (6: 151)

● ... ذَٰلِكُمْ وَصَّىٰكُم بِهِۦ لَعَلَّكُمْ تَذَكَّرُونَ ﴿١٥٢﴾

... thus does He (God) command you, that you may remember. (6: 152)

(سورة الأنعام) ● ... ذَٰلِكُمْ وَصَّىٰكُم بِهِۦ لَعَلَّكُمْ تَتَّقُونَ ﴿١٥٣﴾

... thus does He (God) command you, that you may be righteous. (6: 153)

(سورة مريم) ﴿٣١﴾ ● ... وَأَوْصَىٰنِي بِٱلصَّلَوٰةِ وَٱلزَّكَوٰةِ مَا دُمْتُ حَيًّا

and [God] has enjoined on me prayer and charity as long as I [Jesus (pbuh)] live. (19: 31)

(سورة النساء) ● ... ﴿١١﴾ يُوصِيكُمُ ٱللَّهُ فِىٓ أَوْلَٰدِكُمْ

93

God directs you as regards your Children's (Inheritance). (4:11)

● ثُمَّ كَانَ مِنَ ٱلَّذِينَ ءَامَنُواْ وَتَوَاصَوْاْ بِٱلصَّبْرِ وَتَوَاصَوْاْ بِٱلْمَرْحَمَةِ ۝

(سورة البلد)

Then will he be of those who believe, and enjoin patience, (constancy, and self-restraint), and enjoin deeds of kindness and compassion. (90:17)

III. Series of Commandments

1. First Commandment

A. Arabic Text

الْحَارِثَ الْأَشْعَرِيَّ قَالَ: أَنَّ النَّبِيَّ صَلَّى اللَّهُ عَلَيْهِ وَسَلَّمَ قَالَ إِنَّ اللَّهَ أَمَرَ يَحْيَى بْنَ زَكَرِيَّا بِخَمْسِ كَلِمَاتٍ أَنْ يَعْمَلَ بِهَا وَيَأْمُرَ بَنِي إِسْرَائِيلَ أَنْ يَعْمَلُوا بِهَا وَإِنَّهُ كَادَ أَنْ يُبْطِئَ بِهَا فَقَالَ عِيسَى إِنَّ اللَّهَ أَمَرَكَ بِخَمْسِ كَلِمَاتٍ لِتَعْمَلَ بِهَا وَتَأْمُرَ بَنِي إِسْرَائِيلَ أَنْ يَعْمَلُوا بِهَا فَإِمَّا أَنْ تَأْمُرَهُمْ وَإِمَّا أَنْ آمُرَهُمْ فَقَالَ يَحْيَى أَخْشَى إِنْ سَبَقْتَنِي بِهَا أَنْ يُخْسَفَ بِي أَوْ أُعَذَّبَ فَجَمَعَ النَّاسَ فِي بَيْتِ الْمَقْدِسِ فَامْتَلَأَ الْمَسْجِدُ وَتَعَدَّوْا عَلَى الشُّرَفِ فَقَالَ إِنَّ اللَّهَ أَمَرَنِي بِخَمْسِ كَلِمَاتٍ أَنْ أَعْمَلَ بِهِنَّ وَآمُرَكُمْ أَنْ تَعْمَلُوا بِهِنَّ أَوَّلُهُنَّ أَنْ تَعْبُدُوا اللَّهَ وَلَا تُشْرِكُوا بِهِ شَيْئًا وَإِنَّ مَثَلَ مَنْ أَشْرَكَ بِاللَّهِ كَمَثَلِ رَجُلٍ اشْتَرَى عَبْدًا مِنْ خَالِصِ مَالِهِ بِذَهَبٍ أَوْ وَرِقٍ فَقَالَ هَذِهِ دَارِي وَهَذَا عَمَلِي فَاعْمَلْ وَأَدِّ إِلَيَّ

94

فَكَانَ يَعْمَلُ وَيُؤَدِّي إِلَى غَيْرِ سَيِّدِهِ فَأَيُّكُمْ يَرْضَى أَنْ يَكُونَ عَبْدُهُ كَذَلِكَ وَإِنَّ اللَّهَ أَمَرَكُمْ بِالصَّلاةِ فَإِذَا صَلَّيْتُمْ فَلَا تَلْتَفِتُوا فَإِنَّ اللَّهَ يَنْصِبُ وَجْهَهُ لِوَجْهِ عَبْدِهِ فِي صَلاتِهِ مَا لَمْ يَلْتَفِتْ وَأَمُرُكُمْ بِالصِّيَامِ فَإِنَّ مَثَلَ ذَلِكَ كَمَثَلِ رَجُلٍ فِي عِصَابَةٍ مَعَهُ صُرَّةٌ فِيهَا مِسْكٌ فَكُلُّهُمْ يَعْجَبُ أَوْ يُعْجِبُهُ رِيحُهَا وَإِنَّ رِيحَ الصَّائِمِ أَطْيَبُ عِنْدَ اللَّهِ مِنْ رِيحِ الْمِسْكِ وَأَمُرُكُمْ بِالصَّدَقَةِ فَإِنَّ مَثَلَ ذَلِكَ كَمَثَلِ رَجُلٍ أَسَرَهُ الْعَدُوُّ فَأَوْثَقُوا يَدَهُ إِلَى عُنُقِهِ وَقَدَّمُوهُ لِيَضْرِبُوا عُنُقَهُ فَقَالَ أَنَا أَفْدِيهِ مِنْكُمْ بِالْقَلِيلِ وَالْكَثِيرِ فَفَدَى نَفْسَهُ مِنْهُمْ وَأَمُرُكُمْ أَنْ تَذْكُرُوا اللَّهَ فَإِنَّ مَثَلَ ذَلِكَ كَمَثَلِ رَجُلٍ خَرَجَ الْعَدُوُّ فِي أَثَرِهِ سِرَاعًا حَتَّى إِذَا أَتَى عَلَى حِصْنٍ حَصِينٍ فَأَحْرَزَ نَفْسَهُ مِنْهُمْ كَذَلِكَ الْعَبْدُ لَا يُحْرِزُ نَفْسَهُ مِنَ الشَّيْطَانِ إِلا بِذِكْرِ اللَّهِ قَالَ النَّبِيُّ صَلَّى اللَّهُ عَلَيْهِ وَسَلَّمَ وَأَنَا آمُرُكُمْ بِخَمْسٍ اللَّهُ أَمَرَنِي بِهِنَّ السَّمْعُ وَالطَّاعَةُ وَالْجِهَادُ وَالْهِجْرَةُ وَالْجَمَاعَةُ فَإِنَّهُ مَنْ فَارَقَ الْجَمَاعَةَ قِيدَ شِبْرٍ فَقَدْ خَلَعَ رِبْقَةَ الإِسْلامِ مِنْ عُنُقِهِ إِلا أَنْ يَرْجِعَ وَمَنْ ادَّعَى دَعْوَى الْجَاهِلِيَّةِ فَإِنَّهُ مِنْ جُثَا جَهَنَّمَ فَقَالَ رَجُلٌ يَا رَسُولَ اللَّهِ وَإِنْ صَلَّى وَصَامَ قَالَ وَإِنْ صَلَّى وَصَامَ فَادْعُوا بِدَعْوَى اللَّهِ الَّذِي سَمَّاكُمُ الْمُسْلِمِينَ الْمُؤْمِنِينَ عِبَادَ اللَّهِ. (الترمذي)

B. English Translation

Al-Harith al-Ash'ari narrated: *The Prophet (pbuh) said: 'Allah commanded Yahia [the Son of Prophet Zakariya] to follow five demands, and for him to order the Children of Israel to follow [them], but he nearly hesitated [to fulfill the command]. So Jesus told [him]:'Allah has commanded you [Yahia] with five demands to follow and to order the Children of Israel to follow them. So, either you order them or I will'. Then Yahia told [Jesus]: If you precede me [in fulfilling the action], I fear I would be disgraced or get chastised. So, he [Yahia] gathered the people in Jerusalem, the house of worship became full and they stood by the terrace [to listen to him]. So He told [them]: 'Allah commanded me to follow five demands and [asked me] to order [all of] you to follow [them]. The first one is that you worship Allah and not associate with Him anything. The parable of the one who associate [anything] with Allah is like a man who bought a slave from his own wealth, with gold or money. He then tells him [i.e. to the slave]: here is my house and here is my work [for you], so work and perform for me; but [the slave] would instead work for another person other than his master. So who among you [O my people] would be content to have a slave like this? Allah also demanded to perform prayer, so, when you pray, don't turn around, for Allah focuses His Face toward His servant when he is praying as long as he [the servant] doesn't turn around [get distracted]. Allah also demanded that you fast; for, the parable of that is like a man who belongs to a group [of people]. That man has a packet of musk that everyone enjoys its [nice] scent; and the scent of a fasting person is [even] more pleasurable in the sight of Allah than the scent of musk. Allah [also] demanded from you to give charity. For the parable of this is like a man who is held captive by the enemy. [The enemy] ties his hands all the way to his neck and brings him forward to behead him. [At this point], he said: 'I will redeem him [or myself] from you [i.e. the enemy] with little or large [any amount of my money], so he [indeed] saved himself from them. And Allah demanded that you remember Him for, the parable of this is like a man who is hastily chased by the enemy until he reaches an impenetrable fortress, by then, he would have saved himself from them [the enemy]. Similarly, the servant doesn't protect himself from Satan without remembering Allah.' The Prophet (pbuh) [then] said: 'I demand from you five things that Allah had demanded from me [to follow]: that you listen and*

obey [your leader as long as he is not committing any mischief],
that you struggle [for the sake of Allah] (i.e. jihad), that you
migrate [from Makkah to Madinah, or from the land of unbelievers
to the land of believers, or from prohibited actions to good deeds],
and that [you stay with your] group [righteous people]; for,
whoever distances himself the span of a hand from the group, it is
like he took off the noose of Islam from his neck (a noose is a rope
used to tighten an animal) unless he comes back; for indeed,
whoever goes back to the time of disbelief (Jahiliyyah), he becomes
from the [burning] collected rocks of the hellfire'. A man then
said: 'O Messenger of Allah, even if that [man ends up] praying
and fasting?' the Prophet (pbuh) said: 'even if he prayed and
fasted, so [o companions] proclaim the calls of Allah who named
you Muslims, believers and worshippers of Allah." (Tirmidhi)

2. Second Commandment

A. Arabic Text

قال سويد الأزدي : وفدتُ سابع سبعةٍ من قومي على رسول الله
صلى الله عليه وسلم، فلمّا دخلنَا عليه وكلمناهُ اعجبهُ ما رأى من
سمتنا وَ زينّا، فقال : " من انتم؟ "، فقلنا: مؤمنون. فقال : " إن
لكلِّ قول حقيقة، فما حقيقةُ قولكم، وصدقُ إيمَانِكُم ؟ " فقلنا : خمسَ
عشرةَ خصلة، خمس آمنا بها، وخمس عمِلنا بها، وخمس تخلقنا
بها في الجاهلية، ونحن عليها للآن، فإن كرهتها تركناها .
فقال عليه الصلاة والسلام: " فاذكرُوا مَا عِندَكُم" فقالوا : أما خمس
الإيمان فهي:أن نؤمنَ باللهِ، وملائكتِهِ، وكتبه ورسلِهِ، والبعثِ بعد

97

الموتِ. وأما خمسُ العملِ فهي: ان نشهدَ ان لا إلهَ إلا اللهُ وأن
محمداً عبدُهُ ورسولَه، وأن نقيمَ الصلاةَ، ونؤتي الزكاةَ، ونصومَ
رمضانَ، ونحجُ البيتَ ان استطعنا اليه سبيلاً. وأما خمسُ الجاهليةِ
فهي : الشكرُ عند الرخاء، والصبرُ عند البلاء، والرضا يمُرِّ
القضاء، والصدقُ والثباتُ عند الحربِ واللقاء، وتركُ الشماتةِ
بالأعداء . ومن عظم سُرور النبي صلى الله عليه وسلم بهم
وبإيمانهم النَقي وفطرتهم السليمة، قال لهم:" أنتمُ حُكماءُ، عُلماءُ،
فقهاء، كِدتُم ان تكونُوا انبيَاء، وأنَا أزيدُكم خمساً ليتمَّ لكم عشرونَ .
إن كُنتُم كما تَقولُونَ، فلا تَجمَعُوا مَا لا تَأكُلُونَ وَلا تَبنُوا مَا لا
تَسكُنُون، وَلا تَتَنَافَسُوا في شَيءِ انتُم عَنهُ غَداً زَائِلُونَ، واتقوا اللهَ
الذي اليهِ تُرجَعُونَ، وعليهِ تُعرَضُونَ وارغَبُوا فيمَا انتُم عَليهِ
تُقدِمونَ، وفيهِ تُخَلَّدونَ" . أخرجه أبو نعيم في الحلية، والبيهقي في
الزهد والخطيب في التاريخ

B. English Translation

Narrated by Sawayd al-Azady: *"I was sent with a group of seven from my community to the Messenger of Allah (pbuh). When we entered [to meet him] and talked to him, he was pleased with our appearance and our dress. He said: 'Who are you?' we replied: 'we are believers.' He said: 'for every statement, there is evidence, so, what is the evidence of your statement and of the sincerity of your faith?' We said: "[There are] fifteen characteristics: five of which we believe in, five of which we practice, and five of which we acquired prior to Islam [Jahiliyah], but we still adhere to. [However], should you hate them, we will abandon them.*

[The Prophet] peace be upon him then said: 'convey to me what you have.' They said: as to the five we believe in, they are: that we believe in Allah, His angels, His books, His Messengers, and resurrection after death.

As to the five we practice, they are: we bear witness that there is no deity [worth of worshipping] other than Allah, and that Muhammad is His Servant and Prophet, we perform prayers, we give Zakat, we fast during Ramadan, and we [go to] pilgrimage to the House [of Allah] if we are able to.

As to the five of the Jahiliyah period, they are: to be grateful during [times of] ease, to be patient during troubles, to be content [even] during adverse fate, to be sincere and steadfast during battle and [when] meeting [the opponent], and to refrain from rejoicing at the misfortune of the enemy.

The Prophet (pbuh) was so pleased with their pure faith and prim nature that he told him about: 'you are [indeed] wise people, knowledgeable, and jurists. You are nearly prophets. I shall add [another] five characteristics to make [your fifteen qualities] twenty. If you are what you are saying, therefore don't accumulate what you don't eat, don't build what you don't live in, don't compete amongst yourselves on a matter that you will leave behind, be conscious of Allah Whom you will go back to, and be judged in front of, and prefer the things that you [are interested] to have permanently, and in which you will live in eternity.

(Extracted by Abou Naeem in al-Huliyah, al-Bayhaqi in az-Zuhd, and al-Khatib in the at-Tareekh).

3. Third Commandment

A. Arabic Text

عن أبي ذر رضيَ اللّه عنهُ قالَ :

قلتُ يا رسولَ اللّهِ ما كانت صحفُ ابراهيمَ ؟ قالَ : "كَانَت امثالاً
كُلّهًا .. أيهِا المَلكُ المسلّطُ المُبتلى المغرورُ: إني لم ابعثُّكَ لتجمعَ
الدُّنيا بَعضَهَا على بَعضٍ، ولكنّي بَعثتُكَ لتَرُدَّ عَنّي دَعوةَ المَظلومِ،
فَإني لا أرُدّهَا وإن كَانت مِن كَافِرٍ. وَعَلى العَاقِل مَا لم يَكُن مَغلُوبًا
عَلى عَقلِهِ ان يكونَ لهُ سَاعَات : فسَاعَة يُنَاجِي فيهَا ربَّهُ، وسَاعَة
يُحَاسِبُ فِيهَا نَفسَهُ، وسَاعَة يَتَفَكّرُ فِيها في صُنُع اللهِ عَزَّ وجَلَّ،
وسَاعَة يَخلُو فِيها لِحَاجَتِه مِنَ المطعَمِ والمَشرَبِ ". " وعَلى العَاقِل
أن لا يَكُونَ ظَاعِنًا إلا لثلاثٍ : تَزَوُّدٍ لِمعَادٍ، أو مَرمَةٍ لِمعَاشٍ، او
لذةٍ في غَيرِ مُحَرّمٍ....

وعَلى العَاقِل: ان يَكُونَ بَصِيراً بِزمَانِهِ، مُقبلاً عَلى شَأنِهِ، وحَافِظاً
لِلسَانِهِ، ومَن حَسِبَ كَلامَهُ مِن عَملِهِ قلَّ كلامه إلاَّ فِيمَا يَعنِيه"، قلت
يا رسولَ اللّه فما كانت صحف موسى عليه السلام؟ قال : " كانت
عِبراً كُلّها. عَجِبتُ لِمَن ايقنَ بالمَوتِ ثُمَّ هُوَ يُفرحُ، عَجِبتُ لِمَن ايقنَ
بالنَّارِ ثُمَّ هُوَ يَضحَكُ، عَجِبتُ لِمَن أيقنَ بالقَدَرِ ثُمَّ هُوَ يَنصَبُ،
عَجِبتُ لِمَن رأى الدُّنَيا وتَقلّبِهَا بأهلِهَا ثُمَ اطمأنَّ اليهَا، عَجِبتُ لِمَن
أيقنَ بالحِسابِ غَداً ثُم لا يَعملُ". قلتُ : يَا رَسُولَ اللهِ أوصِني. قالَ :
" أوصِيكَ بتَقوى اللهِ فإنَّهَا رَأسُ الأمرِ كُلّهِ" . قلتُ : يَا رَسُولَ اللهِ
زدني. قالَ: "عَليكَ بتَلاوَةِ القُرآن وذِكرِ اللهِ عَزَّ وجَل، فإنّه نُورٌ لكَ
فِي الأرضِ وذُخرٌ لكَ فِي السمَاءِ ". قلتُ : يَا رَسُولَ اللهِ زدني.
قالَ: " إيّاكَ وكَثرةَ الضحِكِ فإنّهُ يُميتُ القلبَ، ويذهَبُ بنُور

الوَجهِ...". قلتُ : يَا رَسُولَ اللهِ زِدني. قالَ: " عَليكَ بِالجِهَادِ فإنَّهُ
رَهبَانِيةُ أُمَّتِي" . قلتُ : يَا رَسُولَ اللهِ زِدني. قالَ: " أَحِبّ المَسَاكِينَ
وَجَالِسهُم ". قلتُ : يَا رَسُولَ اللهِ زِدني. قالَ: " أنظر الى مَن هُوَ
تَحتَكَ وَلاَ تَنظُر الى مَن هُوَ فوقَكَ فإنَّهُ أجدَرُ أن لا تَزدَري نِعمة اللهِ
عَليكَ ". قلتُ : يَا رَسُولَ اللهِ زِدني. قالَ: " قُل الحقَّ وإن كَانَ مُرّاً
". قلتُ : يَا رَسُولَ اللهِ زِدني. قالَ: " لِيَرُدَّكَ عَن النَاسِ مَا تَعلمُهُ
مِن نَفسِكَ وَلاَ تَجِد عَلَيهم فِيمَا تَأتِي، وَكَفَى بكَ عَيباً أن تَعرفَ مِنَ
النَّاسِ مَا تَجهَلُهُ مِن نَفسِكَ وَتَجِدُ عَلَيهم فِيمَا تَأتِي". ثم ضربَ بِيدِهِ
عَلى صَدري فقال : " يَا أَبَا ذرّ لاَ عَقلَ كَالتَّديير وَلاَ وَرَعَ كَالكَفّ
وَلاَ حَسَبَ كَحُسن الخُلُق ". (رواه ابن حِيان في صحيحه،
والحاكم، وقال صحيح الإسناد) .

B. English Translation

Abu Dharr (may Allah be pleased with him) narrated: *"I said:
'O Messenger of Allah, what were the scrolls of Abraham?' He
replied: 'they were all parables ... O arrogant reigning king under
tribulation: I didn't send you to amass the [resources of the] earth,
but I sent you instead to protect me from the invocation [of God] of
the oppressed [person] for I never turn it down even if it came
from a disbeliever. As to the prudent [person] who has control
over his mind, he must [dedicate] times [for certain actions]: a
time to confide in his Lord, a time to be accountable [for his
actions], a time to reflect of the creation of Allah almighty, and a
time to seclude himself for his [personal] needs for food and drink.
The prudent ought not be attached [to things] except for three
aspects: getting prepared to [face] an opponent, or restoring
livelihood, or seeking leisure from something which is not
prohibited. The prudent ought to be observant of his times, aware*

of his affairs, watchful of his speech. Whoever is vigilant of his speech over his actions will [actually] decrease his speech and [limit it] to matters that [only] concern him. Then I asked: O Messenger of Allah, what were the scrolls of Moses (pbuh)?He said: 'they were all morals. I am astonished of the [person] who recognizes [the truth about] death but still gets joyful; I am astonished of the [person] who recognizes [the truth about] hellfire but still laughs, I am astonished of the [person] who recognizes [the truth about] fate but still fatigues [himself] with this life; I am astonished of the [person] who sees [the truth about] earthly life and how people fluctuate but still feels secure in it, and I am astonished of the [person] who recognizes [the truth about] the Day of Judgment tomorrow but still doesn't work [hard].' Then I said: 'O Messenger of Allah, give me an advice'. He said: 'I advise you to be conscious of Allah for it is the essence of all things.' I said: 'O Messenger of Allah, tell me more [advice].' He said: '[make sure to] recite the Qur'an and remember Allah Almighty, for it is enlightenment for you on this earth and a reserve for you in Heaven. I said: 'O Messenger of Allah, tell me more (advice).' He said: 'be careful of excessive laughing for it kills the heart and takes away the light [of faith] of the face'... I said: 'O Messenger of Allah, tell me more (advice).' He said: 'struggle [for the sake of Allah - Jihad] for it is the friary of my community [Ummah]. I said: 'O Messenger of Allah, tell me more (advice).' He said: 'be loving to the needy and keep them company'. I said: 'O Messenger of Allah, tell me more (advice).' He said: 'look at the [one] who is below you [in authority, wealth, and power] and don't look at the one who is above you, for it is more appropriate not to belittle the blessing of Allah upon you.

I said: 'O Messenger of Allah, tell me more (advice).' He said: 'tell the truth [or be just] even if is detestable. I said: 'O Messenger of Allah, tell me more (advice).' He said: 'keep off

102

*people's [affairs] from what you know about yourself and don't
find [faults in them] in matters that you commit. Refrain from
faultfinding people based on what you don't know about yourself,
and find [faults in them] that you commit.' Then, he patted my
chest and said: O Abu Dharr: There is no knowledge as much as
management; There is no fear except by stopping (Haram); There
is no recognition except through good manners.* [Reported by Ibn
Habban in his Sahih, and Al-Haakim, and it was said: good
reported]

---

4. Fourth Commandment

A. Arabic Text

فَقَالَ الْعِرْبَاضُ صَلَّى بِنَا رَسُولُ اللَّهِ صَلَّى اللَّهُ عَلَيْهِ وَسَلَّمَ ذَاتَ يَوْمٍ
ثُمَّ أَقْبَلَ عَلَيْنَا فَوَعَظَنَا مَوْعِظَةً بَلِيغَةً ذَرَفَتْ مِنْهَا الْعُيُونُ وَوَجِلَتْ
مِنْهَا الْقُلُوبُ فَقَالَ قَائِلٌ يَا رَسُولَ اللَّهِ كَأَنَّ هَذِهِ مَوْعِظَةُ مُوَدِّعٍ فَمَاذَا
تَعْهَدُ إِلَيْنَا فَقَالَ أُوصِيكُمْ بِتَقْوَى اللَّهِ وَالسَّمْعِ وَالطَّاعَةِ وَإِنْ كَانَ عَبْدًا
حَبَشِيًّا فَإِنَّهُ مَنْ يَعِشْ مِنْكُمْ بَعْدِي فَسَيَرَى اخْتِلَافًا كَثِيرًا فَعَلَيْكُمْ
بِسُنَّتِي وَسُنَّةِ الْخُلَفَاءِ الْمَهْدِيِّينَ الرَّاشِدِينَ تَمَسَّكُوا بِهَا وَعَضُّوا عَلَيْهَا
بِالنَّوَاجِذِ وَإِيَّاكُمْ وَمُحْدَثَاتِ الْأُمُورِ فَإِنَّ كُلَّ مُحْدَثَةٍ بِدْعَةٍ وَكُلَّ بِدْعَةٍ
ضَلَالَةٌ. (أبو داوود)

B. English Translation

Al-Irbad narrated: *One day the Messenger of Allah (pbuh) led us in prayer, then faced us and gave us a lengthy exhortation at which the eyes shed tears and the hearts were afraid.*

A man said: *O Messenger of Allah! It seems as if it were a Farewell Exhortation, so what injunction do you give us? He then said: I enjoin you to be conscious of Allah, and to hear and obey even if it be from an Abyssinian slave. For those of you who live after me will see great disagreement. You must then follow my Sunnah and that of the Rightly-Guided Caliphs. Hold to it and stick fast to it. Avoid novelties, for every novelty is an innovation, and every innovation is a misguide.* (Abou Dawood)

---

5. Fifth Commandment

A. Arabic Text

قال رسول الله صلى الله عليه وسلم :
" أوصاني رَبي بتسع أوصيكم بهَا : أوصانِي بالإخلاص في السرّ
والعلانيةِ، والعدلِ في الرضَا والغضبِ، والقصدِ في الغنى والفقرِ،
وان أعفو عَمَّن ظلمني، وأعطيَ مَن حَرَمَني، وأصِلَ من قَطعَني،
وأن يَكون صَمتي فِكراً، ونُطقي ذِكراً، ونَظري عِبراً".
(رواه رُزَين)

لا إله إلا الله محمد رسول الله

104

B. English Translation

The Messenger of Allah (pbuh) said: *"my Lord has bestowed upon me with nine commandments, and I am commanding you to abide by them. He commanded me to be sincere in private and in public, to be just in times of contentment and anger, to be moderate [in times] of wealth and poverty, to be forgiving to the one who inflicted injustice upon me, to give to the one who deprived me, to rebuild relationship with the one who severed me, to make my silence a time for reflection, my speech a time for remembrance, and my observance [of things] a time for moral.* (Reported by Ruzain)

6. Sixth Commandment

A. Arabic Text

عن إبن عبّاس رضيَ الله عنه قال :

قال رسول الله صلى الله عليه وسلم لرجل وهوَ يَعِظه:

" إغتَنِم خمساً قبلَ خمس: شَبَابِكَ قبلَ هَرَمِك، وَ صِحتكَ قبل سَقَمِكَ، وغِناكَ قبل فقرِكَ، وفراغِكَ قبل شُغلِكَ، وحياتِكَ قبل موتِكَ" .رواه الحاكم وقال صحيح على شرطهما وقال شارح الجامع اسناده حسن

B. English Translation

Ibn Abbas (may Allah be pleased with both of them) said: *"the Messenger of Allah (pbuh) said to a man when he was advising him: 'make use of five before the other five: your youth*

105

before your old age, your health before your sickness, your wealth before your poverty, your free time before your busyness, and your life before your death.' (Reported by al-Hakem)

7. Seventh Commandment

A. Arabic Text

عَنْ ابْنِ عَبَّاسٍ قَالَ كُنْتُ خَلْفَ رَسُولِ اللَّهِ صلَى اللَّهُ عَلَيْهِ وَسَلَّمَ يَوْمًا فَقَالَ يَا غُلَامُ إِنِّي أُعَلِّمُكَ كَلِمَاتٍ احْفَظْ اللَّهَ يَحْفَظْكَ احْفَظْ اللَّهَ تَجِدْهُ تُجَاهَكَ إِذَا سَأَلْتَ فَاسْأَلْ اللَّهَ وَإِذَا اسْتَعَنْتَ فَاسْتَعِنْ بِاللَّهِ وَاعْلَمْ أَنَّ الْأُمَّةَ لَوْ اجْتَمَعَتْ عَلَى أَنْ يَنْفَعُوكَ بِشَيْءٍ لَمْ يَنْفَعُوكَ إِلَّا بِشَيْءٍ قَدْ كَتَبَهُ اللَّهُ لَكَ وَلَوْ اجْتَمَعُوا عَلَى أَنْ يَضُرُّوكَ بِشَيْءٍ لَمْ يَضُرُّوكَ إِلَّا بِشَيْءٍ قَدْ كَتَبَهُ اللَّهُ عَلَيْكَ رُفِعَتْ الْأَقْلَامُ وَجَفَّتْ الصُّحُفُ

قَالَ احْفَظْ اللَّهَ يَحْفَظْكَ احْفَظْ اللَّهَ تَجِدْهُ أَمَامَكَ تَعَرَّفْ إِلَيْهِ فِي الرَّخَاءِ يَعْرِفْكَ فِي الشِّدَّةِ وَإِذَا سَأَلْتَ فَاسْأَلْ اللَّهَ وَإِذَا اسْتَعَنْتَ فَاسْتَعِنْ بِاللَّهِ قَدْ جَفَّ الْقَلَمُ بِمَا هُوَ كَائِنٌ فَلَوْ أَنَّ الْخَلْقَ كُلَّهُمْ جَمِيعًا أَرَادُوا أَنْ يَنْفَعُوكَ بِشَيْءٍ لَمْ يَكْتُبْهُ اللَّهُ عَلَيْكَ لَمْ يَقْدِرُوا عَلَيْهِ وَإِنْ أَرَادُوا أَنْ يَضُرُّوكَ بِشَيْءٍ لَمْ يَكْتُبْهُ اللَّهُ عَلَيْكَ لَمْ يَقْدِرُوا عَلَيْهِ وَاعْلَمْ أَنَّ فِي الصَّبْرِ عَلَى مَا تَكْرَهُ خَيْرًا كَثِيرًا وَأَنَّ النَّصْرَ مَعَ الصَّبْرِ وَأَنَّ الْفَرَجَ مَعَ الْكَرْبِ وَأَنَّ مَعَ الْعُسْرِ يُسْرًا.

B. English Translation

Ibn Abbas narrated: *"I was [riding] behind the Messenger of Allah (pbuh) one day so he said to me: 'O young boy, I am*

106

teaching you words: be mindful of Allah, He will protect you, be mindful of Allah you will find Him in front of you, if you ask, ask Allah, and if you seek help, seek it from Allah. Know that if humanity assembled to benefit you in a matter, it will not be able to do that, except in which Allah had pre-planned it for you, and if humanity gathered to harm you in a matter, it will not be able to except in which Allah had pre-planned it for you. The pens have been lifted and the scrolls have dried up.

In another narration: The Messenger of Allah (pbuh) said: *"be mindful of Allah, He will protect you, be mindful of Allah you will find Him in front of you, recognize Him in times of ease, He will recognize you in times of hardship, if you ask, ask Allah, and if you seek help seek it from Allah. The pen has dried up with how matters will turn out. Know that if all creatures wanted to benefit you in a matter that Allah had not prescribed for you, they will not be able to do it, and know if all creatures wanted to harm you in a matter that Allah has not prescribed, they will not be able to. Know that there is good in being patient over [matters] that you dislike and that prosperity is with patience, and that relief comes with anxiety, and that ease comes with hardship.*

8. Eighth Commandment

A. Arabic Text

عَنْ أَبِي هُرَيْرَةَ رَضِيَ اللَّهُ عَنْهُ قَالَ قَالَ رَسُولُ اللَّهِ صَلَّى اللَّهُ عَلَيْهِ
وَسَلَّمَ اسْتَوْصُوا بِالنِّسَاءِ فَإِنَّ الْمَرْأَةَ خُلِقَتْ مِنْ ضِلِعٍ وَإِنَّ أَعْوَجَ

شَيْءٍ فِي الضِّلَعِ أَعْلاهُ فَإِنْ ذَهَبْتَ تُقِيمُهُ كَسَرْتَهُ وَإِنْ تَرَكْتَهُ لَمْ يَزَلْ
أَعْوَجَ فَاسْتَوْصُوا بِالنِّسَاءِ.
(البخاري)

B. English Translation

Abu Huraira (may Allah be pleased with him) narrated: *"Allah's Messenger (pbuh) said: 'Treat women kindly, for a woman is created from a rib, and the most curved portion of the rib is its upper portion, so, if you should try to straighten it, it will break, but if you leave it as it is, it will remain crooked. So treat women kindly.'"* (Bukhari)

9. Ninth Commandment

A. Arabic Text

عَنْ ابْنِ عُمَرَ رَضِيَ اللَّهُ عَنْهُمَا قَالَ قَالَ رَسُولُ اللَّهِ صَلَّى اللَّهُ عَلَيْهِ
وَسَلَّمَ مَا زَالَ جِبْرِيلُ يُوصِينِي بِالْجَارِ حَتَّى ظَنَنْتُ أَنَّهُ سَيُوَرِّثُهُ.
(البخاري)

B. English Translation

Ibn Umar (may Allah be pleased with both of them) narrated: *"the Messenger of Allah (pbuh) said: ' Angel Gabriel has [not ceased to] advise me to [take] care of the neighbor [to the point] where I thought he was going to make him a [legal] heir [of my property].* (Bukhari)

10. Tenth Commandment

A. Arabic Text

عن أبي ثعلبة الخُشيّ جُرثُوم بن نَاشر رضي الله عنه عن رسول الله صلى الله عليه وسلم قال: " إنّ اللهَ تعالى فَرَضَ فرائِضَ فلا تضيّعُوُها، وَحَدّ حدوداً فلا تَعتَدوهَا، وحَرّمَ اشياءَ فلا تنتهكوهَا، وسَكَّت عن أشياء رَحمة لكُم غير نسيانٍ فلا تبحثوا عنها". حديث حسن، رواه الدّار قطني وغيره

B. English Translation

Abi Tha'labah al-Khushany Jurthoom bin Nashir (may Allah be pleased with him) narrated: "the Messenger of Allah (pbuh) said: *'Allah has made [certain matters] obligatory, so don't lose them, and He set limits so don't transgress them, and He has prohibited [certain] actions so don't violate them, and He has overlooked [certain] things as a [gesture] of mercy for you not as a matter of forgetfulness, so don't seek them.'"*. (Ad-Daraqutni)

---

11. Eleventh Commandment

A. Arabic Text

عَنْ مُعَاذِ بْنِ جَبَلٍ أَنَّ رَسُولَ اللَّهِ صَلَّى اللَّهُ عَلَيْهِ وَسَلَّمَ أَخَذَ بِيَدِهِ وَقَالَ يَا مُعَاذُ وَاللَّهِ إِنِّي لَأُحِبُّكَ وَاللَّهِ إِنِّي لَأُحِبُّكَ فَقَالَ أُوصِيكَ يَا

مُعَاذُ لا تَدَعَنَّ فِي دُبُرِ كُلِّ صَلاةٍ تَقُولُ اللَّهُمَّ أَعِنِّي عَلَى ذِكْرِكَ
وَشُكْرِكَ وَحُسْنِ عِبَادَتِكَ. (أبو داوود)

B. English Translation

Mu'adh Ibn Jabal narrated that the Messenger of Allah (pbuh) took him by his hand and said: *"'O Mu'adh, by Allah I love you [for the sake of Allah], by Allah I love you [for the sake of Allah]', then he said: 'I advise you O Mu'adh never to abandon after every prayer [to say]: O Allah! Assist me in remembering You, in thanking You, and in worshipping You properly'"*. (Abou Dawood)

---

12. Twelve Commandment

A. Arabic Text

عَنْ أَبِي هُرَيْرَةَ أَنَّ رَسُولَ اللَّهِ صَلَّى اللَّهُ عَلَيْهِ وَسَلَّمَ قَالَ:
"إِذَا مَاتَ الإِنْسَانُ انْقَطَعَ عَنْهُ عَمَلُهُ إلا مِنْ ثَلاثَةِ أَشْيَاءَ مِنْ
صَدَقَةٍ جَارِيَةٍ أَوْ عِلْمٍ يُنْتَفَعُ بِهِ أَوْ وَلَدٍ صَالِحٍ يَدْعُو لَهُ."
(أبو داوود)

B. English Translation

Abu Hurairah (may Allah be pleased with him) narrated that the Messenger of Allah (pbuh) said: *"When a human being passes away, his deeds are over except through three things [he leaves after his death]: a perpetual charity, a useful knowledge or a righteous child praying for him."*

Chapter (12)   Orations Of The Prophet

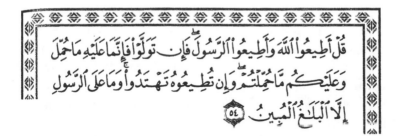

An-Nur: Lights

Say: "Obey Allah, and obey the Messenger: but if you turn away, he is only responsible for the duty placed on him and you for that placed on you. If you obey him, you shall be on right guidance. The Messenger's duty is only to preach the clear (message)". (24:54)

111

I. Introduction

Prophet Muhammad (pbuh) received the Message from Allah (swt) at the age of forty (40) years. He was instructed to deliver that Message to all the people of the world. He listened to Allah (swt), and he started delivering the Message to his local people. In every occasion, he tried his best to give a speech reminding people to believe in the Oneness of Allah (swt). Even after he migrated to the City of Madina, he continued giving speeches and orations to the local people. His Orations were recorded by his own companions and spread all of over the world. Muslims of today do enjoy reading those Orations and Speeches of the Prophet (pbuh). They try to understand their meanings, and try to apply those meanings in their daily life.

In a period of 23 years of being a Prophet, he delivered a good number of Orations, Speeches, Friday Khutbah, Advices, Recommendations, and Commandments. It is not easy to put them all at one time in one chapter. It is left up to the readers to read them, to enjoy their meanings, to inspire the readers and then to apply them in their public and private life. The credits and rewards are from Allah (swt) to those who pass these teachings to others. May Allah bless us all. Ameen.

Al-An'am

Say: "With Allah is the far-reaching (i.e. conclusive) argument. If He had willed, He would have guided you all." (6:149)

An-Nisaa'

$$ ۞ أُوْلَـٰٓئِكَ ٱلَّذِينَ يَعْلَمُ ٱللَّهُ مَا فِى قُلُوبِهِمْ فَأَعْرِضْ عَنْهُمْ وَعِظْهُمْ وَقُل لَّهُمْ فِىٓ أَنفُسِهِمْ قَوْلًۢا بَلِيغًا ۞ $$

Those are the ones of whom Allah knows what is in their hearts, so turn away from them but admonish them and speak to them a far-reaching (effective) word. (4:63)

Al-Qamar

$$ ۞ حِكْمَةٌۢ بَٰلِغَةٌۖ فَمَا تُغْنِ ٱلنُّذُرُ ۞ $$

Extensive wisdom – but warning does not avail (them) (54:5)

II. Preface To Khutbah

A. Arabic Text

عن جابر، رضي الله عنه، قال: كان رسول الله صلى الله عليه وسلم، إذا خطبَ احمرت عيناهُ، وعَلا صَوتُهُ، واشتدَّ غضبُهُ، حتى كأنه منذرُ جيشٍ يقولُ: " **صبَّحكُم ومسَّاكُم**" ويقولُ: " **بُعثتُ أنا والساعة كهاتَين**" ويقرنُ بينَ اصبَعَيه، السبابةِ والوسطى ويقولُ:

113

" أمَّا بعدُ ، فإن خيرَ الحديثِ كتابُ الله، وخيرَ الهدي هديُ محمدٍ،
صلى الله عليه وسلم، وشرَّ الأمور محدثاتُهَا، وكلَّ بدعةٍ ضلالةٌ "

B. English Translation

*Jaber (may Allah be pleased with him) narrated that when the
Messenger of Allah (pbuh) used to sermonize (or preach), his eyes
became red, his voice got louder, his anger increased (i.e. he
became passionate), almost as if he was warning an army saying:
"...Good morning and good evening.." and he would say: "I was
sent with the Hour (i.e. End of Time) like those [two]", joining his
index and middle fingers together, then he would say then: the
best speech is the Book of Allah, and the best guidance is the
guidance of Muhammad (pbuh); for indeed, the most evil actions
are novelties (i.e. introducing new actions into the religion), and
every innovation [leads to] misguidance.*

III. The Opening Of Khutbah

A. Arabic Text

افتتاح خطب الرسول

عن ابن قتيبة في عيون الأخبار:
تتبعت خطب رسول الله صلى الله عليه وسلم، فوجدت أوائل
اكثرها:
" الحمد لله نحمده ونستعينه ونؤمن به، ونتوكل عليه، من يُهده
الله فلا مضلَّ له، ومن يضلل فلا هادي له، واشهد ان لا إله إلاَّ
الله وحده لا شريك له".

114

ووجدت في بعضها:
" أوصيكم عبادي بتقوى الله، وأحثّكم على طاعته" .
ووجدت كل خطبة مفتاحها الحمد، إلا خطبة العيد فإنّ مفتاحها
التكبير.
(عيون الأخبار - م2: ص 231)

B. English Translation

Abu Qutaybah states in `Uyunul-Akhbar: *"I had followed [traced] the Orations of the Messenger (pbuh) and found that most of them started with: 'All praise is due to Allah, we praise Him, we seek His Assistance, we believe in Him, and we depend on Him. Whomever Allah guides, there is no [one] who [can] mislead him, and whomever He misleads, there is no [one] who [can] guide him, and I bear witness that there is no deity except Allah who has no partner.'*

I have also found in some of them [i.e. the Orations] [the following]: '*I entrust you, o my followers that you be conscious of Allah and I urge you to obey Him*'.

I have also found that every oration starts with the praise [of Allah] except the one during Eid which starts with Glorifying Him. (Uyunul-Akhbar – p231)

115

IV. A Series of Orations

• First Speech In Makkah

A. Arabic Text

أول خطبة خطبها بمكة حين دعا قومه

حمد الله واثنى عليه، ثم قال:

" إن الرائد لا يكذب أهله، والله لو كذّبت الناس كلهم ما كذبّتكم،
ولو غررتُ الناس جميعاً ما غررتكم، والله الذي لا إله إلاّ هو إني
لرسول الله اليكم خاصة، والى الناس كافة، والله لتموتنَّ كما
تنامون، ولتبعثنَّ كما تستيقظون، ولتحاسبنَّ بما تعملون،
ولتجزونّ بالإحسان إحساناً، وبالسوء سوءاً، وإنها لجنة ابداً أو
نارٌ أبداً ".

(السيرة الحلبية 272/1، والكامل لإبن الأثير27/2) .

B. English Translation

*He praised Allah and paid tribute to him then said: "A leader
(or pioneer or an exemplary person) doesn't [accuse] his family
i.e., those who are close in kin] of lying, and by Allah, even if I
were to accuse all people of lying, I wouldn't accuse you; and if I
were to deceive all people I still wouldn't deceive you. By Allah
who is the only deity, I am indeed the Messenger of Allah to you in
particular and to all mankind in general. By Allah you shall die
like you sleep and you shall be resurrected like you wake up, and
you shall be held accountable for what you do. You shall be
rewarded for kind acts [that you do] with kindness and for the*

harmful acts [that you do] with harm. And indeed, it is [there will either be] an eternal paradise or an eternal hellfire.
(As-Sirah al-Halabiyyah 1/272 & al-Kamel by Ibn Kathir)

• First Oration In Madina

A. Arabic Text

<u>خطبته صلى الله عليه وسلم في اول جمعة جمّعها في المدينة</u>

الحمد لله احمده واستعينه واستغفره وأستهديه وأومن به ولا أكفره وأعادي من يكفره، واشهد ان لا إله إلاّ الله وحده لا شريك له وأن محمداً عبده ورسوله، أرسله بالهدى والنور والموعظة، على فترة من الرسل، وقلة من العلم، وضلالة من الناس، وانقطاع من الزمان، ودنوّ من الساعة، وقرب من الأجل، من يُطع الله ورسوله فقد رَشَدَ، ومن يعصها فقد غوى وفرط، وضلّ ضلالاً بعيداً.

أوصيكم بتقوى الله فإنه خير ما أوصى به المسلمُ المسلم، أن يحضّه على الآخرة، وأن يأمره بتقوى الله، فاحذروا ما حذّركم الله من نفسه، ولا افضل من ذلك نصيحة، ولا افضل من ذلك ذكراً، وإن تقوى الله لمن عمل به على وجل، ومخافة من ربّه، عون صدق على ما تبغون من امر الآخرة، ومن يصلح الذي بينه وبين الله من امره في السر والعلانية لا ينوي بذلك إلاّ وجه الله يكون له ذكراً في عاجل امره، وذخراً فيما بعد الموت، حين يفتقر المرء الى ما قدّم، وما كان من سوى ذلك " يودّ لو انّ بينها

117

وبينه أمداً بعيداً، ويحذّركم الله نفسه، والله رؤوف بالعباد".
والذي صدّق قوله، وأنجز وعده فلا خلف لذلك، فإنه يقول عزّ
وجل: " ما يبدّل القول إليّ وما أنا ظلّام للعبيد" . فاتقوا الله في
عاجل أمركم وآجله، في السرّ والعلانية، فإنه من يتقّ الله يكفّر
عنه سيئاته ويعظم له اجراً، ومن يتقّ الله فقد فاز فوزاً عظيماً،
وإن تقوى الله يوقيّ مقته، ويوقيّ عقوبته، ويوقيّ سخطه، وإن
تقوى الله يبيّض الوجوه، ويرضي الربّ ويرفع الدرجة.

خذوا بحظكم ولا تفرّطوا في جنب الله، قد علّمكم الله كتابه، ونهج
لكم سبيله، ليعلم الذين صدقوا وليعلم الكاذبين، فأحسنوا كما
احسن الله اليكم، وعادوا أعدائه، وجاهدوا في الله حقّ جهاده،
هو اجتباكم وسمّاكم المسلمين، ليهلك من هلك عن بيّنة، ويحيا
من حيّ عن بينة، ولا قوة إلا بالله، فاكثروا ذكر الله، واعملوا لما
بعد اليوم، فإنه من يصلح ما بينه وبين الله يكفيه الله ما بينه
وبين الناس، ذلك بأن الله يقضي على الناس، ولا يقضون عليه،
ويملك من الناس ولا يملكون منه، الله أكبر ولا قوة إلا بالله العليّ
العظيم.
(تاريخ الطبري 294/2).

B. English Translation

*All praise is due to Allah, I praise Him; I seek His help; I ask
for His forgiveness and I ask for His guidance. I worship Him and
I don't disbelieve Him. I make animosity with the one who
disbelieves in Him. I bear witness that there is no deity but Allah,
the only One, Who does not have any associate. I also bear witness
that Muhammad is His servant and His Messenger. Allah sent him*

with guidance, enlightenment, and good advice. He was sent after other prophets [had come before him], when there was deficiency in knowledge [about proper religious matters] and misguidance among people. He was sent [in a period of time] when there was discontinuity in historic events, when the End of Time was approaching, and when death became closer. Whoever obeys Allah and His Messenger has attained wisdom, and whoever disobeys them would have deviated from the straight path, would have been negligent, and would have gone astray.

I advise you to have Taqwa of Allah, for indeed, the best advice from a Muslim to another [Muslim] is to encourage him to remember the Hereafter and to command him to have Taqwa of Allah. So be aware of what Allah has warned you about Himself; there is no better advice and no better reminder than this. The Taqwa of Allah is for the one who acts with apprehension from his Lord, so that he truly gets what he desires from the Hereafter. Anyone who is righteous in the matters between himself and Allah, in privacy and in public, (for the sake of Allah), will have [good] reputation in his earthly life, and provisions with Allah in the Hereafter, especially when a person is in [dire] need for every good deed he has done. Anything else he performs has no bearing for him. "He wishes that there was long ways between him and the Hereafter [to catch up on good deeds], but Allah warns you [in advance] about Himself, and Allah is Most Clement towards his servants." For Allah, who is indeed truthful to His statement and Who undoubtedly fulfills His promise, says: "The Word that comes from Me cannot be changed and I do not commit the least injustice to My servants." Therefore, have Taqwa of Allah in your immediate and future deeds, in private and in public. Whoever has Taqwa, Allah will forgive his sins and will magnify his rewards. Whoever has Taqwa, he would have greatly succeeded, for Taqwa

119

protects the person from the abomination and the wrath of Allah; The Taqwa of Allah purifies the faces, pleases the Lord, and raises the rank of the person.

Make use of your fortune and don't transgress the limits of Allah. It is He Who taught you His Book and paved His path for you, so that the sincere [people] and the liars may learn. So, do good like Allah had done good to you. Be hostile to His enemies, and strive in the path of Allah for it is the best kind of struggle. It is He Who selected you and named you Muslims. Let the one who perishes perish in clearness, and let the one who survives survive in clearness. There is no power except that of Allah; so, increase your remembrance of Allah, and do good deeds for the Hereafter. Anyone who improves his relation with Allah, Allah will suffice him in whatever was between himself and people, because it is Allah Who judges people and they don't judge Him, it is He Who possesses people and they cannot possess Him. Allah is the greatest, and there is no power except in Allah, the Almighty.
(Tarikh at-Tabari 2/294)

Dome of the Rock in Jerusalem

120

• First Friday Khutbah In Madina

My talk to you is about the first Khutbah by the Prophet Muhammad (pbuh) for the first Jumu'ah. In an Arabic book entitled "Nations and Kings." By Imam Abu Jaafar Muhammad Bin Jareer El-Tabari, Vol. 2, pp. 115, it is reported that the first Khutbah was delivered by Prophet Muhammad (pbuh) on the first Jumu'ah prayed by Muslims in Madina. This Khutbah was given mainly to Banu Salem Ben Awf. Because of its importance and its significance, the Khutbah is translated and presented here with its original Arabic text.

The main theme of the Khutbah is that every Muslim should cleanse and purify himself/herself; that we should improve our relations with Allah Ta'ala; that we should have Taqwa; that we should be good and kind to Muslims and to the rest of mankind; and that we should make use of this world and prepare ourselves for the Hereafter.

The Khutbah is very concise, informative but educational, precise and to the point, historic and useful; practical and up-to-date. Finally it is needed by every Muslim to live a few moments with the Prophet talking to us in a holy day such as Friday, and on a sacred occasion such as the Friday prayer.

A. Arabic Text

أول خطبة خطبها بالمدينة

كانت اول خطبة خطبها رسول الله صلى الله عليه وسلم حين قدم الى المدينة أن قال : " أما بعد، أيها الناس، فقدّموا لأنفسكم، تعلمنّ والله ليصعقنّ ثم ليدعن غنمه ليس لها راع، ثم ليقول له

121

ربّه وليس له ترجمان ولا حاجب يحجب دونه: ألم يأتِك رسولي
فبلّغك، وآتيتك مالاً وافضلت عليك؟ فما قدمت لنفسك؟ فلينظرنّ
يميناً وشمالاً فلا يرى شيئاً، ثم لينظرنّ قدامه فلا يرى غير
جهنّم، فمن استطاع ان يقي وجهه من النار ولو بشق تمرة
فليفعل، ومن لم يجد فبلكمة طيبة، فإنها تجزي الحسنة عشر
أمثالها الى سبعمائة ضعف، والسلام عليكم ورحمة الله
وبركاته".

B. English Translation

*The first speech that the Messenger of Allah (pbuh) delivered
in Madinah was when he said: Then: O people, offer yourself
[something beneficial], by Allah, you know indeed that He will
strike, then He will let His herd (i.e. human beings) [be left]
without a shepherd (i.e., a guardian); then the Lord will tell him
(each human being) - in a time when there is no one to interpret or
to stand as a separator (i.e.: between Allah and the servant):
"didn't my Messenger come to you and relate to you [My
Message], [didn't I] provide you wealth and bestow favor upon
you? So, what did you (i.e., human being) offer to yourself? So, let
[each one] look to his right and left sides but he won't see
anything, then, let him look in front of him and not be able to see
anything [other than] hell. So, whoever is able to protect his face
from the hellfire, even it was through [offering to people] a morsel
of date, let him do it, and whoever is not able [to find the morsel of
date], then let him [say to others] a kind word; indeed, a [kind] act
is rewarded ten to seven hundred times its worth, and may the
peace, mercy, and blessing of Allah be bestowed upon you."*

122

• Speech In Badr

A. Arabic Text

<u>خطبته صلى الله عليه وسلم في بدر</u>

.... بعد ان حمد الله واثنى عليه، أما بعد :

" فإني أحثّكم على ما حثّكم عليه الله، وأنهاكم عمّا نهاكم عنه، فإن الله عظيم شأنه يأمر بالحق، ويحب الصدق، ويعطي على الخير اهله على منازلهم عنده، به يذكرون وبه يتفاضلون. وإنكم قد اصبحتم بمنزل الحق، لا يقبل الله فيه من احد إلأ ما ابتغي به وجهه، وإن الصبر في مواطن البأس ممّا يفرّج الله به الهم ويُنجي به من الغمّ وتدركون النجاة في الآخرة.... فيكم نبيّ الله يحذّركم ويأمركم، فاستحيوا اليوم ان يطلع الله عزّ وجل على شيء من امركم يمقتكم عليه، فإن الله يقول:

(لمقتُ الله اكبر من مَقتكم انفسكم) .

انظروا الذي امركم به في كتابه، وأراكم من آياته وأعزّكم به بعد ذلّة، فاستمسكوا به يرضى به ربكم عنكم وأبلو ربكم في هذه المواطن امراً تستوجبوا الذي وعدكم به من رحمته ومغفرته، فإن وعده حقّ وقوله صدق، وعقابه شديد، وإنّما أنا وأنتم بالله الحي القيوم، إليه لجأنا ظهورنا، وبه اعتصمنا وعليه توكلنا، واليه المصير، يغفر الله لي وللمسلمين.

B. English Translation

After praising and thanking Allah (swt), he said: *"Indeed I urge you to do what Allah (swt) has urged you to do. And I forbid you from what He has forbidden you to do. Indeed Allah's (swt) matter is great. He commands by the truth and He loves honesty/integrity, and He rewards the people of good, according to their degrees with Him, with good; the people of good are remembered, and in good they are classified in degrees. Verily, you have achieved the status of truthfulness – Allah (swt) will not accept any deed from anyone except what is pure and sincere for the sake of Allah (swt). And patience/perseverance in the situations of hardship is one of the causes by which Allah (swt) eases distress and saves (rescues) from stress, and you will attain salvation in the Hereafter.*

Amongst you is a Prophet of Allah who warns and commands you. So today, you ought to feel ashamed toward Allah (swt) of committing anything that Allah (swt) hates you for – since Allah (swt) says: 'the Hate of Allah is greater than the hate among yourselves.'

Look at what Allah has ordered you to follow in His book, and what He has shown you of His signs, and at what He has honored you with after you were humiliated. So, stick to it, your Lord will be pleased with you by doing so. And do your best sincerely to our Lord in these situations (of war), you will be deserving to what He has promised you from His mercy and His forgiveness. For His promise is truth, and His saying is honesty, and His punishment is severe.

And I and you are dependent on Allah, the eternally living, to Him we have sought refuge with our lives, and with Him we have sought protection, and on Him we have depended and to Him is the return. May Allah forgive me and all of the Muslims."

• Speech During Uhud

I. Introduction

My talk to you is about the Prophet's Khutbah on the Day of Uhud. A battlefield took place next to the mountain of Uhud in the neighborhood of the city of Madina. The date was during the month of Shawwal in the third year of Hijra.

This Khutbah was very important in the history of Islam, and its prominence is very significant in our daily life. Hence, we are including it in this book.

The Prophet (pbuh) said the following in his Khutbah on the day of Uhud:

A. Arabic Text

خطبته صلى الله عليه وسلم يوم أُحُد

قام عليه الصلاة والسلام فخطب الناس فقال:

أيها النـاس، أوصـيكم بمـا اوصـاني الله فـي كتابـه، مـن العمـل بطاعته، والتناهي عن محارمه، ثم إنكم اليوم بمنزل أجر وذخر لمن ذكر الذي عليه، ثم وطّن نفسـه علـى الصبر واليقين، والجدّ والنشاط، فإن جهاد العدو شديد كربـه، قليل مـن يصبر عليـه، إلا من عزم على رشده، إن الله مع من أطاعه، وإنّ الشيطان مع من عصاه، فاستفتحوا اعمالكم بالصبر على الجهاد والتمسوا بذلك ما وعدكم الله، وعليكم بالذي أمركم بـه، فإنّي حريص علـى رشدكم.

125

إن الإختلاف التنازع والتثبيط من امر العجز والضعف، وهو ممّا لا يحبّه الله، ولا يعطي عليه النصر.

ايها الناس، أنه قَذف في قلبي أن من كان على حرام فرغب عنه ابتغاء ما عند الله، غفر له ذنبه، ومن صلى على محمد صلاة صلى الله عليه وملائكته عشراً، ومن احسن وَقعَ اجره على الله في عاجل دنياه، او في آجل آخرته، ومن كان يؤمن بالله واليوم الآخر، فعليه الجمعة يوم الجمعة، إلا صبياً او امرأة أو مريضاً أو عبداً مملوكاً، ومـن اسـتغنى عنها اسـتغنى الله عنـه، والله غنـيّ حميد.

ما أعلم من عمل يقربكم الى الله إلا وقد امرتكم به، ولا أعلم من عمل يقربّكم الى النـار إلا وقد نهيتكم عنـه، وإنـه قد نفثَ الروح الأمين في روعي انه لن تموت نفسي حتى تستوفي اقصى رزقها لا ينقص منه شيء وإن أبطأ عنها، فاتقوا الله ربّكم، وأجملوا في طلب الـرزق، ولا يحملـنّكم استبطاؤه علـى ان تطلبـوه بمعصية ربّكم، فإنـه لا يقدر علـى مـا عنـد إلا بطاعتـه، قد بيّن لكم الحلال والحرام، غير ان بينهما شبهاً من الأمر لم يعلمها كثير من الناس إلا من عصم، فمن تركها حفظ عرضه ودينه، ومن وقع فيها كـان كالراعي الى جنب الحمى اوشك ان يقع فيه، وليس ملك إلا وله حمى، ألا وإن حمى الله محارمه، والمؤمن من المؤمنين كـالرأس من الجسد، اذ اشتكى تداعى اليه سائر جسده، والسلام عليكم.

(جمهرة خطب العرب – الجزء الأول)

126

B. English Translation

He [the prophet] (pbuh) stood up and delivered a speech to the people saying:

"O people! I wish to command you with what Allah commanded me in His Book: To obey Him in action and to forbid yourselves from committing what He has prohibited. Today, you are in a state of reward and a treasure as to the One you mention His name. When a person has made up his mind, he is to be patient and certain, and is to be firm and active. The fight of an enemy is indeed very distressful, and in fact, very few people are able to withstand it, except those who commit to it with their wisdom [maturity]. Surely Allah is with those who obey Him, and Satan is with those who disobey Him [i.e. disobey Allah]. So, begin your actions with perseverance and struggle and seek what Allah had promised you, and fulfill that which Allah had commanded you. I am keen to guide you [i.e. give you proper knowledge to attain wisdom]. Indeed, disagreement, dispute, and discouragement stem from incompetence and weakness. Allah doesn't like this [attitude], and will not give victory [success].

O people, it was put in my heart that whoever was committing forbidden acts and has shunned it away for the pleasure of Allah, his sins will be forgiven. Whoever says prayers on Muhammad, Allah and His angels will bless him ten times. Whoever does good, Allah will reward him in this world or in the hereafter. Whoever believes in Allah and the hereafter, let him perform theFriday prayer (Jumuah Salat) on Friday, unless he is a child, or a woman, or sick, or a slave [possessed by a master]. Whoever abandons it [Friday prayer], Allah will abandon him and he is worthy of all praise.

Any act that I am aware of that would bring you closer to Allah, I have commanded you to do, and any act that I am aware of that would bring you closer to hellfire, I have commanded you not to do. The trustworthy spirit (Jibril) has reassured me that no soul [i.e., no person] dies until it receives its maximum [i.e. entire] provision [sustenance] without diminishing anything out of it, even if [the delivery of the provision] is delayed. So, have Taqwa in Allah , your Lord, and be courteous and general when asking for provisions [sustenance]. Don't commit any sins because of His delay to answer your Du'a as there is nothing to be obtained of what He has decreed except through obedience to Him.

He has shown you what is permissible [Halal] and what is prohibited [Haram]. However, there are items that are doubtful where many people are not able to differentiate between them [i.e., if they were allowed or prohibited] except those who have been protected. So, whoever leaves [the doubtful things] aside, will preserve his honor and his religion, and whoever falls into the doubtful items is like a shepherd close to the fence area where he is on the verge of falling. There is no ruler without protection; in fact, the shield of protection from Allah is His forbidden [acts]. The believer to another believer is like the head to the body; when it ills, the entire body comes to protect it. And [may Allah's] peace be upon you.

(Jamharat Khutab al-Arab – Vol. 1)

• Khutbah For Ramadan

A. Arabic Text

<u>رمَضَان مبارك</u>

عن سلمان رضي الله عنه قال:
خطبنا رسول الله صلى الله عليه وسلم، في آخر يوم من شعبان
قال:
" يا أيها الناسُ، قد أظلّكم شهرٌ عظيمٌ مباركٌ، شهرٌ فيهِ ليلة خيرٌ
من ألف شهر، شهرٌ جعل الله صيامه فريضةً، وقيامه تطوّعاً، من
تقرّب فيه بخصلة، كان كمن أدى فريضة فيما سواه، ومن أدّى
فريضة فيه، كان كمن أدّى سبعين فريضة فيما سواه، وهو شهر
الصبر، والصبر ثوابه الجنة، وهو شهر المواساة، وشهرٌ يزاد
في رزق المؤمن فيه، من فطر فيه صائماً، كان مغفرة لذنوبه،
وعتق رقبته من النار، وكان له مثل أجره، من غير ان ينقص
من اجره شيء".

قالوا: " يا رسول الله، ليس كلنا يجد ما يُفطر الصائم"
فقال رسول الله صلى الله عليه وسلم: "يعطي الله هذا الثواب لمن
فطر صائماً على تمرة، أو شربة ماء ، او مذقة لبن . وهو شهر
أولهُ رحمة، ووسطهُ مغفرة، وآخره عتق من النار. فاستكثرا فيه
من اربع خصال:

خصلتين ترضون بهم ربكم، وخصلتين لا غناء بكم عنهما.
فأما الخصلتان اللتان ترضون بهم ربكم: فشهادة ان لا إله الله،
وتستغفرونه، وأما الخصلتان اللتان لا غناء بكم عنهما :
فتسألون الله الجنة، وتعوذون به من النار.
ومن سقى صائماً سقاه الله من حوض شربة لا يظمأ بعدها حتى
يدخل الجنة".
(رواه ابن خزيمة في صحيحه).

B. English Translation

The following Khutbah was delivered by Prophet Muhammad
(pbuh) on the eve of Ramadan. Although it is short, it is concise,
informative and educational. It provides instructional models to the
Muslims to be followed and to be practiced in their daily lives and
especially during the month of Ramadan. Because of its
importance and because it was spoken by the Prophet Muhammad
(pbuh) himself on a notable occasion, the meaning of the Khutbah
was translated and included in this series of Khutab.

It was narrated by Salman the Persian (may Allah be pleased
with him) that the Messenger of Allah (pbuh) delivered a Khutbah
on the last day of [the month of] Sha'ban. The Prophet said: *"O
you people! A great and a blessed month has arrived for you. A
month that contains a night which is better than a thousand
months.*

*Allah made fasting during this month an obligation
[fareedah], and made the extra prayers voluntary.*

Anyone who comes closer to Allah through good deed during this month is as if he performed an obligatory duty (Fareedah) during times other than Ramadan, and he who performs an obligatory duty during the month [of Ramadan] is as if he had performed seventy duties in another month. It is the month of patience, and the reward for patience is Paradise. it is the month of empathy [i.e., visiting the poor, the sick and the needy so as to share their sorrows]. It is a month when the provision [nourishment, sustenance and income] of the believer augments, and they are blessed.

Anyone who provides food to break fast [at Iftar] to a fasting individual [is rewarded with] his sins getting forgiven and is saved from hellfire. He is also rewarded with the same reward [of the individual fasting] without reducing the latter's reward [in any respect]."

Some of the followers of the prophet said: "Not all of us are able to find food [to offer] to a fasting individual so that he may break his fast"

The messenger of Allah (pbuh): said: 'Allah will reward [the person who offers food] to the fasting individual [to break his fast] even if it was a [single piece of] date or a sip of water, or a taste of milk. It is a month whose beginning [segment] is mercy (Rahmah), its middle [segment] is forgiveness, and its last [segment] is freedom from hellfire. So, increase in yourself four habits: two by which you will please your Lord, and the other two that are indispensable to you. The two habits that you please your Lord with are to bear that there is no deity but Allah and that you seek his forgiveness. As to the [other] two habits that are indispensable to you, they are to ask for you to ask Allah for paradise and to seek

His protection from hellfire... And whoever gives a drink to a fasting individual at Iftar time, Allah will give him a drink from the prophet's fountain upon which he will not feel thirsty until he enters paradise."

In bringing this Khutbah to your attention, we hope and pray to Almighty Allah that we will benefit from it and we will act according to its teachings so that Allah and His messenger be pleased with us all. Ameen. Let us ask Almighty Allah for forgiveness.

(Reported in the authentic collection of Khuzayma)

- ## Speech In Al-Khayf

A.   Arabic Text

خطبته صلى الله عليه وسلم بالخيف

وخطب بالخيف من مِنى فقال:

" نضّر الله عبداً سمع خطبتي فوعاها، ثم ادّعاها الى من لم يسمعها، فربّ حامل فقه لا فقه له، وربّ حامل فقه الى من هو افقه منه، وثلاثٌ لا يغلّ عليهن قلب المؤمن: إخلاص العمل لله، والنصيحة لأولي الأمر، ولزوم الجماعة، إن دعوتهم تكون من ورائه، ومن كان همّه الآخرة جمع الله شمله، وجعل غناه في قلبه، وأتته الدنيا وهي راغمة، ومن كان همّه الدنيا فرقّ الله أمره، وجعل فقره بين عينيه، ولم يأته من الدنيا إلاّ ما كُتب له "

(إعجاز القرآن ص 112)

132

B. English Translation

He delivered a speech at al-Khayf in Mina and said: *"May Allah bestow His grace on His servant who hears my speech and understands it well, and who conveys it to those who have not heard it, for a bearer of knowledge may have no knowledge, and a bearer of knowledge may convey it to one who is more knowledgeable.*

And there are three things where the heart of a believer will never experience discomfort with: Sincerity in deed for Allah, advice to those in authority, and staying within the Muslims unified group – their call will be including Him.

And whoever his concerns is the Hereafter, Allah will fix his affairs, establish richness in his heart, and cause the worldly life to come to him against its will. And whoever his concern is this worldly life, Allah will disperse his affair, make poverty right before his eyes, and will never get from this worldly life except what had already been written for him.
(I'jaz al-Qur'an p. 112)

• Speech After `Asar

A. Arabic Text

ومن خطبه صلى الله عليه وسلم أنه خطب بعد العصر فقال:

"ألا إنّ الدنيا خضرةٌ حلوةٌ، ألا وإن الله مستخلفكم فيها فناظرٌ كيف تعملون، فاتقوا الدنيا، واتقوا النساء، ألا لا يمنعنّ رجلاً مخافة الناس ان يقول الحقّ اذا علمه" .

133

ولم يزل يخطب حتى لم تبق من الشمس إلا حمرة على اطراف السعف فقال: **"إنه لم يبق من الدنيا فيما مضى إلاً كما بقي من يومكم هذا فيما مضى "** . إعجاز القرآن ص 113)

B. English Translation

"Indeed this life is lush and beautiful. Indeed Allah is making you his vicegerents in it and will see how you will act. So be mindful with life, and be mindful of women. No believer should fear what people might say [about him] when he tells the truth when he learns it."

The [prophet (pbuh)] kept speaking until the sun [was setting] and nothing was left from it except some redness [it was reflecting] at the leaves [of the palm trees]. "Indeed, what is remaining from this life [in comparison to] what had already passed, is like what is remaining from this day [light] [in comparison to] what had already passed from it."
(I'jaz al-Quran p.113)

• Other Speeches

A. Arabic Text

خطبة له عليه الصلاة والسلام

" ان الحمد لله، احمده واستعينه، نعوذ بالله من شرور انفسنا، وسيئات اعمالنا، ومن يهد الله فلا مُضلَّ له ومن يضلل فلا هادي له، واشهد ان لا إله إلاَّ الله وحده لا شريك له .

134

إن احسـن الحـديث كتـاب الله، قـد أفلـح مـن زيّنـه الله فـي قلبـه،
وأدخله في الإسلام بعد الكُفر، واختاره على من سواه من احاديث
النـاس، أنـه اصدق الحديث وابلغه. أحبّوا مـن احبّ الله، وأحبّوا
الله مـن كـل قلـوبكم ولا تملّـوا كتـاب الله وذكـره، ولا تقـوّا عليـه
قلـوبكم، اعبدوا الله ولا تشـركوا بـه شيئاً، اتقوا الله حتـى تقاتـه،
وصدّقوا صـالح مـا تعملون بـأفواهكم، وتحابّوا بـروح الله بـينكم،
والسلام عليكم ورحمة الله وبركاته ".

B. English Translation

*"Praise is due to Allah, I praise Him and I seek His help, we
seek refuge with Allah from the evils of ourselves [soul], and from
the sins of our deeds. Whomever is guided by Allah, no one can
lead him astray, and whomever is misguided by Allah, no one can
guide him. I bear witness that there is no deity but Allah alone,
without partners.*

*The best speech is the Qur'an. He is truly successful the one
whom Allah beautified his heart with the Qur'an, and made him a
Muslim after he was in disbelief, and chose the Qur'an over the
rest of people's talk. It is [the Qur'an] the truest of speech and the
most eloquent.*
*Love whoever loves Allah and love Allah with all your hearts.
Do not get bored of the Book of Allah and of remembering it and
do not let your hearts harden with it.*

*Worship Allah and associate nothing with Him. Have Taqwa
of Allah the pious way and fulfill the good [deeds] of what you
promise with your mouths, turning it into action. Love one another*

with the spirit of Allah among yourselves, and may the peace, the
mercy of Allah and His blessings be upon you.

• General Speech

A. Arabic Text

<u>ومن خطب الرسول صلى الله عليه وسلم</u>

خطب رسول الله صلى الله عليه وسلم ذات يوم فأثنى على طوائف
المسلمين خيراً، ثم قال: **" مـا بـال اقوام لا يفقّهون جيرانهم ولا
يعلّمونهم ولا يعظونهم ولا ينهونهم؟ ومـا بـال اقوام لا يتعلّمـون
مـن جيرانهم ولا يتفقّهـون ولا يتّعظون؟ والله ليعلمنّ قـوم مـن
جيرانهم ويتفقهون ويتعظون او لأعجلتهم العقوبة!".**

ثم نزل رسول الله صلى الله عليه وسلم فقال قوم : من ترونـه عنى
بهؤلاء؟ قال: الأشعريين هم قوم فقهاء ولهم جيران جفاة من اهل
المياه والأعراب. فبلغ ذلك الأشعريين فاتوا رسول الله صلى الله
عليه وسلم فقالوا: يا رسول الله! ذكرت اقواماً بخير وذكرتنا بشر
فما بالنا؟ فقال: **" ليلعمن قـوم جيرانهم وليعظنهم وليـأمرنهم
ولينهونهم، وليتعلمن قوم من جيرانهم ويتعظون ويتفقهون. أو
لأعجلتهم العقوبة في الدنيا"،** فقالوا : يا رسول الله ! انفطن
غيرنا؟ فأعاد قوله عليهم، وأعادوا قولهم: أنفطن غيرنا؟ فقال ذلك
أيضاً، فقالوا: أمهلنا سنة، فأمهلهم مدة ليفقهونهم .

B. English Translation

One day, the messenger of Allah (pbuh) delivered a speech. He [first] praised a group of Muslims and then said: "What is the matter with folks who do not educate their neighbors about Islam, do not teach them the religion, do not admonish them and do not stop them from [committing] evil? And what is wrong with folks who do not get educated from their neighbors, do not learn from them and do get admonished from them? By Allah, either some folks [ought to] learn from their neighbors and get knowledge and admonition from them or the punishment of Allah will fall on them sooner rather than later." Then the messenger (pbuh) ended his speech and some people asked him: "Whom do you think he is referring to?" He said: "Al-Ashariyyeen [a Muslim group], a very knowledgeable group of people who have neighbors who are harsh, who live by waters along with Bedouins. When they [al-Ashariyyeen] knew about that [the prophet's speech], they came to the messenger of Allah (pbuh) and said: "O Messenger of Allah, you have spoken highly of some other folks, but critically of us, so what's our fault?" He said: "Either some folks educate their neighbors about Islam and admonish them and order them to do good and forbid them from committing evil or, punishment of Allah will fall upon them in this life." They said: "O messenger of Allah, shall we make others aware [of that]?" He repeated what he said. They repeated what they said: "Shall we make others aware?"

He said the same thing again. They said: give us a year period to do that. Then he gave them some time to educate their neighbors.

• Another Speech

A. Arabic Text

<u>ومن خطب الرسول صلى الله عليه وسلم</u>

خطب النبي صلى الله عليه وسلم في عصر يومٍ من الأيام، فكان ممّا قاله لهم:

"إن بني آدم خلقوا على طبقات شتى،ألا وإن منهم البطيء الغضب السريع الفيء، والسريع الغضب سريع الفيء، والبطيء الغضب بطيء الفيء، فتلك بتلك، ألا وإنّ منهم بطيء الفيء سريع الغضب، ألا وخيرهم بطيء الغضب السريع الفيء، وشرّهم سريع الغضب سريع الفيء.

ألا ومنهم حسن القضاء، حسن الطلب، ومنهم سيء القضاء حسن الطلب، منهم سيء الطلب حسن القضاء، فتلك بتلك.

ألا وإن الغضب جمرة في قلب ابن آدم. أما رأيتم الى حمرة عينيه وانتفاخ أوداجه، فمن احسن بشيء من ذلك فليلصق بالأض" (أي فليبق مكانه).

B. English Translation

One afternoon, the prophet (pbuh) delivered a speech. A portion of what he said was: "the children of Adam were created in various ranks. Truly among them are those who get angry slowly yet are fast in giving; [another category is] those who get angry fast and also give fast, [another category is] those who get angry slowly and give slowly, [and another category is] those who get angry fast but give slowly. So, each quality makes up for the other. But truly the best among them is the one who does not get

138

angry fast yet is fast in giving and the worst among them is the one who gets angry fast and is fast in giving.

Truly among them [children of Adam] are the just [fair] and kind when they ask for a favor. [Another category is] those who are unjust [unfair] yet are kind when they ask for a favor. [Another category is] those who ask for favors unkindly but are just [fair]. Each quality makes up for another.

But truly, anger is a burning coal in the heart of the child of Adam. Haven't you seen the redness in his eyes and the enlargement in the veins [when he is angry]? Whoever experiences such a feeling (anger) should be glued to the ground [i.e. should remain where he is.]

• Speech At The Wedding Of Fatima

A. Arabic Text

<u>خطبة النبي صلى الله عليه وسلم في زواج السيدة فاطمة</u>

" الحمـد لله المحمـود بنعمتـه، المعبـود بقدرتـه، المرهـوب مـن عذابه، المرغوب في عنده، النافذ أمره في سمائه وأرضـه، الـذي خلق الخلق بقدرتـه، وميّز هم بأحكامـه، وأعزّ هم بدينـه، وأكرمهم بنبيهم محمد صلى الله عليه وسلم، ثم إن الله جعل الصـاهرة نسباً لاحقاً، وأمـراً مفترضـاً، ووشـج بـه الارحام، وألزمـه الأنـام، قـال تبارك اسمه وتعالى ذكره (هو الذي خلق مـن المـاء بشراً فجعلـه نسباً وصـهراً وكـان ربّك قـديراً)، فـأمر الله يجري الـى قضـائه،

139

ولكل قضاء قدر ولكل قدرأجل، (يمحو الله ما يشاء ويُثبت وعنده أمُّ الكتاب).

ثم ان امرني الله ان أزوج فاطمـة الـى علـي بن أبـي طالـب، وقد زوجته إيّاها على اربعمائة مثقال فضة، إن رضي علي بذلك".

(جمهرة خطب العرب ـ الجزء الثالث)

B. English Translation

Praise be to Allah, the Praised by His blessing, the Worshipped by his Power, the Feared due to His punishment, the desired for what he has, the one whose order is fulfilled in heaven and earth. The one who created the creation with his power and distinguished them [his creation] with his laws, and dignified them with religion, and honored them with their prophet Mohammad, then verily Allah has ordained to be a later relation connecting people, and on assumed matter and he made wombs connected through marriage, and made marriage obligatory to humans, he blessed his name ,and glorified his remembrance, has said [he is the one who created of water a human being and then made him kin and in law and your lord has been absolutely powerful] the order of Allah is transmitted to his destiny, and for each a due measure, and for each due measure is a time (Allah deletes what he wishes and affirms, and with him is the mother of the book).

And Allah caused me to marry Fatimah to Ali, son of Abee Talib, and I have married her to him for a dowry of 400 pieces of silver if he accepts that. (Jamharat Khutab al-Arab, Vol 3)

• General Speech

A. Arabic Text

<u>ومن خطبه عليه الصلاة والسلام</u>

" أيها الناس ان لكم معالم فإنتهوا الى معالمكم، وأن لكم نهاية فانتهوا الى نهايتكم، فإن العبد بين مخافتين، أجل قد مضى لا يدري ما الله فاعل فيه، وأجل باق لا يدري ما الله قاض فيه، فليأخذ العبد من نفسه لنفسه، ومن دنياه لآخرته، ومن الشبيبة قبل الكبر، ومن الحياة قبل الممات، فالذي نفس محمد بيده : ما بعد الموت من مستعتب، وما بعد الدنيا من دار إلا الجنة أو النار " . (تهذيب الكامل 5/1، أعجاز القرآن 110)

B. English Translation

O mankind, you have landmarks [guidelines], so return to these landmarks [guidelines] [i.e., don't transgress boundaries] and you have an end, so return to that end. The servant [of Allah] is between two fears: Time that has already passed, he doesn't know what Allah is going to do about it [about an individual's own past actions], and time that is yet to come, he doesn't know what Allah is planning for it. So, the servant [of Allah] should take from his own self for himself [his own benefit], and from his own world [on this earth] for his hereafter, and from his youth before he gets older, and from life before death. I swear by the One the soul of Muhammad is in His hand [i.e. Allah], there is no excuse (chance) after death, and there is nothing after this life except paradise or hell. (Tahdheeb al-Kamil 5/1, I'jaz al Qur'an 110)

• Another General Speech

A. Arabic Text

<u>ومن خطبه عليه الصلاة والسلام</u>

" يا أيها الناس، كأنّ الموت فيها على غيرها قد كُتب، وكأن الحق فيها على غيرنا قد وَجَب، وكأنّ الذي يشيّع من الأموات سفر، عما قليل إلينا راجعون، نبوّئهم أجداثهم، ونأكل من تراثهم، كأنّا مخلدون بعدهم، ونسينا كل واعظة، وأمِنا كل جائحة، طوبى لمن شغله عيبه عن عيون الناس، طوبى لمن انفق مالاً أكتسبه من غير معصية، وجالس اهل الفقه والحكمة، وخالط أهل الذلّ والمسكنة، طوبى لمن زكت وحسنت خليقته، وطابت سريرته، وعزل عن الناس شرّه، طوبى لمن انفق الفضل من ماله، وامسك الفضل من قوله، ووسعته السنّة، ولم تستهوه البدعة". (صبح الأعشى 213/1).

B. English Translation

O people, it seems as if death in this life has been prescribed [only] for others [not you], and as is if being just with one another has been decreed [only] to others [to abide by but not you], and as if the buried dead ones are travelers away. But shortly, we will all join each other, we place them in their graves, and we eat what they have left behind as if we will live forever after them. We have forgotten every admonishment and we felt secure from every calamity. Glad tidings to the one who is busy with his own shortcomings away from others' shortcomings. Glad tidings to the one who is spending his wealth [in good cause] having earned it lawfully. [Glad tidings] to the one who has been in the company of people of understanding [knowledge] and wisdom, and who interacted with people of humility and modesty.

Glad tidings to the one whose manners are pure and good, and whose inside heart is upright, who isolated his own evil from people. Glad tidings to whoever spends [in good cause] the leftover of his money and who withholds the extra [unnecessary speech] of his talk, and who has applied my tradition (sunnah), and who was not attracted to any innovations.
(Subh al-A'sha 213/1)

• General Speech

A. Arabic Text

<u>خطبة له عليه الصلاة والسلام</u>

" ألا ايها الناس توبوا الى الله قبل ان تموتوا، وبادروا الأعمال الصالحة قبل ان تُشغلوا، وصِلوا الذي بينكم وبين ربّكم بكثرة ذكركم له، وكثرة الصدقة في السرّ والعلانية، تُرزقوا وتُؤجروا وتنصروا، واعلموا ان الله – عزّ وجلّ – قد افترض عليكم الجمعة في مقامي هذا، في عامي هذا، في شهري هذا، الى يوم القيامة. حياتي ومن بعد موتي، فمن تركها وله إمام، فلا جَمَعَ الله شمله ولا بارك له في امره، ألا ولا حجّ له ، ألا ولا صوم له، ألا ولا صدقة له، الا ولا برّ له، ألا ولا يؤم إعرابي مهاجراً، ألا ولا يؤم فاجر مؤمناً ، ألا ان يقهره سلطان يخاف سيفه او سوطه" .
(إعجاز القرآن ص 110)

143

B. English Translation

Truly O mankind, repent to Allah before you die and rush to good deeds before you get pre-occupied. Connect what is between you and your Lord by remembering Him frequently, and by often [giving] charity in secret and public. Then you will be provided with [good] livelihood, you will be rewarded, and you will be supported [victorious]. Know that Allah the Almighty has decreed the Friday prayer upon you while I am on this pulpit, during this year, in my presence, during this month, inmy presence until the Day of Judgment, while I am alive and after my death. Whoever doesn't perform it while he has an Imam [masjid], may Allah unsettle his life and un-bless his affair. Truly, [that person] has no hajj (pilgrimage) [i.e. his hajj is not acceptable], truly he has no fasting [his fasting is not acceptable], truly he has no charity [his charity is not acceptable], and truly he has no good deed to be accepted. Truly, no desert man (Bedouin) [who lacks knowledge] should lead an immigrant in prayer. Truly no Bedouin [i.e. someone who is not knowledgeable about religion] shall lead the prayer of an immigrant [someone who did the first migration with the prophet], and not disobedient shall lead a [pious] believer, unless he (the believer) fears the sword [being killed] or the whip of the powerful leader.
(I'jaz al-Qur'an p 110)

لا إلٰهَ إلّا الله مُحَمّدٌ رَسُولُ الله

لا إله إلا الله محمد رسول الله

144

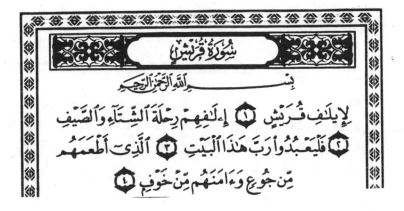

Quraish: Custodian of the Ka'bah

For the familiarity of the Quraish, their familiarity with the journeys by winter and summer, let them worship the Lord of this House, Who provides them with food against hunger, and with security against fear (of danger). (106: 1-4)

145

• Speech At The Liberation Of Makkah

A. Arabic Text

خطبته صلى الله عليه وسلم يوم فتح مكة

وقف على باب الكعبة ثم قال:

" لا إله إلا الله وحده لا شريك له، صدق وعده، ونصر عبده ، وهزم الأحزاب وحده، ألا كل مأثرة أو دم أو مـال يُدّعى فهوتحت قدمي هاتين، إلا سدانة البيت وسقاية الحجّ، ألا وقتيل الخطأ مثل العمد بالسوط والعصا، فيهمـا الديّة مغلّظة (مئة من الإبل) منها اربعـون خلفة فـي بطونهـا أولادهـا. يا معشـر قـريش إن الله قـد اذهب عنكم نخوة الجاهلية وتعظمها بالآباء، النـاس مـن آدم وآدم خلق من تراب، ثم تلا (يا ايها الناس إنّا خلقنـاكم مـن ذكر وانثى وجعلنـاكم شـعوباً وقبائـل لتعـارفوا إنّ أكـرمكم عنـد الله اتقـاكم) الآية، يا معشـر قريش ويا أهل مكة : مـا ترون إني فاعل بكم ؟ قالوا: خيرٌ، أخٌ كريمٌ ابن اخ كريم، ثم قـال : إذهبوا فأنتم الطلقاء " . (تاريخ الطبري : 120/3، وسيرة ابن هاشم 273/2).

B. English Translation

[The prophet] (pbuh) stood at the gate of the Ka'bah then said: "There is no deity but Allah, the only one with no partner; He fulfilled His promise, He gave support [and victory] to His servant, and alone He defeated the parties. Truly any vengeance or murder or possession that is claimed, is under my own two feet, except for the maintenance of the Ka'bah and for serving water to the pilgrims. Truly the accidental murder is like intentional use of

146

whip and stick, there unbearable diyyah [blood money – compensation] is one hundred of camels, forty of them [need to] be pregnant [their offspring in their litter (belly)].

O people of Quraysh. Verily Allah has taken away from you the pride of the era of Ignorance (Al-Jahiliyyah) and its bragging of its forefathers [ancestry]. All humans are from Adam and Adam was created from dust. Then he recited verse 49:13: O Mankind, we created you from a single pair of a male and a female, and we have made you nations and tribes that you may get to know one another. Indeed, the best among you in Allah's eyes is the most righteous.

O people of Quraysh and residents of Makkah, what do you think I'll do to you? They said: "Only good, you are a good brother, and a son of a good brother". Then he said: "You may disperse with full freedom."

(History of al-Tabari: 120/3 and the Seerah of Ibn Hisham 273/2)

• Speech At Tabuk

I. Introduction

Tabuk is a city in Northern part of Arabian Peninsula. Nine years after Hijra (Migration) of the Prophet (pbuh) to Madina, and in the month of Rajab (the Seventh of the Lunar Calendar), the Battle of Tabuk was to take place. It was summer time, and weather was very hot. It was brought to the attention of the Prophet (pbuh) that the Romans sent forty thousand (40,000) soldiers to get rid of the Prophet (pbuh) and the Muslims.

The Prophet (pbuh) recruited his companions. About thirty-thousands (30,000) accepted to go with him. Abu Bakr donated all his wealth while Omar donated fifty percent of his wealth. Muslims did not have enough horses or camels to ride on. They tried to share riding among themselves. Some of the hypocrites had false excuses and did not go with the Prophet (pbuh). One may read Surah Tawbah (Repentance) and see the detail information about them.

It took the Prophet and his companions two months to come back from this trip. The good thing about it was that the commander of the Roman army was afraid to enter into war. An agreement was signed by the leader of the Roman Army to live peacefully under the rules of Islam.

II. Arabic Text

<u>فى خطبته صلى الله عليه وسلم بتبوك وصلاته</u>

حمد الله واثنى عليه بما هو اهله، ثم قال: أما بعد، فإن اصدق الحديث كتاب الله، وأوثق العرى كلمة التقوى، وخير الملل ملة إبراهيم، وخير السنن سنة محمد، واشرف الحديث ذكر الله، واحسن القصص هذا القرآن، وخير الأمور عوازمها، وشر الامور محدثاتها، وأحسن الهدي هدي الانبياء، واشرف الموت قتل الشهداء، وأعمى العمى الضلالة بعد الهدى، وخير الأعمال ما نفع، وخير الهدى ما أتبع، وشر العمى عمى القلب، واليد العليا خير من اليد السفلى، وما قلّ وكفى خيرٌ مما أكثر وألهى، وشرّ المعذرة حيث يحضر الموت، وشرّ الندامة يوم القيامة،

148

ومن الناس من لا يأتي الجمعة إلا دبراً، ومنهم من لا يذكر الله إلا هجراً، ومـن أعظم الخطايـا اللسـانُ الكـذاب، وخير الغنى غنى النفس، وخير الزاد التقوى، وراس الحكم مخافة الله عز وجل، وخير ما وقر في القلوب اليقين، والإرتياب من الكفر، والنياحة من عمل الجاهلية، والغلول من جثا جهنم، والسكر كي من النـار، والشِعرُ من ابليس، والخمر جماع الإثم، وشر المأكل مـال اليتيم، والسعيد من وُعِظ بغيره، والشقيّ مـن شقي في بطن امـه. وإنمـا يصير احدكم الى موضع اربعة اذرع، والأمر الى الآخرة، ومـلاك العمل خواتمه. وشر الروايا روايا الكذب، وكل مـا هو آت قريب. وسباب المؤمن فسوق، وقتاله كفر، وأكل لحمه من معصية الله، وحرمة ماله كحرمة دمـه، ومـن يتألَّ على الله يكذبّه، ومن يغفر يُغفر له، ومن يَعفُ، يعفُ الله عنه، ومن يكظم الغيظ يـأجُرهُ الله، ومن يصبر على الرزيـة يعوضّه الله، ومن يبتغ السمعة، يُسمّع الله به، ومن يتصبّر، يُضعف الله لـه، ومـن يعص الله (ثم استغفر ثلاثاً)

وذكر أبو داوود فـي "سننه" مـن حـديث ابـن وهـب: أخبرنـي معاوية، عن سعيد بن غزوان، عن ابيـه انـه انزل بتبوك، وهـو حاج، فإذا رجل مقعد، فسألته عن أمره، قال: سأحدّثك حديثاً، فلا تُحدثّ به ما سمعت اني حيّ: أن رسول الله صلى الله عليه وسلم نزل بتبوك الى نخلة، فقال: "هذه قبلتنا"، ثم صلى اليه، قال: فأقبلـت وانـا غـلامٌ اسعى، حتى مـررت بينـي وبينـه، فقال: فاستفتحوا اعمالكم بالصبر على الجهاد والتمسوا بذلك ما وعدكم الله، وعليكم بالـذي أمـركم بـه، فإنـي حـريص علـى رشـدكم. إن

149

الإختلاف التنازع والتثبيط من امر العجز والضعف، وهو ممّا لا يحبّه الله، ولا يعطي عليه النصر.

ايها الناس، أنه قُذف في قلبي أن من كان على حرام فرغب عنه ابتغاء ما عند الله، غفر له ذنبه، ومن صلى على محمد صلاة صلى الله عليه وملائكته عشراً، ومن احسن وَقعَ اجره على الله في عاجل دنياه، او في آجل آخرته، ومن كان يؤمن بالله واليوم الآخر، فعليه الجمعة يوم الجمعة، إلا صبياً او امرأة أو مريضاً أو عبداً مملوكاً، ومن استغنى عنها استغنى الله عنه، والله غنيّ حميد.

ما أعلم من عمل يقربكم الى الله إلا وقد امرتكم به، ولا أعلم من عمل يقربّكم الى النار إلا وقد نهيتكم عنه، وإنه قد نفثَ الروح الأمين في روعي انه لن تموت نفسي حتى تستوفي اقصى رزقها لا ينقص منه شيء وإن أبطأ عنها، فاتقوا الله ربّكم، وأجملوا في طلب الرزق، ولا يحملنّكم استبطاؤه على ان تطلبوه بمعصية ربّكم، فإنه لا يقدر على ما عند إلا بطاعته، قد بيّن لكم الحلال والحرام، غير ان بينهما شبهاً من الأمر لم يعلمها كثير من الناس إلا من عصم، فمن تركها حفظ عرضه ودينه، ومن وقع فيها كان كالراعي الى جنب الحمى اوشك ان يقع فيه، وليس ملك إلا وله حمى، ألا وإن حمى الله محارمه، والمؤمن من المؤمنين كالرأس من الجسد، اذ اشتكى تداعى اليه سائر جسده، والسلام عليكم.

(جمهرة خطب العرب – الجزء الأول)

III. English Translation

After praising Allah, he said: *"Verily the most veracious discourse is the Book of Allah. The most trustworthy handhold is the word of piety. The best of the religions is the religion of Ibrahim. The best of the precedents is the precedent of Muhammad. The noblest speech is the invocation of Allah. The finest of the narratives is this Qur'an. The best of the affairs is that which has been firmly resolved upon. The worst in religion are those things which are created without sanction. The best of the ways is the guidance of the Prophets. The noblest death is the death of a martyr. The most miserable blindness is waywardness after guidance. The best of actions is that which is beneficial. The best guidance is that which is put into practice. The worst blindness is the blindness of the heart.*

The upper hand is better than the power hand [i.e. the hand which gives charity is better than the one which receives it]. The little that suffices is better than what is abundant and alluring. The worst apology is that which is tendered when death approaches. The worst remorse is that which is felt on the day of Resurrection.

There are some people who come to Friday prayer with hesitance and delay, others remember Allah with reluctance. A lying tongue [i.e. a person who lies] is among the gravest sins; the most valuable wealth is the contentment of the heart, and the best provision is that of piety. The highest wisdom is the fear of Allah, the Almighty and the Great. The best thing to be cherished in the hearts is faith [conviction], and doubt is a part of disbelief [infidelity].

151

Impatient wailing and fulsome laudation of the dead is an act of ignorance. Betrayal leads one to the fire of hell. Drunkenness amounts to burning. [Obscene] poetry is the work of the devil. Wine is the mother of all evil. The worst thing eaten is the property [wealth - belongings] of the orphan. The joyful is the one who receives admonition from others, and the overbearing is the one who is overbearing in his mother's womb.

Each one of you must resort to a place of your cubit [grave]. Your affairs would de decided ultimately in the next life. The ultimate action is the one done at the end of one's life. The worst narratives are those [based on] lies, and everything that will occur is actually approaching. Insulting the believer is lewdness, murdering [a believer] is an act of disbelief. To backbite is [an act of] disobedience of Allah. Inviolability [and sacredness] of his [the believer's] property is like that of his blood.

He who [falsely] swears by Allah, in fact falsifies Him. He who pardons others is himself granted pardon [from Allah]. He who forgives others, is forgiven [by Allah for his sins]. He who suppresses his rage is rewarded [by Allah], and whoever is patient in a calamity, Allah makes it up for him. He who acts only for fame and reputation, Allah disgraces him. He who shows patience and forbearance, Allah doubles his reward. He who disobeys Allah, Allah chastises him.

I seek the forgiveness of Allah
I seek the forgiveness of Allah
I seek the forgiveness of Allah"

152

خُطْبَةُ حِجَّةِ الْوَدَاعِ

• Farewell Hajj Khutbah

I.   Preface

Pilgrimage in Islam was prescribed during the 9th year of the Islamic Hijra or 632 C.E. The Prophet (pbuh) of Islam deputed Abu Bakr to lead the pilgrims to perform Hajj. He went with 300 people and performed the rites of Hajj.

During the 10th year of Hijra, the Prophet (pbuh) left Madina on the 26th of Zul Qi'dah with an average of 90,000 Muslims who joined him to perform Hajj. On the 9th day of Zul Hijjah the Prophet (pbuh) left Makkah to Arafat with a group of Muslims who exceeded 115,000. At Mount of Mercy (Al-Rahmah), the Prophet (pbuh) mounted his camel, and addressed the Muslims while Raabiah Ibn Umaiyah Ibn Khalaf was repeating after the Prophet sentence by sentence.

This khutbah was the last one that the Prophet delivered. The Hajj performance to Makkah and Arafat was the only one and the last one that the Prophet did. For this reason, the speech that he gave was called khutbathul Wida': The Farewell Speech, the Farewell Khutbah, The Farewell Sermon, or the Farewell Address.

Because of its importance and its significance, because of its topics covered, because of its universality, and because of its values and of its principles, the author wishes to submit some reflections about the Farewell Speech of the Prophet (pbuh).

A. Arabic Text

" اليوم أكملت لكم دينكم وأتممت عليكم نعمتي ورضيت لكم الإسلام ديناً " (سورة المائدة -3)

" الحمد لله نحمده ونستعينه ونتوب اليه، ونعوذ بالله من شرور انفسنا ومن سيئات اعمالنا، من يَهدِ الله فلا مضل له، ومن يضلل فلن فلا هادي له، واشهد ان لا إله إلاّ الله وحده لا شريك له، واشهد ان محمداً عبده ورسوله.

أوصيكم عباد الله بتقوى الله، وأحثّكم على طاعته، واستفتح بالذي هو خير.

أما بعد ايها الناس، اسمعوا منّي أبيّن لكم، فإني لا أدري لعلّي لا ألقاكم بعد عامي هذا، في موقفي هذا.

أيها الناس، أن دماءكم، وأموالكم وأعراضكم، حرام عليكم الى ان تلقوا ربّكم، كحرمة يومكم هذا، في شهركم هذا، في بلدكم هذا. ألا هل بلّغت ؟ اللهم فاشهد.

فمن كانت عنده امانة فليؤدها الى من ائتمنه عليها.

وإنّ ربا الجاهلية موضوع، ولكن لكم رءوس اموالكم، لا تظلمون ولا تُظلمون . قضى الله انـه لا ربا، وإن اول ربا ابدأ بـه، ربى عميّ العباس بن عبد المطلب.

وإن دماء الجاهلية موضوعة، وإن أول دم نبدأ بـه، دم عامر بن ربيعة بن الحارث بن عبد المطلب.

وإن مآثر الجاهلية موضوعة، غير السدانة والسقاية.

والعَمد قود، وشبه العمد ما قتل بالعصا والحجز، وفيه مائة بعير. فمن زاد فهو من اهل الجاهلية، ألا هل بلّغت ؟ اللهم فاشهد.

أما بعد ايها الناس! إنّ الشيطان قد يئس ان يعبد في ارضكم هذه. ولكنـه قـد رضـي ان يُطـاع فيمـا سـوى ذلك، ممّـا تحقرون مـن اعمالكم، فاحذروه على دينكم.

أيها الناس ! إنمّا النسيء زيادة في الكفر، يضلّ بـه الذين كفروا. يحلّونه عاماً ويحرّمونه عاماً، ليواطئوا عدة مـا حرّم الله، فيحلّوا ما حرم الله، ويحرّموا ما أحلّ الله. وإن الزمـان قد استدار كيوم خلق كهيئته يوم خلق الله السموات والارض، "وإن عدة الشهور عنـد الله إثنـا عشـر شـهراً فـي كتـاب الله يـوم خلق السمـاوات والأرض، منهـا اربعـة حُرمّ" ثلاثـة متواليـات وواحدٌ فـردٌ: ذو القعدة وذو الحجـة ومُحـرّم ورجبُ مُضـر، الـذين بـين جمـادى وشعبان.

ألا هل بلّغت ؟ اللهم فاشهد.

أما بعد أيها الناس! إن لنسائكم عليكم حقاً ولكم عليهنّ حق : لكم عليهنّ ان لا يـوطئن فرشكم غيركم، ولا يُدخلن أحداً تكرهونـه بيوتكم إلاّ بإذنكم، ولا يـأتين بفاحشـة، فإن فعلن، فإنّ الله قد اذن لكم ان تعضلوهنّ وتهجروهنّ في المضاجع، وتضربوهنّ ضرباً غيـر مبّـرح، فـإن انتهـين واطعنكم، فعلـيكم رزقهـن وكسـوِّهن بالمعروف.

واستوصوا بالنساء خيراً فإنهن عندكم عوان، لا يملكن لأنفسهنّ شيئاً، وإنكم أخذتموهنّ بأمانـة الله، واستحللتم فـروجهنّ بكلمـة الله، فاتقوا الله في النسـاء واستوصوا بهنّ خيراً. ألا هل بلّغت ؟ اللهم فاشهد.

أيها النـاس! إنمـا المؤمنـون أخوة، ولا يحلُّ لامرئ مـالُ أخيـه إلاّ عن طيب نفس منه .

ألا هل بلّغت ؟ اللهم فاشهد.

فلا ترجعُنّ بعدي كفاراً يضرب بعضكم رقاب بعض. فإني تركت فيكم ما إن أخذتم به لن تضلّوا بعده: كتاب الله وسنّة نبيه. ألا هل بلّغت ؟ اللهم فاشهد.

أيها النّاس! إنّ ربّكم واحد وإنّ أباكم واحد. كلكم لآدم، وآدم من تراب، أكرمكم عند الله اتقاكم، وليس لعربي على عجمي فضل إلاّ بالتقوى. ألا هل بلّغت ؟ اللهم فاشهد. قالوا: نعم. قال: فليّبلغ الشاهدُ الغائب.

أيها النّاس! إنّ الله قد قسم لكل وارث نصيبه من الميراث، ولا يجوز لوارث وصيةً، ولا يجوز وصية في اكثر من الثلث. والولد للفراش وللعاهر الحجر. مَن ادّعى الى غير ابيه أو تولّى غير مواليه فعليه لعنة الله والملائكة والنّاس اجمعين، لا يُقبل منه صرف ولا عدل. والسلام عليكم .

II.   Farewell Hajj Khutbah

Since it is impossible to write all about the subjects of the Prophet's Sirah, it is better to include here The Khutbah of the Farewell Hajj of the Prophet (pbuh).

B. English Translation

O people! listen well to my words, for I do not know whether I will meet you again on such an occasion in the future.

O people! Your lives and your properties will be inviolate until you meet your Lord. The safety of your lives and of your properties will be as inviolate as this sacred day and sacred *month. Remember that you will indeed meet your Lord, and that He will indeed reckon your deeds. Thus do I warn you. Whoever of you is keeping a trust of someone else will return that trust to its rightful owner. All Riba obligations will henceforth be waived. Your capital, however, is yours to keep. You will neither inflict nor suffer inequity. Allah (swt) has judged that there will be no Riba and that all the Riba due to `Abbas ibn Abd Al-Muttalib will henceforth be waived. Every right arising out of homicide in pre-Islamic days is henceforth waived. And the first such right I waive is that arising from the murder of Rabi'ah Al-Harith ibn `Abd Al-Muttalib.*

O People! the devil has lost all hope of ever being worshipped in this land of yours. Nevertheless, he still is anxious to determine the lesser of your deeds. Beware of him, therefore, for the safety of your religion.

O people! Changing or tampering with the calendar is evidence of great unbelief and confirms the unbelievers in their misguidance. They indulge in it one year and forbid it the next in order to make permissible. The pattern according to which the time reckoned is always the same. With Allah (swt), the months are twelve in number. Four of them are sacred. Three of these are successive and one occurs singly between the months of Jumada and Sha'ban.

O people! to you a right belongs with respect to your women, and to your women a right with respect to you. It is your right that they not fraternize either any one of whom you do not approve, as well as never to commit adultery. But if they do, then Allah (swt) has permitted you to isolate them within their homes and to chastise them without cruelty. But if they abide by your right, then to them belongs the right to be fed and clothed in kindness. Do treat your women well and be kind to them, for they are your partners and committed helpers. Remember that you have taken them as your wives and enjoyed their flesh only under Allah's (swt) trust and with His permission. Reason well, therefore, O people! and ponder my words which I now convey to you. I am leaving you with the Book of Allah (swt), the Sunnah of His Prophet (saw). If you follow them, you will never go astray.

O people! harken well to my words. Learn that every Muslim is a brother to every Muslim, and that the Muslims constitute one brotherhood. Nothing will be legitimate to a Muslim which belongs to a fellow Muslim unless it was given freely and willingly. Do not, therefore, do injustice to your own selves.

O Allah (swt)! Have I conveyed Your Message?

III.   General Reflections

The charter of human rights was laid down by Islam for over 1,400 years, long before the UN charter* was written. The charter of human rights in Islam was recognized, emphasized and applied in the daily life of the Muslim Ummah. The human rights preached, taught and practiced by the Prophet of Islam surpassed those of every nation and every society.

The farewell address of the first President of the United States of America Mr. George Washington was delivered in 1796. It emphasized that there should be no entanglement of foreign alliances. He talked about trade and commerce, about being free and independent, and about being proud to be Americans. His farewell address was written by Mr. Madison and then rewritten by

Mr. Hamilton. George Washington gave his farewell address so as to retire and to spend the rest of his life on his farm; unlike Prophet Muhammad (pbuh) who maintained his responsibility until the last minute of his life.

The former president of the USA Mr. James Carter (1977-1980) championed the concept of human rights. In reality he was championing only for the dissident Jews of Russia. He did not care much for the rest of the world. He did not even care enough for the homeless, jobless, shelter less, foodless, and penniless Americans who lived on the streets of America throughout the years of their lives and through the winter freezing seasons.

It was only in the 60's that late President Lyndon B. Johnson signed the bill of Civil Rights Act** in the USA. While in South Africa, even until 1998, the black majority were denied of their human and civil rights. They are segregated, discriminated and denied their human rights by the white minority regime.

President Ronald Reagan was very much concerned about the Human Rights of the dissident Jews of Russia. In his meeting with Secretary General Michael Gorbachev in Reykjavik, Iceland, October 11-12, 1986, the two sides agreed to pursue future discussion of Soviet emigration and the reunification of divided families. Mr. Reagan forgot about the separated families of the world including his own citizens. He was even helping some other countries who became belligerent and in turn killed thousands of innocent civilians in their own homes.

The most astonishing incident and the double standard situation is that of Rev. Jessie Jackson. In his meeting with Mr. Gorvachev in Reykjavik, Iceland, 1986, he also was concerned about the dissident Jews of Russia. It seems he forgot or he overlooked the miserable situation of his own people and those of his own racial background. He tried to forget the life in the slum areas and the ghettos. It is good to be concerned for others who are thousands of miles away, but it would be nobler of him, as a presidential candidate and as a Reverend, to talk and to help his own citizens.

The Farewell Khutbah of the Prophet (pbuh) covers all aspects of life. It is the best charter of guidance to mankind for social justice, racial harmony, and international peace with people of other societies. The Prophet enjoined virtue, piety, modesty, and brotherhood of mankind irrespective of color, race, nationality, ethnic background or language. The topics of his Khutbah marked a turning point in the history of the world. He showed the way to amity and to a well civilized behavior. He established an ideal, but a practical, an eternal, and a universal system of values and principles. He also laid down a pattern of conduct based on divine will and injunctions.

IV.   Final Remarks

The "Farewell Khutbah" of Prophet Muhammad (pbuh) was indeed addressed to all mankind at all times and for all generations. It encompasses many aspects of life (general and specific). He laid down the foundation of morality, chastity, modesty, justice, equality, brotherhood, and accountability. He abolished economic exploitation, human enslavement, paganism, transgression and all systems that contradict with the systems of Allah.

He demanded that the congregating Muslims should deliver his message to all mankind. Accordingly they did deliver the message. For this reason the message of Islam has spread through the centuries to every corner of the world. The number of the Muslims has exceeded one and half billion people.

The Final Address of the Prophet (pbuh) should be in everyone's home, library, office, classroom, car, UN offices, the White House, and in all public transport and public places. It should be taught in schools, and its principles and values are to be followed by all segments of society. Then and only then, people will enjoy their life.

The Sacred Mosque of the Prophet in Madina

---

*The Charter of UN signed at San Francisco on June 1945 as the League of Nations.
** The Civil Rights Act (P.L. 88-352) was signed by President Johnson on July 2, 1964

• Speech During His Illness;
Prior to His Death

<u>خطبته صلى الله عليه وسلم في مرض موته</u>

عن الفضل بن عبّاس قال:

جاءني رسول الله صلى الله عليه وسلم، فخرجت إليه فوجدته موكوعاً قد عصب رأسه، فقال: **" خُذْ بيدي يا فضل"**، فأخذت بيده حتى جلس على المنبر، ثم قال : ناد في الناس، فاجتمعوا اليه، فقال:

" أما بعد، أيها الناس فإني احمد اليه الله الذي لا إله إلاّ هو، وإنه قد دنا منّي خُفوق ما بين اظهركم، فمن كنت جلدت له ظهراً، فهذا ظهري فليستقد منه، ومن كنت شتمت له عرضاً، فهذا عرضي فليستقد منه، ومن أخذت له مالاً، فهذا مالي فليأخذ منه، ولا يخشى الشحناء من قبلي، فإنها ليست من شأني، ألا وان احبّكم اليّ من اخذ مني حقاً ، إن كان له، أو حلّلني فلقيت ربّي وأنا طيب النفس، وقد ارى ان هذا غير مغن غني حتى أقوم فيكم مراراً " .

ثم نزل فصلى الظهر، ثم رجع فعاد الى مقالته الأولى، فادعى عليه رجل بثلاثة دراهم فأعطاه عوضها ثم قال: **" أيها الناس، من كان عنده شيء فليؤده ولا يقل فضوح الدنيا، ألا وإنّ فضوح الدنيا أهون من فضوح الآخرة "**، ثم صلى على اصحاب أحد واستغفر لهم ثم قال: **" إنّ عبداً خيّره الله فيما بين الدنيا وبين ما عنده فاختار ما عنده"** ، فبكى أبو بكر، وقال : **" فديناك بأنفسنا وآبائنا"** .   (تاريخ الطبري 2: 192 والكامل لإبن أثير 2: 254)

162

His Speech (pbuh) During His Illness Prior to His death

Al-Fadl ibn Abbas said: "The Messenger of Allah (pbuh) came to me and I noticed that he was sick, and wrapped to his head. He said to me: 'hold with my hand', Fadl, and I held his hand until he sat on the pulpit, then he said: 'call the people to gather' – the people gathered and he said: 'Now, O people, I am truly expressing my praise to Him, Allah the one that there is no deity but Him; and truely the disappearance of what is before you [i.e. my death] is getting closer to me, so whoever I have lashed his back, here is my back so he can take his right – and whoever that I had verbally abused his honor, here is my honor and let him take his right, and whoever I have taken a piece of property from, here is my property and let him take his right, and should never have hatred from my side. Truly, the most beloved among you to me is the one who takes his right from me if he has a right on me, or forgives me (exempts me) so that I may meet my Lord in good spirit – and I may see this is not good enough 'the regret for justice' until I repeat it several times.'

Then he left the forum and prayed Dhuhr, then he came back and repeated his first request, and a man claimed three dirhams from the prophet who gave him its equivalent. Then he said: 'O people, whoever owes something should give it back and not think of the embarrassment of this life – truly, the embarrassment of this life is a lot easier than the embarrassment of the Hereafter.' Then he prayed for the companions of the Battle of Uhud and asked forgiveness for them – and then he said: 'verily a servant [of Allah], Allah has given him a choice between this life and what Allah has, and the servant has chosen the latter'. Abu Bakr cried and said: 'we sacrifice ourselves and our fathers for you'.
(History of al-Tabari 192:2 and al-Kamil by Ibn Atheer 254-2)

Chapter (13)   Prophet's Supplications

Al-Ahzab: The Confederates

Muhammad is not the father of any of your men, but (he is) the Messenger of Allah, and the Seal of the Prophets: and Allah has full knowledge of all things. O you who believe! Remember Allah, with much remembrance; and Glorify Him morning and evening. He it is Who sends Blessings on you, as do His angels, that He may bring you out from the depths of Darkness into Light: and He is full of Mercy to the Believers. (33:40-43)

In this Section there is a small list of Du`aa' recited by the Prophet (pbuh) on different occasions. They are reported here in their original Arabic texts as well as the transliterated forms and their English meaning. Such Du`aa' could be of great help to the Khateebs and to the individual Muslims. Not all of them are to be used only on Friday. They are meant for different occasions in the life of the individual as well as the Jumu'ah.

• Supplication in Fajr Salat

دُعَاءُ ٱلْفَجْرِ

اللَّهُمَّ اهْدِنِي فِيْمَنْ هَدَيْتَ ، وَعَافِنِي فِيْمَنْ عَافَيْتَ ، وَتَوَلَّنِيْ فِيْمَنْ تَوَلَّيْتَ ، وَبَارِكْ لِيْ فِيْمَا أَعْطَيْتَ ، وَقِنِيْ شَرَّ مَا قَضَيْتَ. فَإِنَّكَ تَقْضِيْ وَلَايُقْضَى عَلَيْكَ. إِنَّهُ لَايَذِلُّ مَنْ وَالَيْتَ. تَبَارَكْتَ رَبَّنَا وَتَعَالَيْتَ .

Allahumma ihdinee feeman hadaita, wa 'afinee feeman 'afaita, wa tawallanee feeman tawallaita, wa barik lee feeman a'ataita, waqincc sharra ma qadaita, fa innaka taqdee wala yuqda alaika, innahu la yazillu man walaita, tabarakta wa ta 'alaita.

O Allah! Guide me among those whom You have guided aright and preserve me among those whom You have preserved, and befriend me among those whom You have befriended, and bless me in what You have granted me, and protect me from the evil of what You have judged; for surely You judge and none can judge against You; surely

165

he whom You befriend is not disgraced. Blessed are You our Lord, and Exalted.

• Supplication for Forgiveness

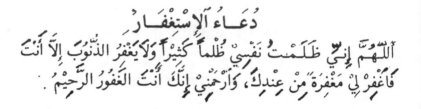

Allahuma innee zalamtu nafsee zulman katheeran, wa la yaghfiruz-zonooba illa anta. Faghfirlee maghfiratan min'indika, warhamnee innaka antal ghafurur raheeem.

O Allah! I have been greatly unjust to myself and none grant protection against faults but You; therefore, protect me with a protection from Yourself, and have mercy on me, surely You are the Forgiving, the Merciful.

• Supplication after Salat

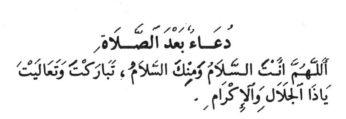

166

Allahumma antassalamu, wa minkassalamu, tabarakta ya thaljalali wal ikram.

O Allah! You are the fountainhead of peace and from You is peace; You are blessed, O! Lord of Glory and Honor.

• **Supplication for Distress**

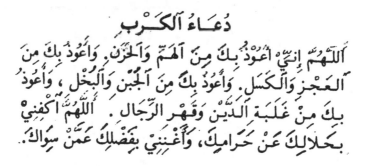

Allahuma inni A'uthu Bika minal hammni wal hazan; wa A'uthu Bika minal 'ajzi wal kassal; wa A'uthu Bika minal jubni wal bukhli; wa A'uthu Bika min ghalabatid daini wa qahrir rijali. Allahummak finee bi halalika 'an haramika; wa aghninee be Fadlika 'amman siwaka. Allahuma inni A'uthu Bika min 'Azabil qabri; wa Athoozu Bika min fitnatil mahya, wa fitnatil mamati. Allahuma inni A'uthu Bika minal ma'thami wal maghrami.

O Allah! (swt) I come under Your refuge from anxieties and grief; and betake Your refuge from impotence and inactiveness; and betake Your refuge from cowardice and niggardliness; and betake Your refuge from excessiveness of debt and oppression of people. O Allah! (swt) Suffice legitimate things for me, saving me from the illegitimate and make me independent in subsistence with Your grace from everyone except You. O Allah! (swt) I betake Your refuge from chastisement of the grave; and betake Your refuge from the seduction of anti-Christ from faith in You; and betake Your refuge from hardships of life and afflictions at the time of death. O Allah (swt)! I betake refuge from sins and debt.

• Supplication after Azan

دُعَـاءٌ بَعْدَ الأَذَانِ

أَللّٰهُمَّ رَبَّ هٰذِهِ ٱلدَّعْوَةِ ٱلتَّامَّةِ، وَٱلصَّلاَةِ ٱلقَائِمَةِ، آتِ مُحَمَّدًا ٱلْوَسِيلَةَ والفَضِيلَةَ، وَٱبْعَثْهُ اللهمَّ ٱلمَقَامَ ٱلمحمودَ الذِي وَعَدْتَهُ

Allahumma rabba Hathihid-da'watit-tammati wassalatil qa-imati aati Muhammadanil-wasselata wal-fadeelata wab-ath-hu al-maqamal mahmuda-nillazi wa'adtahu.

O Allah! The Lord of this perfect call and the ever living prayer, grant to Muhammad nearness and excellence and raise him to the position of glory which You have promised him.

• Marriage Sermon

خُطْبَةُ النِّكَاحِ

أَلْحَمْدُ لِلَّهِ، وَنَحْمَدُهُ وَنَسْتَعِينُهُ وَنَسْتَغْفِرُهُ، وَنَعُوذُ بِاللهِ مِنْ شُرُورِ أَنْفُسِنَا وَمِنْ سَيِّئَاتِ أَعْمَالِنَا، مَنْ يَهْدِهِ اللهُ فَلَا مُضِلَّ لَهُ، وَمَنْ يُضْلِلْهُ فَلَا هَادِيَ لَهُ، وَأَشْهَدُ أَنْ لَا إِلَهَ إِلَّا اللهُ وَأَشْهَدُ أَنَّ مُحَمَّداً عَبْدُهُ وَرَسُولُهُ. يَاأَيُّهَا الَّذِينَ آمَنُوا اتَّقُوا اللهَ حَقَّ تُقَاتِهِ وَلَاتَمُوتُنَّ إِلَّا وَأَنْتُمْ مُسْلِمُونَ. يَاأَيُّهَا النَّاسُ اتَّقُوا رَبَّكُمُ الَّذِي خَلَقَكُمْ مِنْ نَفْسٍ وَاحِدَةٍ وَخَلَقَ مِنْهَا زَوْجَهَا وَبَثَّ مِنْهُمَا رِجَالاً كَثِيراً وَنِسَاءً. وَاتَّقُوا اللهَ الَّذِي تَسَاءَلُونَ بِهِ وَالْأَرْحَامَ إِنَّ اللهَ كَانَ عَلَيْكُمْ رَقِيباً. يَاأَيُّهَا الَّذِينَ آمَنُوا اتَّقُوا اللهَ وَقُولُوا قَوْلاً سَدِيداً يُصْلِحْ لَكُمْ أَعْمَالَكُمْ وَيَغْفِرْ لَكُمْ ذُنُوبَكُمْ، وَمَنْ يُطِعِ اللهَ وَرَسُولَهُ فَقَدْ فَازَ فَوْزاً عَظِيماً .

Alhamdu lillahi, wa nahmaduhu, wa nasta'eenuhu, wa nastaghfiruhu, wa na'udhu billahi min shururi anfusina wa min sayyi'ati a'malina; man yahdihillahu fala mudilla lahu, wa man yudlillhu fala hadiya lahu; wa ash-hadu an la ilaha illallahu, wa ash-hadu anna Muhammadan 'abduhu wa rasuluh; ya ayyuhal-ladheena aamanut-taqul-laha haqqa tuqatihee wa la tumutunna illa wa antum muslimun; ya ayyuhan-ansut-taqu rabbakum-ullathi khalaqaqum min nafsin wahidatin, wa khalaqa minha zawjaha wa baththa minhuma rijalan katheeran wa nisaa-aa, wattaqullahal-ladhi tasa'aluna

169

bihee wal arhama. Innallaha kana 'alaikum raqeeba; ya ayyuhalladheena aamanut-taqullaha wa quloo qawlan sadidaa. Yuslih lakum a'amalakum wa yaghfir lakum dhuzoo bakum; wa man yuti'illaha wa rasulahu faqad faza fawzan azima.

All praise is due to Allah, and we praise Him, and we beseech His help, and we ask His protection, and we betake Allah's refuge from the evils of our animal life and from the bad results of our actions. Whom Allah guides there is none to misguide him, and whom Allah pleases to lead astray, there is no one to guide him; and I bear witness that there is none to be worshipped but Allah; and I bear witness that Muhammad is His servant and His apostle.

O you who believe! Be careful of (your duty to) Allah with the care which is due to Him and die not unless you are Muslims. O people! Be careful of (your duty to) your Lord, Who created you from a single being and created its mate of the same (kind) and spread from these two, many men and women; and be careful of (your duty to) Allah, by whom you demand one of another (your rights) and (to the ties of) relationship; surely, Allah ever watches over you. O you who believe! Be careful of (your duty to) Allah and speak the right word. He will put your deeds into a right state for you, and forgive you your faults; and whoever obeys Allah and His apostle, he indeed has achieved a mighty success.

• Supplication for the Dead

دُعَـاءُ لِلْمَـيِّت

١٢٠٤ ـ وعن أبي هُريرة وأبي قَتَادَةَ ، وأبي إبْرَاهِيمَ الأَشْهَلِيِّ عَنْ أبِيه ـ وَأَبُوه صَحَابيٌّ ـ رضي الله عنهم ، عَنِ النبي صلى الله عليهِ وسلّم أنَّه صَلَّى عَلى جِنَازَةٍ فقال :« اللَّهُمَّ اغْفِرْ لِحَيِّنَا وَمَيِّتِنَا ، وَصَغِيرِنَا وَكَبِيرِنَا ، وَذَكَرِنَا وَأُنْثَانَا ،وَشاهِدِنَا وَغَائِبِنَا . اللَّهُمَّ مَنْ أَحْيَيْتَهُ مِنَّا، فَأَحْيِهِ عَلَى الإِسْلامِ ،وَمَنْ تَوَفَّيْتَهُ مِنَّا، فَتَوَفَّهُ عَلى الإِيمانِ ؛ اللَّهُمَّ لاَتَحْرِمنَا أجْرَهُ، وَلا تَفْتِنَّا بَعْدَهُ » (١) ، رواه الترمذي (٢) من رواية أبي هُرَيْرَةَ وَالأَشْهَلِيِّ ،

Allahummagfhirli hayyina wa mayyitina, wa shahidina wa gha-ibina, wa sagheerina wa kabeerina, wa zakarina wa unthana. Allahumma man ahyaitahu minna fa ahyihi 'alal islam, wa man Tawaffaitahu minna Fatawaffanu 'alal imani; allahumma la tahrimna ajrahu, wala taftinna ba 'dahu.

Allah, forgive our living and our dead, and those of us who are present; and those who are absent, and our little ones and full grown one; and our men and our women. O Allah! Whom You keep alive from among us, keep him alive in Islam and whom You cause to die from among us, make him die with faith (in You). O Allah, do not keep us away from his reward and do not put us in trial after him.

171

• Different Du`aa' in Sujood

The following Du`aa' were recited by the Prophet (pbuh) at different times while he was making Sujood. Each Du`aa' has its own beauty and significance. They are of great help to our relations with Allah (swt) the Creator of the whole universe. The following is a list of a few Du`aa's that were reported on behalf of the Prophet (pbuh).

A. The First Du`aa' Goes as Follows:

Narrated by Ali (May Allah be pleased with him) that the Messenger of Allah (swt) used to say while in Sujood the following:

١ ـ عن علي رضي الله عنه : أن رسول الله صلى الله عليه وسلم كان إذا سجد يقول : « اللهم لك سجدت ، وبك آمنت ، ولك أسلمت ، سجد وجهي للذي خلقه فصوّره فأحسن صُوره ، فشق سمعه وبصره : فتبارك الله أحسن الخالقين. » رواه أحمد ومسلم .

O Allah (swt), I prostrated to you, I believed in You. I submitted to You. I prostrate my face to the One Who molded it in the best shape, and slit its hearing and sight: Glory be to Allah (swt) the Best Creator. (Ahmad and Muslim)

B. The Second Du`aa' Goes as Follows:

Ibn Abbas ® explained the Salat of the Prophet (pbuh) after midnight saying: "Then the Prophet (pbuh) went to perform salat and while in Sujood he said:

٢ – وعن ابن عباس رضي الله عنهما يصف صلاة رسول الله صـــلى الله عليه وسلم في التهجد قال : ثم خرج إلى الصلاة فصلى وجعل يقول في صلاته أو في سجوده : « اللهم اجعل في قلبي نوراً ، وفي سمعي نوراً ، وفي بصري نوراً ، وعن يميني نوراً ، وعن يساري نوراً ، وأمامي نوراً ، وخلفي نوراً ، وفوقي نوراً ، وتحتي نوراً ، واجعلني نوراً

O Allah (swt)! Put light in my heart, light in my hearing, light in my sight, light on my right, light on my left, light in front of me, light behind me, light from under me, and make me light (or make for me light). (Muslim and Ahmad)

C. The Third Du`aa' Goes as Follows:

٣ – وعن عائشة : أنها فقدت النبي صلى الله عليه وسلم من مضجعه فلمسته بيدها ، فوقعت عليه وهو ساجد ، وهو يقول : « رب أعط نفسي تقواها ، وزكها ، أنتَ خيرُ من زكاها ، أنت وليها وَمَولاها » رواه أحمد .

173

Narrated by `Aisha ® that she did not find the Prophet (pbuh) in bed, and found him prostrating and saying:

O my God: give myself its protection (Taqwa), and purify it as You are the Best Purifier, and You are its Master and Protector. (Ahmad)

D. The Fourth Du`aa' Goes as Follows:

٤ – وعن أبي هريرة أن النبي صلى الله عليه وسلم كان يقول في سجوده
« اللهم اغفر لي ذنبي كله ، دقه وجله (١) وأوله وآخره ، وعلانيته وسرّه »
رواه مسلم وأبو داود والحاكم .

Narrated by Abu Hurairah ® that the Prophet (pbuh) used to say while in Sujood:

O Allah (swt)! Forgive all my sins: the smallest and the biggest, the first and the last, and the one in public and the one in private. (Muslim, Abu Dawood, and Al-Hakim)

E. The Fifth Du`aa' Goes as Follows:

٥ – وعن عائشة قالت : فقدت النبي صلى الله عليه وسلم ذات ليلـة
فلمسته في المسجد ، فإذا هو ساجد وقدماه منصوبتان ، وهو يقول : « اللهم
إني أعوذ برضاك من سخطك ، وأعوذ بمعافاتك من عقوبتك ، وأعوذ بـك
منك لا أحصي ثناء عليك أنت كما أثنيت على نفسك » رواه مسلم

Narrated by `Aisha ® that once she did not find the Prophet (pbuh) at night in the house but found him in the Masjid. He was in a state of Sujood saying:

> *O Allah (swt)! I seek refuge in Your pleasure from Your anger; and I seek refuge in Your forgiveness from Your punishment; and I seek refuge in You from You. I don't know how much I should praise You as much as You have done Yourself.* (Muslim)

F.   The Sixth Du`aa' Goes as Follows:

٦ ــ وعنها أنها فقدته صلى الله عليه وسلم ذات ليلة ، فظنت أنه ذهب إلى بعض نسائه ، فتحسسته فإذا هو راكع أو ساجد يقول : « سبحانك اللهــم وبحمدك ، لا إله إلا أنت » فقالت : « بأبي أنت وأمي ، إني لفي شأن وإنك لفي شأن آخر » رواه أحمد ومسلم والنسائي .

Narrated by `Aisha ® that once she did not find the Prophet (pbuh) at home and she thought he left her secretly and went to one of his wives. I looked for him and found him in the Masjid saying while in the state of Rukoo' (Sujood) the following:

> *Glory be to You, O Allah (swt)! and thanks to You! There is no lord worthy of worship except You.*

I replied" "O Messenger of Allah (swt)! You are in a status of my father and mother! I am indeed in a different world (in my thoughts) while you are in another!" (Ahmad, Muslim, and Nisai)

G.   The Seventh Du`aa' Goes as Follows:

٧ ـ وكان صلى الله عليه وسلم يقول وهو ساجد : « اللهم اغفر لي
خطيئتي وجهلي ، وإسرافي في أمري ، وما أنت أعلم به مني . اللهم اغفر لي
جدي وهزلي ، وخطئي ، وعمدي ، وكل ذلك عندي . اللهم اغفر لي مـا
قدمت وما أخرت ، وما أسررت وما أعلنت . أنت إلهي لا إله إلا أنت » .

It was mentioned that the Prophet (pbuh) used to say while in
a state of prostration:

*O Allah (swt)! Forgive me for my mistakes and my
ignorance; for my transgression in my affairs; and in
what You know about me better than me.*

*O Allah (swt)! Forgive me for what is serious and what is
not serious in me; for my mistake and my intention, and
all what is in me.*

*O Allah (swt)! Forgive me for what I made earlier or that
which is to come; and that which I kept secret or which I
made public.*

You are my Lord! There is no Lord except You...

دُعَاءُ الْأَنْبِيَاءِ

Du`aa' Al-Anbiyaa'

I. General

This section is devoted for the Du`aa' of some Prophets and Messengers of Allah (swt). These Du`aa's are taken directly from the Qur'an. In Surah Al-Baqarah (The Cow), Allah (swt) says the following:

وَإِذَا سَأَلَكَ

عِبَادِى عَنِّى فَإِنِّى قَرِيبٌ أُجِيبُ دَعْوَةَ ٱلدَّاعِ إِذَا دَعَانِ
فَلْيَسْتَجِيبُوا لِى وَلْيُؤْمِنُوا بِى لَعَلَّهُمْ يَرْشُدُونَ ﴿١٨٦﴾

When My servants ask you concerning Me, I am indeed close (to them): I respond to the prayer of every suppliant when he calls on Me: Let them also, with a will, listen to My call, and believe in Me: That they may walk in the right way.   **(2:186)**

However, in Surah Al-A'raf (The Heights), Allah (swt) informs us how to make Du`aa'. He says the following:

ٱدْعُوا رَبَّكُمْ تَضَرُّعًا

وَخُفْيَةً إِنَّهُ لَا يُحِبُّ ٱلْمُعْتَدِينَ ﴿٥٥﴾ وَلَا تُفْسِدُوا فِى
ٱلْأَرْضِ بَعْدَ إِصْلَٰحِهَا وَٱدْعُوهُ خَوْفًا وَطَمَعًا إِنَّ رَحْمَتَ
ٱللَّهِ قَرِيبٌ مِّنَ ٱلْمُحْسِنِينَ ﴿٥٦﴾

Call on your Lord with humility and in private: For Allah loves not those who trespass beyond bounds. Do not make mischief on the earth, after it had been set in order, but call on Him with fear and longing (in you hearts): For the Mercy of Allah is (always) near to those who do good. **(7:55-56)**

Moreover, one should state here that the doors of heavens are open twenty –four hours a day through out the whole year. Allah (swt) hears, sees, and records. He knows when, how, and where He gives us what we need. We may ask too much that we cannot handle. All what is needed from us is to make the Du`aa' with honesty, sincerity, and pure intention, i.e., Ikhlas. He also wanted us to call upon Him with: Wholeheartedly, in privacy and with hope and fear. At the same time, He gave us examples of His Prophets and their Du`aa' to Him while in happiness and in sorrows, as well as in distress and difficulty.

II. Prophet Nooh Du`aa'

The first example is Prophet Nooh (phuh). His Du`aa' is mentioned four times in the Qur'an. In Surah Al-Anbiyaa', chapter 21, verse 76; also in Surah As-Saffat, chapter 37, verse 75-79; and in Surah Al-Qamar (The Moon), chapter 54, verse 10-14. However, there is a Surah in the name of Prophet Nooh himself. It is Surah 71 whereby he made his Du`aa' in verses 26-28. He requested Allah (swt) to wipe out the disbelievers completely, because there is no hope in them anymore. The Qur'an recorded the Du`aa' of Prophet Nooh as follows:

178

وَقَالَ نُوحٌ رَّبِّ لَا تَذَرْ عَلَى ٱلْأَرْضِ مِنَ ٱلْكَٰفِرِينَ
دَيَّارًا ۝ إِنَّكَ إِن تَذَرْهُمْ يُضِلُّوا۟ عِبَادَكَ وَلَا يَلِدُوٓا۟ إِلَّا فَاجِرًا
كَفَّارًا ۝ رَّبِّ ٱغْفِرْ لِى وَلِوَٰلِدَىَّ وَلِمَن دَخَلَ بَيْتِىَ
مُؤْمِنًا وَلِلْمُؤْمِنِينَ وَٱلْمُؤْمِنَٰتِ وَلَا تَزِدِ ٱلظَّٰلِمِينَ إِلَّا تَبَارًا ۝

*And Noah said: "O my Lord! Leave not of the
Unbelievers, a single one on earth. For if you do leave
(any of) them, they will but mislead Your devotees,
and they will breed one but wicked ungrateful ones.
"O my Lord! Forgive me, my parents, all who enter
my house in Faith, and (all) believing men and
believing women. (71:26-28)*

III. Prophet Ibrahim Du`aa'

As far as is concerned, he prayed to Allah (swt) to save only
those who followed him. He left it up to Allah to take care of those
who refused to follow him. In Surah Ibrahim, Allah (swt) recorded
the voice and the Du`aa' of Prophet Ibrahim. The Qur'an states
the following.

رَبِّ إِنَّهُنَّ أَضْلَلْنَ كَثِيرًا مِّنَ ٱلنَّاسِ
فَمَن تَبِعَنِى فَإِنَّهُۥ مِنِّى وَمَنْ عَصَانِى فَإِنَّكَ غَفُورٌ رَّحِيمٌ ۝

179

"O my Lord! they have indeed led astray many among mankind; he then who follows my (ways) is of me, and he that disobeys me, -but You are indeed Oft-Forgiving, Most Merciful. (14:36)

IV. Prophet Ayub Du`aa'

As far as Prophet Ayub (pbuh), he was struck with too many problems and calamities. He was also struck with sickness and diseases. Finally, he made his famous Du`aa'. It is a personal Du`aa'. It is a personal Du`aa' about himself and for him. In Surah Al-Anbiya' (The Prophets), Allah (swt) says the following:

﴿ وَأَيُّوبَ إِذْ نَادَىٰ رَبَّهُۥٓ أَنِّى مَسَّنِىَ ٱلضُّرُّ وَأَنتَ أَرْحَمُ ٱلرَّٰحِمِينَ ۝ فَٱسْتَجَبْنَا لَهُۥ فَكَشَفْنَا مَا بِهِۦ مِن ضُرٍّ وَءَاتَيْنَٰهُ أَهْلَهُۥ وَمِثْلَهُم مَّعَهُمْ رَحْمَةً مِّنْ عِندِنَا وَذِكْرَىٰ لِلْعَٰبِدِينَ ۝ ﴾

And (remember) Job, when he cried to his Lord "truly distress has seized me, but You are the Most Merciful of those that are Merciful". So We listened to him: We removed the distress that was on him, and We restored his people to him, and doubled their number,-as a Grace from Ourselves, and a thing for commemoration, for all who serve Us. (21:83-84)

Allah (swt) heard his crying voice, and saved him from all those troubles. Finally, he recovered his health and made him to procreate many children.

V. Prophet Yunus Du`aa'

As far as Prophet Yunus (Zan-Noon) is concerned, he left the people while he was unhappy. He tried to go to another place by boat, but he was thrown into the water. A whale engulfed him. Inside the tummy of the whale, he made his famous Du`aa'. He admitted his mistake by leaving without taking the permission. Allah (swt) saved him and brought him back. Anyone who recites the Du`aa' of Prophet Yunus, Allah will save him/her from troubles. The Du`aa' of Prophet Yunus in Surah Al-Anbiyaa' (The Prophets) goes as follow:

وَذَا ٱلنُّونِ إِذ ذَّهَبَ مُغَـٰضِبًا فَظَنَّ أَن لَّن نَّقۡدِرَ عَلَيۡهِ فَنَادَىٰ فِى ٱلظُّلُمَـٰتِ أَن لَّآ إِلَـٰهَ إِلَّآ أَنتَ سُبۡحَـٰنَكَ إِنِّى كُنتُ مِنَ ٱلظَّـٰلِمِينَ ۞ فَٱسۡتَجَبۡنَا لَهُۥ وَنَجَّيۡنَـٰهُ مِنَ ٱلۡغَمِّ وَكَذَٰلِكَ نُـۨجِى ٱلۡمُؤۡمِنِينَ ۞

And Remember Zun-nun, when he departed in wrath: He imagined that We had no power over him! But he cried through the depths of darkness, "There is no god but You: Glory be to You; I was indeed wrong!" So We listened to him: and delivered him from distress: and thus do We deliver those who have faith. (21:87-88)

VI. Prophet Zakariya Du`aa'

As far as Prophet Zakariya is concerned, his Du`aa' is recorded in Surah Al-Imran (3:35-37); and in Surah Al-Anbiyaa'

(The Prophets), (21:89-90); and in Surah Mariam (19:2-11). His main concern was that he became old, and he wanted an offspring to take over the Message and to deliver it to the people. He wife was barren at that time. She was about 80 years old while he was about 90 years old. While he was praying at the Masjid, he made his famous Du`aa' and Allah (swt) answered him through His angels momentarily. In Surah Al-Anbiyaa', Allah (swt) says the following:

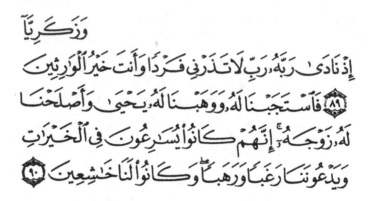

And (remember) Zakariya, when he cried to his Lord: "O my Lord! leave me not without an offspring, though You are the best of inheritors. So We listened to him: and We granted him Yahya: We cured his wife's (barrenness) for him. These (three) were ever quick in doing in good works: they used to call on Us in yearning and awe. And humble themselves before us.
(21:89-90)

VII. Prophet Moosa Du`aa'

As far as Prophet Moosa is concerned, he requested Allah (swt) to get rid of Pharaoh and his people altogether. His famous Du`aa' as a curse is recorded in Surah Yunus. Prophet Moosa said the following:

وَقَالَ مُوسَىٰ

رَبَّنَآ إِنَّكَ ءَاتَيْتَ فِرْعَوْنَ وَمَلَأَهُۥ زِينَةً وَأَمْوَٰلًا فِى ٱلْحَيَوٰةِ ٱلدُّنْيَا رَبَّنَا لِيُضِلُّوا۟ عَن سَبِيلِكَ رَبَّنَا ٱطْمِسْ عَلَىٰٓ أَمْوَٰلِهِمْ وَٱشْدُدْ عَلَىٰ قُلُوبِهِمْ فَلَا يُؤْمِنُوا۟ حَتَّىٰ يَرَوُا۟ ٱلْعَذَابَ ٱلْأَلِيمَ ﴿٨٨﴾ قَالَ قَدْ أُجِيبَت دَّعْوَتُكُمَا فَٱسْتَقِيمَا وَلَا تَتَّبِعَآنِّ سَبِيلَ ٱلَّذِينَ لَا يَعْلَمُونَ ﴿٨٩﴾

Moses prayed: "Our Lord! You have indeed bestowed on Pharaoh and his Chiefs splendor and wealth in the life of the Present, and so, Our Lord they mislead (men) from Your Path. Deface Our Lord the features of their wealth, and send hardness to their hearts, so they will not believe until they see the grievous Chastisement." Allah (swt) said "Accepted is your prayer (O Moses and Aaron)! So stand up straight, and follow not the path of those who know not." (10:88-89)

183

VIII. Prophet Issa Du`aa'

As far as the Du`aa' of Prophet Issa is concerned, it is mentioned in the Qur'an that in the Day of Judgment he will wash out his hands from those who claimed to be his worshippers. The dialogue that will take place between Prophet Issa and Allah (swt) is recorded in Surah Al-Maida (Table Spread). The Qur'an states the following:

وَإِذْ قَالَ ٱللَّهُ يَٰعِيسَى ٱبْنَ مَرْيَمَ ءَأَنتَ قُلْتَ لِلنَّاسِ ٱتَّخِذُونِى وَأُمِّىَ إِلَٰهَيْنِ مِن دُونِ ٱللَّهِ قَالَ سُبْحَٰنَكَ مَا يَكُونُ لِىٓ أَنْ أَقُولَ مَا لَيْسَ لِى بِحَقٍّ إِن كُنتُ قُلْتُهُۥ فَقَدْ عَلِمْتَهُۥ تَعْلَمُ مَا فِى نَفْسِى وَلَآ أَعْلَمُ مَا فِى نَفْسِكَ إِنَّكَ أَنتَ عَلَّٰمُ ٱلْغُيُوبِ ﴿١١٦﴾ مَا قُلْتُ لَهُمْ إِلَّا مَآ أَمَرْتَنِى بِهِۦٓ أَنِ ٱعْبُدُواْ ٱللَّهَ رَبِّى وَرَبَّكُمْ وَكُنتُ عَلَيْهِمْ شَهِيدًا مَّا دُمْتُ فِيهِمْ فَلَمَّا تَوَفَّيْتَنِى كُنتَ أَنتَ ٱلرَّقِيبَ عَلَيْهِمْ وَأَنتَ عَلَىٰ كُلِّ شَىْءٍ شَهِيدٌ ﴿١١٧﴾ إِن تُعَذِّبْهُمْ فَإِنَّهُمْ عِبَادُكَ وَإِن تَغْفِرْ لَهُمْ فَإِنَّكَ أَنتَ ٱلْعَزِيزُ ٱلْحَكِيمُ ﴿١١٨﴾

And behold! Allah will say: "O Jesus the son of Mary! Didn't you say unto men, "take me and my mother for two gods beside Allah (swt)?" he will say "Glory to You never could I say what I had no right (to say). Had I said such a thing. You would have indeed known it. You know what is in my heart, though I know not what is in Yours. For You know in full all that is hidden. "Never said I to them except what You did command me to say, to with, "Worship Allah (swt), my Lord and your Lord': And I was a witness over them while I dwell among them; when You did take me up You were the Watcher over them, and You are a witness to all things. "If you did punish them, they are Your servants: If You do forgive them, You are the Exalted in power, the Wise". (5:116-118)

IX. Prophet Muhammad Du`aa'

Every Prophet made a series of Du`aa'. Some of those Du`aa' were for their personal use or for their communities. Some Du`aa' were for the Hidaya of their communities, or they were against their peoples. Our Prophet Muhammad (pbuh) made all his Du`aa' for the guidance of humanities at large till The Day of Judgment. He was worried and concerned for all of us. He is also worried about all those who are going to accept the Message of Allah (swt), namely Islam. Prophet Muhammad (pbuh) cried when he recited the Du`aa' of Ibrahim and Prophet Issa. The following has been recorded:

Narrated by Abdullah Ibn `Amr Al-Ass (raa) that the Prophet read in Qur'an the Du`a' of Prophet Ibrahim. It is recorded in Surah Ibrahim the following.

رَبِّ إِنَّهُنَّ أَضْلَلْنَ كَثِيرًا مِّنَ ٱلنَّاسِ

فَمَن تَبِعَنِى فَإِنَّهُۥ مِنِّى وَمَنْ عَصَانِى فَإِنَّكَ غَفُورٌ رَّحِيمٌ ٣٦

"O My Lord! They have indeed led astray many among mankind; he then who follows my (ways) is of me, and he that obeys me, but You are indeed Oft-Forgiving, Most Merciful". (14:36)

Then the Prophet read the Du`aa' of Prophet Issa (a.s):

إِن تُعَذِّبْهُمْ فَإِنَّهُمْ عِبَادُكَ
وَإِن تَغْفِرْ لَهُمْ فَإِنَّكَ أَنتَ ٱلْعَزِيزُ ٱلْحَكِيمُ ۝

If you do punish them, they are your servants: If you do forgive them, you are the Exalted in power, the Wise. (5:118)

Then Prophet Muhammad (pbuh) raised his hands and said:

فَرَفَعَ يَدَيْهِ صَلَّى اللَّهُ عَلَيْهِ وَسَلَّمَ وَقَالَ:
((اللَّهُمَّ أُمَّتِي أُمَّتِي، وَبَكَى، فَقَالَ اللَّهُ عَزَّ وَجَلَّ:
يَا جِبْرِيلُ إِذْهَبْ إِلَى مُحَمَّدٍ وَرَبُّكَ أَعْلَمُ فَسَلْهُ مَا يُبْكِيهِ؟ فَأَتَاهُ
جِبْرِيلُ فَأَخْبَرَهُ فَأَخْبَرَهُ رَسُولُ اللَّهِ صَلَّى اللَّهُ عَلَيْهِ وَسَلَّمَ بِمَا قَالَ وَهُوَ
أَعْلَمُ، فَقَالَ اللَّهُ تَعَالَى: يَا جِبْرِيلُ إِذْهَبْ إِلَى مُحَمَّدٍ فَقُلْ: إِنَّا
سَنُرْضِيكَ فِي أُمَّتِكَ وَلَا نَسُوؤُكَ))

— رواه مسلم —

186

O Allah! My Ummah.... my Ummah...and cried. Then Allah (swt) instructed Jibril to go to Muhammad (Allah (swt) knows) and asked why he is weeping. When Jibril came to the Prophet he told him about the reason (Allah (swt) knows). Allah (swt) said to Jibril: Go to Muhammad and inform him that He is going to please you with your Ummah and He will not hurt you with them." Muslim

X. Final Remarks

Prophet Muhammad (pbuh) was chosen by Allah (swt) to be sent to humanity at large until the Day of Judgment. He was sent as a Guide, as a Role Model and as a Mercy. It was Allah (swt) Who molded him, trained him, guided him, and made him pure and innocent. One can say that Prophet Muhammad (pbuh) is the Summation, Culmination and Purification of all the previous Prophets and Messengers. He never cursed his opponents or his enemies. On the contrary, he used to pray to God to guide them, or if not, then Allah (swt) will guide their children. Indeed this is what happened. Nowadays there are about 1.9 Billion Muslims in the world. Slowly but surely Islam is spreading all over the world through peaceful ways by Muslims behaviors, manners, and attitudes. We pray for a better future. Ameen.

187

Chapter (15)   Letter To The King Of Ethiopia

يَـٰٓأَيُّهَا ٱلرَّسُولُ بَلِّغْ مَآ أُنزِلَ إِلَيْكَ مِن رَّبِّكَ وَإِن لَّمْ تَفْعَلْ فَمَا بَلَّغْتَ رِسَالَتَهُۥ وَٱللَّهُ يَعْصِمُكَ مِنَ ٱلنَّاسِ إِنَّ ٱللَّهَ لَا يَهْدِى ٱلْقَوْمَ ٱلْكَٰفِرِينَ

Al-Ma`ida: The Table Spread

O Messenger! Proclaim the (message) which has been sent to you from your Lord, if you did not, you would not have fulfilled and proclaimed His Mission. And Allah will defend you from men (who mean mischief) For Allah guides not those who reject Faith. (5:67)

I. Introduction

My talk to you is about the Prophet's letter to the King of Ethiopia Al-Najashi. The message of the Prophet in his letter was to invite the King to accept Islam. The information was straight and concise. He praised him and reminded him about Jesus and his mother Mary. He asked him how much respect is given to them in the Qur'an. He asked him to become obedient to the Creator, namely Allah (swt). Due to its importance in our daily life, and because we should follow the tradition and the footsteps of our beloved Prophet (pbuh). We are including his letter in this book of Al-Khutab.

The letter of the Prophet (pbuh) reads in English as follows:

"In the Name of Allah, the Merciful, the Beneficent. From Muhammad, the Messenger of Allah to the King of Ethiopia, Al-Najashi Al-Assham.

You are in peace. I send you the greetings of Allah. There is no God but Himself. He is the Sovereign, the Holy One, the Source of Peace, the Guardian of Faith, the Preserver of Safety. I bear witness that Jesus, the son of Mary is the spirit of Allah and His Word. He bestowed it to Mary the devoted, the good and the virgin. She carried Jesus. Allah created him from His Spirit and His breath as He created Adam with His Hand and His Breath.

I invite you to Allah the Unique Who has no partner; and to continue to obey Him; and that you follow me, and believe in what I received. I am the Messenger of Allah.

189

I sent you my cousin Jaafar with a group of Muslims. When he reaches you, give them settlement and don't be an obstinate transgressor. I invite you and your soldiers to Allah. I have already informed (you) and advised (you). Accept my advice.

And peace is on those who accepted guidance.

إلَى النَّجَاشِيِّ مَلِكِ الْحَبَشَةِ

بِسْمِ اللهِ الرَّحْمَنِ الرَّحِيمِ

مِنْ مُحَمَّدٍ رَسُولِ اللهِ ، إِلَى النَّجَاشِيِّ الأَصْحَمِ مَلِكِ الْحَبَشَةِ .

سِلْمٌ أَنْتَ ، فَإِنِّي أَحْمَدُ إِلَيْكَ اللهَ [الَّذِي لاَ إِلَهَ إِلاَّ هُوَ] ، الْمَلِكُ ، الْقُدُّوسُ ، السَّلاَمُ ، المُؤْمِنُ ، المُهَيْمِنُ ، وَأَشْهَدُ أَنَّ عِيسَى بْنَ مَرْيَمَ رُوحُ اللهِ وَكَلِمَتُهُ ، أَلْقَاهَا إِلَى مَرْيَمَ البَتُولِ الطَّيِّبَةِ الحَصِينَةِ ، فَحَمَلَتْ بِعِيسَى ، فَخَلَقَهُ اللهُ مِنْ رُوحِهِ وَنَفْخِهِ ، كَمَا خَلَقَ آدَمَ بِيَدِهِ وَنَفْخِهِ .

وَإِنِّي أَدْعُوكَ إِلَى اللهِ وَحْدَهُ لاَ شَرِيكَ لَهُ ، وَالْمُوَالاَةُ عَلَى طَاعَتِهِ ، وَأَنْ تَتَّبِعَنِي ، وَتُؤْمِنَ بِالَّذِي جَاءَنِي ، فَإِنِّي رَسُولُ اللهِ .

وَقَدْ بَعَثْتُ إِلَيْكَ ابْنَ عَمِّي جَعْفَراً ، وَنَفَراً مَعَهُ مِنَ الْمُسْلِمِينَ .

فَإِذَا جَاءَكَ فَأَقْرِهِمْ ، وَدَعِ التَّجَبُّرَ ، فَإِنِّي أَدْعُوكَ وَجُنُودَكَ إِلَى اللهِ ، فَقَدْ بَلَّغْتُ وَنَصَحْتُ ، فَاقْبَلُوا نُصْحِي .

وَالسَّلاَمُ عَلَى مَنِ اتَّبَعَ الْهُدَى .

190

Chapter (16)   Prophet's Treatment Of Non-Muslims

I. General

This chapter is devoted to a special group of Non-Muslims, namely those who are called Christians (Catholics, Protestants, others) and Jews. Such groups are considered in Islam to be People of the Book. People of the Book are looked upon by Muslims as God-fearing, God-loving, and God-conscious.

Although Islam is the most recent religion sent by God to mankind, it is a complete and a total way of life. Islam, Christianity, and Judaism are rooted in the Abrahamic Religion. Muslims are to respect, honor, protect, and defend non-Muslims present in the Islamic state. They are to see that non-Muslims are living in peace and harmony within Muslim territories. In Surah Al-Imran Allah (swt) says to the Prophet of the Book, the following:

قُلْ يَٰٓأَهْلَ ٱلْكِتَٰبِ تَعَالَوْاْ إِلَىٰ كَلِمَةٍ سَوَآءٍ بَيْنَنَا وَبَيْنَكُمْ أَلَّا نَعْبُدَ إِلَّا ٱللَّهَ وَلَا نُشْرِكَ بِهِۦ شَيْـًٔا وَلَا يَتَّخِذَ بَعْضُنَا بَعْضًا أَرْبَابًا مِّن دُونِ ٱللَّهِ فَإِن تَوَلَّوْاْ فَقُولُواْ ٱشْهَدُواْ بِأَنَّا مُسْلِمُونَ ٦٤ يَٰٓأَهْلَ ٱلْكِتَٰبِ لِمَ تُحَآجُّونَ فِىٓ إِبْرَٰهِيمَ وَمَآ أُنزِلَتِ ٱلتَّوْرَىٰةُ وَٱلْإِنجِيلُ إِلَّا مِنۢ بَعْدِهِۦٓ أَفَلَا تَعْقِلُونَ ٦٥ هَٰٓأَنتُمْ هَٰٓؤُلَآءِ حَٰجَجْتُمْ فِيمَا لَكُم بِهِۦ عِلْمٌ فَلِمَ تُحَآجُّونَ فِيمَا لَيْسَ لَكُم بِهِۦ عِلْمٌ وَٱللَّهُ يَعْلَمُ وَأَنتُمْ لَا تَعْلَمُونَ ٦٦ مَا كَانَ إِبْرَٰهِيمُ يَهُودِيًّا وَلَا نَصْرَانِيًّا

وَلَكِن كَانَ حَنِيفًا مُّسْلِمًا وَمَا كَانَ مِنَ ٱلْمُشْرِكِينَ ۝

إِنَّ أَوْلَى ٱلنَّاسِ بِإِبْرَٰهِيمَ لَلَّذِينَ ٱتَّبَعُوهُ وَهَٰذَا ٱلنَّبِىُّ وَٱلَّذِينَ

ءَامَنُوا ۖ وَٱللَّهُ وَلِىُّ ٱلْمُؤْمِنِينَ ۝ وَدَّت طَّآئِفَةٌ مِّنْ أَهْلِ ٱلْكِتَٰبِ

لَوْ يُضِلُّونَكُمْ وَمَا يُضِلُّونَ إِلَّا أَنفُسَهُمْ وَمَا يَشْعُرُونَ ۝ يَٰٓأَهْلَ

ٱلْكِتَٰبِ لِمَ تَكْفُرُونَ بِـَٔايَٰتِ ٱللَّهِ وَأَنتُمْ تَشْهَدُونَ ۝

O People of the Book! Come to common terms as between us and you: That we worship none but Allah; that we associate no partners with Him; that we erect not, from among ourselves, lords and patrons other than Allah. If then they turn back, say you: "Bear witness that we (at least) are Muslims (bowing to Allah's will)". You people of the Book! Why you dispute about Abraham, when the Torah and the Gospel were not revealed till after him? Have you no understanding? Ah! you are those who fell to disputing (even) in matters of which you had some Knowledge! But why you dispute in matters of which you have no knowledge? It is Allah Who knows, and you who know not! Abraham was not a Jew nor yet a Christian; but he was Upright, and bowed his will to Allah's (which is Islam). And he joined not gods with Allah. Without doubt, among men, the nearest of kin of Abraham, are those who follow him, as are also this Prophet and those who believe and Allah is the Protector of those who have faith. It is the wish of a section of the People of the Book to lead you astray. But they shall lead astray (not you), but themselves, and they do not perceive! You people of the Book! Why do you reject the Signs of Allah, of which you are (yourselves) witnesses? (3:64-70)

II. Jews

A. During the life of Prophet Muhammad, the Jews in Madina had a synagogue and an educational institute by the name of Bait-Al-Madras. He preserved it as well as he protected them.

B. The Prophet of Islam made several treaties with the Jews. One of those messages that he wrote is the following:

In the name of God, Most Gracious, Ever Merciful. This message is from Muhammad, Messenger of God. Verily, whoever follows us from the Jews shall have the help and the aid; and shall neither be victim of injustice, nor taken vengeance upon. The Jews of the children of Awf are safe with the Faithful. They have their religion and the Muslims theirs and themselves, except those who oppress or sin; they will forfeit themselves and their families. The Jews of Bani Al-Najjar, of Bani Al-Harith, of Bani Saaedah, of Bani Aws and of Bani Belanah are Jews like the others.

III. Christians

A. The Prophet honored the Christians of Najran from Yemen who visited him in his own mosque in Madina. The Christians prayed according to Christian fashion inside the mosque, while the Prophet and his followers prayed in Muslim tradition.

193

B. The Prophet respected the autonomy of the Christian churches. The nomination and the appointment of bishops and priests were left to the Christian community itself.

C. Prophet Muhammad promoted cooperation between Muslims and Christians in the political arena as well. The Prophet selected a non-Muslim and delegated him as his Ambassador to Negus, the King of Ethiopia. The name of that Ambassador was `Amr-ibn-Umaiyah-ad-Damri.

D. During the days of the Prophet, there were two super powers, the Persians and the Romans. The Romans adopted Christianity while the Persians adopted Godless beliefs. Those two super powers were at wars with each other. During that period, Muslims were a small minority in the Arabian Peninsula. They prayed to Almighty God that the Romans would win the war against the Atheistic community. The feelings and the beliefs of the Muslims were based on the fact that the Romans were part of the People of the Book. (See Qur'an Chapter 30- Verses 1-7)

E. The Prophet (pbuh) sent a message to the Monks of Saint Catherine in Mount Sinai. The English translation of that document is as follows:

This is a message written by Muhammad Ibn Abdullah, as a covenant to those who adopt Christianity, far and near, we are behind them. Verily, I defend them by myself, the servants, the helpers, and my followers, because Christians are my citizens; and by Allah! I hold out against anything that displeases them. No compulsion is to be on them. Neither are their judges to be changed from their jobs, nor their monks from their monasteries.

194

No one is to destroy a house of their religion, to damage it, or to carry anything from it to the Muslims' houses. Should anyone take any of these, he would spoil God's covenant and disobey His Prophet. Verily, they are my allies and have my secure charter against all that they hate. No one is to force them to travel or to oblige them to fight. The Muslims are to fight for them. If a female Christian is married to a Muslim, this is not to take place without her own wish. She is not to be prevented from going to her church to pray. Their churches are to be respected. They are neither to be prevented from repairing them nor the sacredness of their covenants. No one of the nation is to disobey this covenant till the Day of Judgment and the end of the world.

IV. Pagans of Makkah

1. Prophet Muhammad, liberated Makkah from idol worshippers and it became a Muslim City. At the time of his victory he declared that whoever was an enemy taking refuge in the house of their leader, Abu Sufiyan, was considered safe. He would be protected by Muhammad and his followers. Abu Sufiyan was the worst enemy to Muhammad and to the Muslims until that moment. It was unbelievable to Abu Sufiyan that he and his soldiers were treated with honor and dignity, in the face of defeat.

2. During the liberation of Makkah, the captured enemies were imprisoned. The Prophet could have killed them all without mercy, if he wished. Instead he looked at them and asked:

What do you think I am going to do with you?

They replied:

195

You are a generous brother and a son of a generous brother.

He told them:

Go home free.

V. Final Remarks

The Prophet thus gave the best example to his enemies who tortured and persecuted him. They even attempted to kill him and eventually forced him to leave Makkah. Therefore, he migrated to Madina with his followers. The Prophet was sent by Allah (swt) to all human beings irrespective of color nationality, ethnicity, gender, race, creed or religion. He came as a Mercy and a Guide to all. Many non-Muslims accepted Islam, and accepted the Prophet as the Final Prophet and Final Messenger of Allah (swt). When he performed his Hajj (pilgrimage), he had about 124,000 Muslims performing Hajj rituals with him. In the year of 2005, the number of Muslims in the world is 1.9 billions.

Allah is Beautiful, He Likes Beauty;
Prophet says the truth.

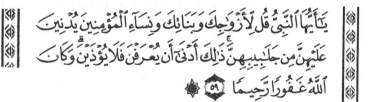

يَـٰٓأَيُّهَا ٱلنَّبِىُّ قُل لِّأَزْوَٰجِكَ وَبَنَاتِكَ وَنِسَآءِ ٱلْمُؤْمِنِينَ يُدْنِينَ عَلَيْهِنَّ مِن جَلَـٰبِيبِهِنَّ ۚ ذَٰلِكَ أَدْنَىٰٓ أَن يُعْرَفْنَ فَلَا يُؤْذَيْنَ ۗ وَكَانَ ٱللَّهُ غَفُورًا رَّحِيمًا ٥٩

Al-Ahzab: The Confederates

O Prophet! Tell your wives and daughters and the believing women that they should cast their outer garment over their persons (when out of doors): that is most convenient. That they should be known (as such) and not be molested. And Allah is Oft-Forgiving, Most Merciful. *(33:59)*

I. General

My talk to you this time is about a subject which is very dear to every human being. It is about "What Prophet Muhammad (pbuh) said about Women." The subject is important because Prophet Muhammad was a Prophet, a Messenger and a Leader to mankind. As such he has to receive revelation from Allah related to all mankind. He, as a Messenger, has to deliver the message and he, as a leader, has to teach, to train, to educate and to lead mankind to the straight path.

The topic about "What Prophet Muhammad (pbuh) said about Women" is important because women comprise half of the society if not more than half. In the U.S.A. woman is considered to be "The Boss." In the twentieth (20th) century we talk about Woman's Liberation Movement, the Civil Rights Movement fighting for Equal Rights Amendments (ERA), the Human Rights move by the President of the U.S.A., and many other moves and organizations in this direction.

In reality, a woman is the person who has in her hands the capacity, the instinct and the natural way of life to prepare, and to bring up the future leaders to mankind. She is the one who molds the child to become the best or the worst leader in the world.

Because Prophet Muhammad (pbuh) was a Prophet, a Messenger, and a Leader, and because he was able to train leaders for mankind from men and women, it would be pertinent to consult his sayings and get the wisdom to be followed in our daily lives.

For these reasons and others, I have selected the subject of "What Prophet Muhammad Said About Women." However, the subject is too big to be covered in one article or in one talk, so I wish to restrict it to the idea of "Treatment." Although a good number of verses from the Qur'an have been stated about her treatment, I will, for the time being, restrict my selections to the Hadith so as to be within the limits of this talk or article.

II. Prophet's Sayings

Prophet Muhammad (pbuh) knew that woman is very important in the society. She is to play a very effective role as a mother, a wife, a daughter, a sister, an aunt and a grandmother. In each aspect of her life, Prophet Muhammad (pbuh) has spoken the wisdom of Ultimate Truth for her. He knew she is the one who molds, who trains and who makes the future generation and the future leader to mankind. Therefore, she has to be treated kindly and to be trained properly. Many sayings of the Prophet have been reported on this subject among which are the following:

A. Concerning the composition of woman in society, the Prophet says:

النسَـاء شَـقائـق الرجَـال

"Women are the other halves of men."

B. Concerning their treatment, it has been reported by Abu Hurairah ® that the Prophet (pbuh) said:

(.. واسـتوصوا بالنساء خيرًا ـ ... فاسـتوصوا بالنساء خيرًا)

199

"And you are recommended to treat women with the best... and indeed you are advised to treat women with goodness."

C. Concerning man's treatment to woman, it has been reported that Prophet Muhammad (pbuh) said:

خَيركُم خَيركُم لنسائه وَأَنَا خَيركم لِنسائي

The best amongst you are those who are best to their wives, and I am the best to my wives."

D. Concerning her treatment with gentleness, Prophet Muhammad (pbuh) said:

(رفقـــاً بـــالقـــواريـــر ...)

Be kind with the soft and gentle ones (females)."

E. Concerning her responsibility at home, it was reported by Abdullah that Prophet Muhammad (pbuh) said:

(... والمـــرأة راعية على بيت زوجها وهي مسؤولة ...)

"And woman is a leader on her husband's house and she is accounted for that...."

F. Concerning their preference and their position in paradise, they were given the preference over their husbands in this world and in the Hereafter. It was reported that Prophet Muhammad (pbuh) said:

(... أمك أمك ثم أباك الجنة تحت أقدام الأمهات ..)

"Your mother, your mother, and mother and then your father, indeed paradise is under the feet of the mothers."

G. Women are not supposed to obey their husband when ordered to disobey Allah. They are to obey and to please Allah first and foremost. It has been reported that Prophet Muhammad (pbuh) said:

لاتطيــع المـــرأة زوجها في

A woman does not obey her husband in disobedience to Allah."

H. Concerning her right from her husband it was reported by Abdullah bin 'Amer bin Al-Ass that Prophet Muhammad (pbuh) said:

(.. وان لزوجك عليك حقًا..)

"... and to your wife you have a duty and a responsibility."

III. Conclusion

From the above collection of the sayings of Prophet Muhammad (pbuh) on the subject, one may conclude the following:

1. Woman is to be raised properly when she is young as a daughter.
2. She is to be treated very kindly.
3. She is to lead a happy life at home as a wife and a mother.

4. She is to raise her children properly so that she will be a good teacher, a good leader, a good trainer, a good mother and a good grandmother.
5. She is to be rewarded in this world as well as in the Hereafter.

May I request you to play your effective role in molding and in bringing up a new generation and a new group of leaders who are more than half of the society. These in turn are to shape up the future leaders of mankind. In so doing, you have played your role perfectly; you have benefited from the teachings of the leader, Prophet Muhammad (pbuh), and you will be rewarded by Allah (swt) Almighty for your efforts. Ameen. Let us ask Almighty Allah forgiveness.

Light upon Light!

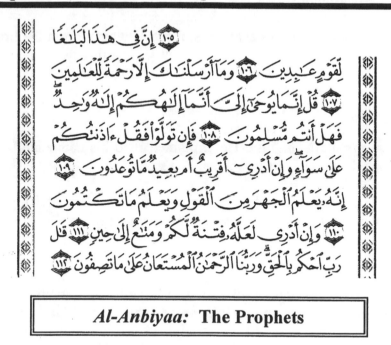

القرآن عَن لِسَان مُحَمَّد ﷺ

Chapter (18)   About The Qur'an From Muhammad

Al-Anbiyaa: The Prophets

Verily in this (Qur-an) is a Message for people who would (truly) worship Allah. We sent you not, but as a Mercy for all creatures. Say: what has come to me by inspiration is that your God is One God: Will you therefore bow to His will (in Islam)? But if they turn back, Say: I have proclaimed the Message to you all alike and in truth; but I know not whether that which you are promised is near or far. "It is He Who knows what is open in speech and what you hide (in your hearts). I know not but that it may be a trial for you, and a grant of (worldly) livelihood (to you) for a time. Say: O my Lord! You Judge in truth! "Our Lord Most Gracious is the One Whose assistance should be sought against the blasphemies you utter! (21:106-112)

I. Introduction

The subject of this chapter is about the Qur'an from the lips of Prophet Muhammad (pbuh). It is well known that the Qur'an was revealed in the Arabic language to Prophet Muhammad as a Mercy, a Guide, a Glad Tiding and a Warning.

The Prophet memorized the Qur'an totally and lived in it every minute of his life. He explained it to his companions and helped them to live its teachings; and so they did.

The Prophet spoke about the Qur'an, by advising his companions to learn it, to recite it, to memorize it, to live it and to believe in it as a revealed book from the Ultimate Truth, namely Allah.

In this short talk I would like to bring to your attention some of the sayings of Prophet Muhammad (pbuh) about the Qur'an, so that we will be inspired and motivated in our daily lives. In so doing we will, Insha Allah, be able to practice the teachings of Allah without difficulty.

II. Reading and Recitation

Concerning the reading, recitation and chanting of the Qur'an, Prophet Muhammad (pbuh) said the following:

A. The Qur'an as a Savior

The Prophet encouraged the Muslims to read the Qur'an so that it will be a witness and a savior for them in the Day of Judgment. He said in this regard:

عَن أبي ـــ أُما مَة رضيـــ الله عنه :

" اقـــرءوا القُــرآن فإنه يأ تــ يوم القيامة شفيعاً "

ـ رواه مسلم ـ

Abu Umaimah narrated that the Messenger of Allah said:

"Read the Qur'an so that it will be an intercessor for you on the Day of Judgement." Muslim

B. Reading is a Blessing

The Prophet encouraged the Muslims to read the Qur'an so that they will be rewarded by Allah for every Surah, for every Ayah, for every word (Kalimah) and for every letter (Harf) they read, The Prophet (pbuh) said:

عن ابن مَسـعود رَضيـــ الله عنه :

" مَن قـــرأ أحـــرفاً من كتاب الله فله حسنة ، والحسنة بعشر أمثالها لا أقول الــمّ حرف ولكن الف حرف ولام حرف وميم حرف "

ـ رواه الترمذي ـ

"Anyone who reads one letter from the Book of Allah will have a blessing and reward; and each good thing is equal to ten rewards ; I don't say: Alif Lam Meem is a letter, but Alif is one letter; Lam is a letter and Meem is a letter."

C. Chanting the Qur'an

The Prophet encouraged the Muslims to recite the Qur'an in a chanting and in a beautiful voice. He said:

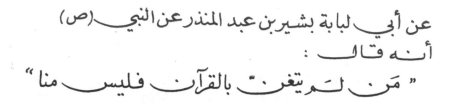

عن أبي لبابة بشير بن عبد المنذر عن النبي (ص)
أنه قال :
" مَن لَم يَتغَن بالقرآن فليس منا "

Abu Lubabah 'Abu Al-Mundzir narrated that the Prophet said:

D. Recitation with Difficulty

The Prophet encouraged Muslims to read the Qur'an even if they find it difficult, as it is a blessing from Allah to read it. Those whose mother tongue is other than Arabic may find it difficult to recite the Qur'an. For them is a better reward indeed. In this respect the Prophet (pbuh) said:

عن عائشة رضي الله عنها : قالت
قال رسول الله صلى الله عليه وسلم : الذي يقرأ القرآن
وهو ماهر به مع السَفرة الكِرام البَرَرة ، والذي
يَقرأ القرآن وَيَتَعْتَع فيه وهو عليه شاق له
أجران "

ـ متفق عليه ـ

206

"Anyone who recites the Qur'an and is an expert in it will in the Hereafter be with the Ambassadors (Messengers) of Allah who are the noblest and the most honest; and anyone who recites the Qur'an with difficulty and hard pronunciation will have a double reward and blessings." Agreed

III. Reading and not Reading

Concerning those who read the Qur'an or those who do not read the Qur'an, the Prophet compared them in similitude and examples, some of which are the following:

A. A Reciting Believer

A believer who recites the Qur'an is like a citron having a sweet fragrance and good taste.

B. A Non-Reciting Believer

A believer who does not read the Qur'an is like a date fruit which has no fragrance but has a sweet taste.

C. A Hypocrite Reciter

A hypocrite who recites the Qur'an may impress the audience only, but not Allah. His similitude is like that of a fruit which has a good smell but a bitter taste.

D. A Hypocrite Non-Reader

If a person, who is considered to be a hypocrite or a non-believer, does not read the Qur'an, then he is like a colocynth. It does not have a good smell and it has a bitter taste.

All these four categories of people have been mentioned by Prophet Muhammad (pbuh) and have been summarized in one beautiful Hadith which is 'Agreed' as follows:

عن أبي موسى الأشعري :

" مَثـل المؤمن الذي يَقْرأ القرآن مثل الأُتْرُجَة ، ريحها طيّب وطعـمها طيّب ، ومَثل المؤمن الذي لا يقـرأ القرآن كمثل التَمَرة لاريح لها وطعـمها حـلو ، ومثل المنافق الذي يَقْرأ القرآن كمثل الريحانة ريحها طيّب وطعمها مُرّ ، ومثل المنافق الذي لا يقرأ القرآن كمثل الحنظلة ليس لها ريح وطعمها مُرّ. - متفق عليه -

"The similitude of a believer who reads the Qur'an is like that of a citron (Atrijah) that smells good and taste good; the similitude of a believer who does not read the Qur'an is like a date fruit which does not have a good smell but it tastes good; the similitude of a hypocrite who reads the Qur'an is like a basil (Rayhana) which does have a good smell but it does taste bitter; and the similitude of a hypocrite who does not read the Qur'an is like a colocynth (Hanzalah) which does not have good smell and it does taste bitter".

IV. Final Remarks

Finally, I would like to remind you of what the Prophet (pbuh) said about those who have not memorized anything from the Qur'an. The Prophet (pbuh) said:

208

عَنِ ابْنِ عَبَّاسٍ رَضِيَ اللهُ عنه :
" إِنَّ الَّذِي لَيْسَ فِي جَوْفِهِ شَيْءٌ مِنَ القُرْآنِ كَالبَيْتِ الخَرِبِ "
ـ رواه الترمذي .

*"The one who has nothing from the Qur'an in his
heart is like a deserted and demolished house.*
Al-Tirmidhi

Therefore, may I request you kindly to do your best to read the
Qur'an daily so that it will be a witness for you and a savior in the
Day of Judgment. We hope and we pray that each one of us will
try his/her best to be closer and closer to Allah by reading His
words, namely the Qur'an. Remember that the Qur'an is a special
message from Allah to each one of us personally. Allah wants each
one of us to communicate with Him directly and quite often.
Remember that the best language to communicate with Allah is
His own favorite chosen language; namely the language of the
Qur'an. Remember that one Muslim lady in the early history of
Islam never spoke anything for forty years in her daily life except
quotations from the Qur'an. We hope and we pray that we, the
contemporary Muslims of the 21st century, will realize our need for
the daily reading of the Qur'an.

Since we don't have radio or T.V. stations owned and
operated by Muslims, we are deprived and denied the spiritual
need to listen to the recitation of the Qur'an. The best thing for us
to do as Muslims who are living in a non-Muslim society, would
be to obtain tapes or records to hear the recitations of the Qur'an in
the houses, offices and cars while we are driving. These days we
can use CD, DVD, and other means such as internet. One may

209

have satellites to observe and listen to Salat in Madina city of the Prophet and in Ka'bah in the city of Makkah. There is no excuse anymore. Remember that we live in a complex society and everything is working like a machine. We might end up having mental break-downs. One of the best ways to obtain and uplift spiritually would be to read the Qur'an daily with a chanting voice. One may join a group of Muslims who meet together in a Masjid whereby they read the Qur'an one chapter after the other. Moreover, a Muslim scholar will explain the meanings of what was recited so that they will benefit from what they read, and then apply its meaning in their private and public life. May Allah bless us. May Allah guide us and may Allah bring us closer to Him. Ameen.

Let us ask Almighty Allah for forgiveness.

The Mountain of Light where Angel Gabriel appeared to Muhammad

Chapter (19)   **Cave Hiraa'**

بِسْمِ اللّٰهِ الرَّحْمٰنِ الرَّحِيمِ

مُّحَمَّدٌ رَّسُولُ اللَّهِ ۚ وَالَّذِينَ مَعَهُ أَشِدَّاءُ عَلَى الْكُفَّارِ رُحَمَاءُ بَيْنَهُمْ ۖ تَرَاهُمْ رُكَّعًا سُجَّدًا يَبْتَغُونَ فَضْلًا مِّنَ اللَّهِ وَرِضْوَانًا ۖ سِيمَاهُمْ فِي وُجُوهِهِم مِّنْ أَثَرِ السُّجُودِ ۚ ذَٰلِكَ مَثَلُهُمْ فِي التَّوْرَاةِ ۚ وَمَثَلُهُمْ فِي الْإِنجِيلِ كَزَرْعٍ أَخْرَجَ شَطْأَهُ فَآزَرَهُ فَاسْتَغْلَظَ فَاسْتَوَىٰ عَلَىٰ سُوقِهِ يُعْجِبُ الزُّرَّاعَ لِيَغِيظَ بِهِمُ الْكُفَّارَ ۗ وَعَدَ اللَّهُ الَّذِينَ آمَنُوا وَعَمِلُوا الصَّالِحَاتِ مِنْهُم مَّغْفِرَةً وَأَجْرًا عَظِيمًا ﴿٢٩﴾

Al-Fath: Victory

Muhammad is the Messenger of Allah; and those who are with Him are strong against Unbelievers, (but) compassionate amongst each other. You will see them bow and Prostrate themselves (In prayer), seeking Grace from Allah and (his) Good Pleasure, on their faces are their marks, (being) the traces of their prostration. This is their similitude in the Taurat; and their similitude in the Gospel is: like a seed which sends forth its blade, then makes it strong; it then becomes thick, and it stands on its own stem, (filling) the sowers with wonder and delight. As a result, it fills the Unbelievers with rage at them. Allah has promised those among them who believe and do righteous deeds forgiveness, and a great reward. (48:29)

I. Introduction

Cave Hiraa' is a cave on the top of a mountain next to Makkah. It is known as Jabal An-Noor: Mountain of Light. It takes more than one hour to climb the mountain in order to reach the cave.

Our beloved Prophet Muhammad (pbuh) used to go to that cave to meditate, contemplate and reflect. He did not like the lifestyle of the people of Makkah. He could not accept their manners, behaviors, attitude, and even their methods of worship. The people in Makkah were steeped in ignorance. They worshipped so many idols, and they were eating unsacrificed carrion. They used to commit abominations, and the strong would devour the weak. There are other bad things they used to do such as burying their own daughters alive as it was shameful to have daughters.

II. Revelation

After the Prophet married Khadijah (r) he continued going to that cave to reflect and to request Allah to guide his people. After fifteen years of going up-and-down to Cave Hiraa', Allah (swt) sent him Angel Jibril (r) in the shape of a human being dressed all in white. Angel Jibril embraced Muhammad (pbuh) three times requesting him to read what he brought him. The answer was that "I am unable to read." Muhammad (pbuh) never went to a teacher in his life. He was unlettered, but he was the most honest and truthful person in his society. He was known as Assadiq Al-Amin. He was a wise person at the same time.

Finally, Angel Jibril told Muhammad the following few Ayat (verses) in Surah Al-'Alaq:

212

أَقْرَأْ بِأَسْمِ رَبِّكَ الَّذِى خَلَقَ ١ خَلَقَ الْإِنسَـٰنَ مِنْ عَلَقٍ ٢ أَقْرَأْ وَرَبُّكَ
الْأَكْرَمُ ٣ الَّذِى عَلَّمَ بِالْقَلَمِ ٤ عَلَّمَ الْإِنسَـٰنَ مَا لَمْ يَعْلَمْ ٥

Proclaim! In the Name of your Lord and Cherisher
Who created – Created Man, out of a Leech-like clot.
Proclaim! And the lord is Most Bountiful. He Who
taught the use of the pen. Taught man that which he
knew not. (96:1-5)

. Angel Jibril flew up in the air, and told Muhammad (pbuh) that you are the Messenger of Allah, and I am Jibril. The Prophet raised his eyes towards heaven, and there was his visitant Jibril. He was recognizable but now clearly an Angel, filling the whole horizon. The Prophet tried to look everywhere: east, west, north, south, and Angel Jibril was there filling the horizon. Finally, Jibril disappeared and Muhammad (pbuh) came down to his house.

III. After Revelation

From that time on, Muhammad (pbuh) was selected by Allah (swt) to be the final Prophet and final Messenger to humanity at large. The Prophet came back to his house and explained to his wife Khadijah what had happened to him. He was shivering, and he thought something happened to him. He requested her to cover him by saying: Zammilooni, Zammilooni: Cover me! Cover me! Khadijah went to her cousin, Waraqah, who was then an old man and blind. She told him the story of her husband Muhammad (pbuh). He was so pleased and he said to her: Holy! Holy! By Him in whose Hand is the soul of Waraqah, there has to come to

213

Muhammad (pbuh) the greatest Namoos (the divine Law or Scripture). Verily Muhammad is the Prophet of his people. Bid him rest assured.

IV. Reflections

The first five verses revealed to Prophet Muhammad (pbuh) in Cave Hiraa' need to be studied properly, discussed in detail and presented to the readers accordingly. However, in this chapter we are going to reflect within the limited space available in this book. The following is a summary of Reflections.

1. Knowledge has to be through reading, and the latter cannot be read without a teacher. Prophet Muhammad's (pbuh) teacher was Allah, the Creator of the whole Universe.

2. One should seek knowledge in the Name of Allah (swt). It should be for the pleasure of Allah (swt), and for the benefit of all humanity at large.

3. It should be stated here that Allah (swt) is the Creator of the whole universe including anything and everything.

4. It is Allah (swt) Who created mankind. He created all in the best shape and form. (see Qur'an 95:4). We people are the children of Adam and Eve. None of us are the bi-products of Ape or otherwise. We do not believe in Darwinism of Evolution, but we believe in Creation.

5. God (Allah) created each one from the fertilization of a sperm and an ova to produce the zygot. This in turn acts as a leech-like clot, adhering to the walls of the womb of the mother.

6. At that time no one was able to think or to find out how human beings are created until the discovery of microscopes and other studies of Embryology.

7. Allah (swt) taught people new things in science, technology, industry, social studies, arts, medicine, chemistry, math, computer, and other sciences that we did not know before.

8. To read something one has to have the material in writing through manuscripts. Writing has to be through the use of the pen.

9. No one should abuse any type of writing against humanity at large. One should recognize the sanctity of the pen. If and when someone writes something wrong about other people, he will create commotion and hate. Such thing may lead to fight, and this in turn leads to catastrophe. Therefore, people should think twice or even ten times before writing anything indecent, immoral, or bad about other people, irrespective of color, nationality, ethnic background, or religion.

V.   Final Remarks

No one can claim himself to be a Prophet or a Messenger. The One Who has the right to chose is Allah, Alone. He makes sure that such a person is a role model, and he has been raised with honor and dignity. Allah (swt) makes sure that a messenger is protected by Him. He sends angels to act as bodyguards to the Prophets. For that reason, Prophets are infallible.

Prophet Ibrahim had to go to the roof of his house looking for Allah (swt). Prophet Moosa had to go to the mountain of Toor to receive the Message from Allah. Prophet Muhammad (pbuh) had to go for 15 years to Cave Hiraa' meditating, contemplating and reflecting. Finally, Allah (swt) sent him Angel Jibril in the shape of a human being dressed with white clothing to give him the Message of Allah.

Those Muslims who go to perform 'Umrah and/or Hajj should try to climb the Mountain of Light (Jabal al-Noor). They should try to reach Cave Hiraa' and pray in it. They should stay there for a few hours reflecting and contemplating. They should make Zikr, Tassbeeh, Tahmeed, Tahleel, and Takbeer. Muslims will not appreciate the Message of Islam until and unless they visit the historical places of Revelation in Makkah, Madinah and all other places that the Prophet himself visited for one reason or the other. After visiting those places, then a Muslim will really recognize the beauty of this religion of Islam. We pray to Allah (swt) to give Muslims a golden opportunity to perform 'Umrah and Hajj. We pray also for them to visit the historical places Insha Allah. Ameen.

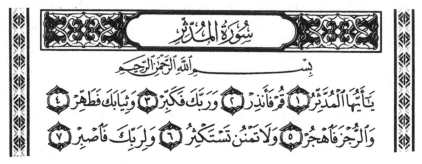

O you wrapped up (in a mantle)! Arise and deliver your warning! And your Lord do you manify! And your garments keep free from stain! And all abomination shun! Nor expect, in giving, any increase (for yourself)! (74:1-6)

216

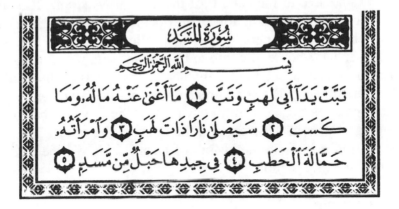

Al-Lahab: The Flame

Perish the hands of the Father of Flame! Perish he!
No profit to him from all his wealth, and all his gains!
Burnt soon will he be in a fire of blazing Flame! His
wife shall carry the (crackling) wood as fuel! A twisted
rope of palm-leaf fiber round her (own) neck! (111:1-5)

I. General

It is a Cave in the suburb of the City of Makkah. It is about 3.5 miles outside Makkah towards Mina, i.e., southeast. It is called Thawr because of a person who was called Thawr Ibn Manat. It takes 1 and 1/2 hours to climb to it. The mountain is composed of three (3) hills attached to one another. The Cave is in the third hill. There are about (54) trails to reach it; sometimes one has to go up and sometimes to go down till one reaches the Cave. It has two (2) openings: One in the front and the other in the back. This Cave has its significance in the history of Islam. This will be discussed in the following section.

II. Importance

It should be mentioned here that during the Hijra (migration) of the Prophet from Makkah to Madina, the Prophet chose to hide himself in that Cave with his companion Abu Bakr. One has to state here that instead of going north towards Madina, he went south towards Mina. The Prophet (pbuh) requested his cousin Ali to stay in the house of the Prophet so as to give all the Trusts back to people's belongings. He also requested Abu Bakr to join him in his Hijra. At the same time Abu Bakr asked his daughter Asmaa' to bring food to the Cave for him and the Prophet. He also asked his son Abdullah to come at night and bring news about the enemies and their plots of searching for the Prophet to be killed.

With the Mercy of Allah (swt), the Prophet and his companion Abu Bakr went to the Cave before sunrise and hid themselves there. Allah (swt) sent a spider and she made a web to cover the entrance to the Cave. At the same time, Allah (swt) sent a pigeon, and it laid her eggs at the main entrance of the Cave.

The Makkans who wanted to kill the Prophet tried to search for where about he was. They went to the house of the Prophet, but they found Ali there. They tried to follow the footsteps. Finally, they arrived at Cave Thawr, but they found the spider web and the pigeon with its eggs. They did not enter the Cave due to the fact of the presence of the spider web and the pigeon. They tried around and above the Cave to look for the Prophet. Meanwhile, Abu Bakr was scared when he saw people from the hole of the Cave. He told the Prophet that if they look through the hole they would be able to find us. The Prophet told Abu Bakr not to be scared. We are two and Allah is with us. He takes care of us. The people of Makkah lost hope and therefore they went back to Makkah. Allah (swt) revealed in Qur'an in Surah Al-Tawbah (Repentance) the following:

إِلَّا تَنصُرُوهُ فَقَدْ نَصَرَهُ ٱللَّهُ إِذْ أَخْرَجَهُ ﴿٣٩﴾ ٱلَّذِينَ كَفَرُوا ثَانِيَ ٱثْنَيْنِ إِذْ هُمَا فِى ٱلْغَارِ إِذْ يَقُولُ لِصَاحِبِهِ لَا تَحْزَنْ إِنَّ ٱللَّهَ مَعَنَا فَأَنزَلَ ٱللَّهُ سَكِينَتَهُ عَلَيْهِ وَأَيَّدَهُ بِجُنُودٍ لَّمْ تَرَوْهَا وَجَعَلَ كَلِمَةَ ٱلَّذِينَ كَفَرُوا ٱلسُّفْلَىٰ وَكَلِمَةُ ٱللَّهِ هِىَ ٱلْعُلْيَا وَٱللَّهُ عَزِيزٌ حَكِيمٌ ﴿٤٠﴾

If you help not your Leader, it is no matter: for God did indeed help him. When the unbelievers drove him out, he had no more than one companion. They two were in the Cave, and he said to his companion, 'Have no fear, for God is with us.' Then God sent down His peace upon him and strengthened him with forces which you saw not, and humbled to the depths the word of the unbelievers, but the word of God is exalted to the heights: for God is Exalted in Might, Wise (9:40).

It was reported that the Prophet took a nap while Abu Bakr could not sleep because he was scared of the enemies to come inside the cave. During the nap-hour, a snake tried to come out of a hole. Abu Bakr immediately put his hand to stop it from coming out. Unfortunately it bit him, and it hurt him so much that tears came down on his face and fell on the face of the Prophet. Our beloved Prophet woke-up to find out what happened. He felt sorry for Abu Bakr. Immediately the Prophet took saliva from his mouth, and put it on the wound, praying for healing. Immediately Abu Bakr was healed, and as if nothing had happened to him.

After three days, the Prophet and Abu Bakr made arrangements to leave the Cave and go north towards the City of Yathrib which became the City of Madina of the Prophet (pbuh).

III. Reflections

One has to recognize the importance of the Cave in the history of the Prophet and in the history of Muslims till the Day of Judgment. The following are some Reflections:

1. If the Makkans were able to find the Prophet they would have killed him and Abu Bakr inside the Cave. They would have brought their heads as a sign of their success.

2. The Message of Islam would have been over at that time. No one would be able to carry the Message, and none of us would have been Muslims.

3. The Prophet made sure that all those who became Muslims should migrate before him. No one leader would do what the Prophet did. Every leader tries to secure his own life with all the bodyguards around him. The Prophet was concerned for the safety of the Muslims much more than his own safety.

4. The Prophet trusted Abu Bakr to be his trustworthy companion in this trip.

5. Abu Bakr ® was smart enough to arrange through his daughter Asmaa' to bring food daily after sunset.

6. Abu Bakr ® was knowledgeable enough to request his son to come daily after sunset with his cattle and sheep after Asmaa': to bring information about the plots of the enemies, and to cover the footsteps of his sister Asmaa'.

7. Abu Bakr was kind enough to make arrangement for their Hijra with a guide to lead them the way to Yathrib.

8. Abu Bakr as a human being was scared when he saw the Makkans around the Cave; but the Prophet had more faith in Allah. He gave him peace of mind at that moment.

9. The Cave of Thawr reminds us of the days of migration, and the days of Hijra. This Hijra reminds Muslims all over the world of the Islamic Calendar.

10. While this Cave reminds us of the Days of Hijra, the Cave of Hiraa' reminds us of the Day of Revelation of Qur'an to Prophet Muhammad (pbuh).

11. To get out of persecution to freedom sometimes one has to run away and hide in a Cave. This reminds us of the youth in Surah Al-Kahf. They ran away from oppression and persecution from the city of Al-Raqeem in Palestine. On their way they hid in a Cave for safety. One may read their story in the Qur'an in Surah Al-Kahf (The Cave) chapter 18.

IV. Final Remarks

Yes indeed! The Cave has its importance in the history of the Prophet as well as in the history of Muslims and Islam. The first Revelation came to the Prophet in Cave Hiraa', and the last Revelation in Makkah before migration came to the Prophet in Cave Thawr.

Muslims are encouraged to read more about the Seerah of the Prophet. They are to go back to the Qur'an and Hadith to understand and to realize their existence now with the Blessings of Allah from the day He sent His beloved Prophet Muhammad (pbuh). We all should be grateful to Allah for making us Muslims, and faithful believers. We should try our best to deliver this Message to Muslims and non-Muslims as well. We pray to Allah to give the opportunity to all to go there to the Holy Land and visit their religious and historical places where the Revelation of the Qur'an came down to Prophet Muhammad. We pray the best for all. Ameen.

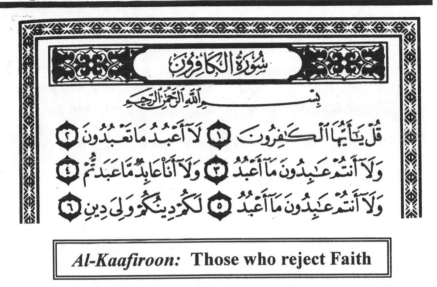

Al-Kaafiroon: Those who reject Faith

O you that reject Faith! I worship not that which you worship, nor will you worship that which I worship. And I will not worship that which you worship nor will you worship that which I worship. To you be your way, and to me mine. (109:1-6)

The following are some of the historical incidents that took place in Madina after the migration of Prophet Muhammad (pbuh).

I.   THE FIRST YEAR

A. Arrival of the Prophet and the welcoming songs.
B. Building of Masjid Qubaa'/First Friday salat and Khutbah.
C. Building the Mosque of the Prophet.
D. Informing people about Islam.
E. Forming a brotherhood bond between Muhajireen and Ansaar
F. Building fraternal bonds between the rich and the poor, between Arabs and non-Arabs, and between the slaves and those who were Free.

II.   THE SECOND YEAR

A. Changing the direction of Qibla from the Sacred Mosque in Jerusalem to Ka'bah on Tuesday, the 15th of Sha'ban.
B. Fasting the month of Ramadan was prescribed.
C. Battle of Badr took place on Friday the 17th of Ramadan.
D. Ali, the cousin of the Prophet, married Fatimah, the daughter of the Prophet.
E. The Prophet married Aisha, the daughter of Abu Bakr.
F. Peace Treaties with local groups were signed.

III.   THE THIRD YEAR

A. Alcohol was prohibited.
B. Battle of Uhud was Saturday, the 7th of Shawwal.
C. Hamzah, the uncle of the Prophet, was killed in the Battle of Uhud.
D. Making agreements with local groups to live in peace and harmony.

IV. THE FOURTH YEAR

A. Story of the Ifk (Scandal) and Revelation about Aisha's innocence.
B. Revelation of Tayammum.
C. Battle of Khandaq (Trench).
D. Inviting neighboring Tribes to the Religion of Islam.

V. THE FIFTH YEAR

A. Salat Al- Khawf (Fear) was taught.
B. Death of Sa'ad Ibn Mu`az.
C. Battle of Bani Quraltha.
D. Sending Ambassadors to International Leaders.

VI. THE SIXTH YEAR

A. Pledge of Al-Radwan was signed.
B. Peace Treaty of Al-Hudaybiya.
C. Hajj (Pilgrimage) was prescribed.
D. Revelation on Tahara (cleanliness from impurities)
E. More Agreements with local tribes
F. Peace Treaties with Christians and Jews

VII. THE SEVENTH YEAR

A. Battle of Khaybar took place.
B. Abu Hurayra accepted Islam.
C. Performance of Umra (Little Hajj) for the first time.
D. Peace Treaty with neighboring Arab tribes.

VIII. THE EIGHTH YEAR

A. Liberation of Makkah from a paganistic society.
B. Zainab, the daughter of the Prophet, died.

C. Battle of Hunayn, in the month of Shawwal, took place.
D. Peace Treaties with Christians and Jews outside Arabia were signed.
E. Sending Ambassadors outside Arabian Peninsula.

IX. THE NINTH YEAR

A. Performance of Pilgrimage under the leadership of Abu Bakr.
B. Death of King Najashi of Ethiopia.
C. Battle of Tabook took place.
D. Death of Umm Kulthoom, the daughter of the Prophet.
E. Death of Abdullah Ibn Sallool, the head of the hypocrites, in the month of Zul Qi'dah.
F. King of Persia was killed, and a woman took over the kingdom.
G. Delegations visiting the Prophet in Madina.
H. More Ambassadors were sent to different countries.

X. THE TENTH YEAR

A. The Farewell Pilgrimage and the khutbah at Arafa.
B. Death of Ibrahim, the son of the Prophet.
C. Many delegations started coming to visit the Prophet.

XI. THE ELEVENTH YEAR

A. Death of the Prophet on Monday, in the month of Rabee' Awwal.
B. Fatimah, the daughter of the Prophet, died six months later.
C. Umm Ayman, the baby-sitter of the Prophet died.
D. Abu Bakr had to assume the leadership of the Muslim Ummah (Caliph).

Chapter (22)   **Madina: City Of The Prophet**

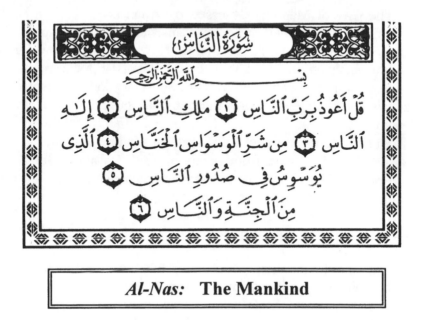

Al-Nas: The Mankind

Say: I seek refuge with the Lord and Cherisher of Mankind, The King (or Ruler) of Mankind, The God (Judge) of Mankind, from the mischief of the Whisperer (of Evil), who withdraws (after his whisper), who whispers into the hearts of mankind, among Jinns and among Men. (114:1-6)

I. Introduction

The City of Madina is blessed by Allah (swt). Allah could have made the Prophet to be born in Madina, raised up till he became a Prophet, and stayed there. However, Allah (swt) gave him Prophethood in Makkah because it was a focal point for business, politics, poetry, pilgrimage and many other reasons. It was also a central point of international business from India, Yemen, Syria and Europe. Moreover, Allah (swt) with His Wisdom, made the Prophet to migrate to Madina after the age of (53) or after (13) years from receiving the Message. But Allah (swt) prepared the Prophet (2) years in advance by allowing him during Israa' and Mi'raaj to visit the City of Madina and pray there. Angel Jibril informed the Prophet at that time, that this City Al-Taibah or Yathrib is going to be his migration.

One should mention here that Abdullah, the father of the Prophet, died there and was buried there. He was on a trip to Syria. While coming back, he felt sick, he died and was buried there. Moreover, the Prophet's uncle did live in Yathrib. They are from the family of Al-Najjar. When the Prophet was (12) years old, he went with his uncle Abu Talib on a trip to Syria. He stopped in Yathrib and visited his uncles. At the same time he visited the grave of his father.

II. Significance

As far as its importance the following are some Ahadith that explain its significance:

1. Anas ® said that he heard the Prophet (pbuh) saying:

٣٤٣ ـ عن أنس قال: سمعت رسول الله ﷺ يقول: «اللهم إجعل بالمدينـة
ضِعْفَيْ ما جعلت بمكة من البركة»(٢٤).

O Allah! Give double Blessings in Madina as much
as You used to give Blessings in Makkah.

2. Sa'ad ® narrated that the Prophet (pbuh) said:

٣٤٤ ـ وفي أفراد مسلم: من حديث سعـد عن النبي ﷺ قال: «لا يثبت أحـدٌ
على لأوَائها وشدتها إلا كنت له شفيعاً يوم القيامة»(٢٥).

Any person who keeps firm while having difficulty by
living in Madina, I will be a Shafee' for him/her in the
Day of Judgment.

3. Abdullah Ibn 'Umar Ibn Al-Khattab ® said that the
Messenger of Allah said:

٣٤٥ ـ عن ابن عمر قال: قال رسول الله ﷺ: «من استطاع أن يموت بالمدينة
فليَمُتْ، فإن من مات بالمدينة شفعت له يوم القيامة»(٢٦).

Whoever can afford to die in the City of Madina let
him do so. Whoever dies in Madina I will be a Shafee' for
him in the Day of Judgment.

4. Another Hadith narrated by Abdullah Ibn 'Umar ® that the
Prophet (pbuh) said:

٣٤٦ ـ عن ابن عمر قال: قال رسول الله ﷺ: «صيام شهر رمضان بالمـدينة
كصيام ألف شهر فيما سواها، وصلاة الجمعة بالمدينة كألف صلاة بما سواها»(٢٧).

Fasting one month in Madina is equal to one thousand months elsewhere; and praying Jumu'ah in Madina is equal to one thousand Salat elsewhere.

5. Another Hadith reported by Abi Thabit ® that the Prophet (pbuh) said:

٣٤٧ ـ عن أبي ثابت قال: قال رسول الله ﷺ: «غبار المدينة شفاء من الجذام»(٢٨).

Dust of Madina is a source of a healing from leprosy.

6. It was narrated by Abu Hurairah ® that the Prophet (pbuh) said:

٣٤٨ ـ عن أبي هريرة قال: قال رسول الله ﷺ: «المدينة قُبّة الإسلام وقلب الإيمان، وما بين الحلال والحرام»(٢٩).

Madina is the Dome of Islam, the Heart of Iman (faith), and it is in-between Lawful and Unlawful.

III. Final Remarks

Yes, indeed the City of Madina is so important and very significant in the history of Islam. It is the City of Migration. That year was considered to be the first year of the Islamic Calendar. It has the Masjid of the Prophet and many other Masajid of the Sahaba of the Prophet. Among them are the following Masajid:

1. Masjid Qubaa'
2. Masjid Abu Bakr Assiddiq

230

3. Masjid 'Umar Ibn Al-Khattab
4. Masjid Othman Ibn 'Affan
5. Masjid Ali Ibn Abi Talib
6. Masjid Bilal Ibn Rabah
7. Masjid Salman Al-Farisi
8. Masjid Sa'ad Ibn Mu'az
9. Masjid Zul Qiblatain
10. Masjid Al-Jumu'ah
11. Masjid Al-Fath
12. Masjid Bani Quraiza
13. Masjid Al-Ghamama
14. Masjid Al-Raaya
15. Masjid Assajda (Abu Zarr)
16. Masjid Assuqiya
17. Masjid Ash-Shaykhain
18. Masjid Al-Manaratain
19. Masjid Ash-Shajara (Al-Meeqat)
20. Masjid Bani Al-Haritha (Al-Mustarah)

Moreover, one recognizes that a good number of the companions died and were buried there in a cemetery called Jannatul Baqee'. Many Muslims all over the world wish to be buried there because of its significance, and because it is close to the Masjid of the Prophet. One more thing that crosses our mind is that even the Battle of Uhud took place there. A good number of Muslims were killed as Martyrs and buried there. Also the Battle of Trench (khandaq) took place in the City of Madina. Therefore, the City of the Prophet is so significant in the Book of Allah. May Allah bless us all. Ameen.

مسجد قباء

Chapter (23)	Masjid Qubaa'

I. General

Masjid Qubaa' is very important in the history of Islam. It was the first Masjid that the Prophet (pbuh) built with his own hands along with his companions immediately after arriving to the city of Yathrib. He prayed in it vocally with his companions. It is located in a village called Qubaa', and it is in the South West suburb of the city of Yathrib. Now it is part of the City of the Prophet i.e. it is part of Madina.

The Muslims remained praying in it till the time of changing the direction of the Qibla. At that time the Prophet (pbuh) came to that Masjid and received revelation to face towards the Ka'bah. From then onward the direction of the Qibla was towards Ka'bah in Makkah.

II. Importance

Being the First Masjid built in Madina after migration from Makkah, indicates how important it was. From persecution and prevention to praying at Ka'bah in Makkah, here the Muslims have had the freedom to pray without harassment. Allah (swt) revealed Ayah in the Qur'an praising that Masjid. In Surah Al-Tawbah (Repentance) Allah (swt) says the following:

لَا تَقُمْ فِيهِ أَبَدًا لَّمَسْجِدٌ أُسِّسَ عَلَى ٱلتَّقْوَىٰ مِنْ أَوَّلِ
يَوْمٍ أَحَقُّ أَن تَقُومَ فِيهِ فِيهِ رِجَالٌ يُحِبُّونَ أَن يَتَطَهَّرُوا
وَٱللَّهُ يُحِبُّ ٱلْمُطَّهِّرِينَ ۝

Never stand you forth therein. There is a mosque whose foundation was laid from the first day on piety; it is more worthy of your standing forth (for prayer) therein. In it are men who love to be purified; and God loves those who make themselves pure (9:108).

After building the new Masjid in the City of Madinah, the Prophet (pbuh) used to visit that Masjid every Saturday, walking or riding so as to pray in it.

1. It was reported through Abdullah Ibn Umar®:

وعنه رضي الله عنهـمـا قـال : «كـان النبي ﷺ يأتي مـسـجـد قبـاء راكباً وماشياً فيصلي فيه ركعتين». (١)

The Prophet (pbuh) used to come to Masjid Qubaa' riding or walking to pray two Rak'at.

2. Also it was reported by Sahl Ibn Hanif that the Prophet (pbuh) said:

وعن سهل بن حنيف(٢) قال : قال رسـول الله ﷺ : « من تطهـر في بيتـه ثم أتى مـسـجـد قبـاء فصلى فيـه صـلاة كـان له كأجـر عـمرة». (٣)

(حديث صحيح) .

Anyone who cleans himself in his house and then comes to Masjid Qubaa' to pray in it, gets reward equal to 'Umrah.

3. Another Hadith reported by Aseed Ibn Hadeer that the
Prophet (pbuh) said:

وعن أسيد بن حضير (٤) وكان من أصحاب النبي ﷺ يحدث عن
النبي ﷺ قال: الصلاة في مسجد قباء كعمرة» . (٥) (حديث
صحيح) .

Salat in Masjid Qubaa' is similar to 'Umrah.

III. Final Remarks

Masjid Qubaa' was the First Masjid built after Migration. The
year of the Hijra started the Islamic Calendar of the Muslims.
Since that day, that year, and the day of building Masjid Qubaa',
Muslims all over the world are still taking their Islamic Calendar
as the Calendar of Hijra. Moreover, Masjid Qubaa' was mentioned
in the Qur'an as the First Day of Hijra, and as the first Masjid that
Muslims should pray in it. The word: "Min Awwali Yawmin"
means from the First Day of Hijra. Allah (swt) in the same Ayah
is encouraging the Prophet and all the Muslims to pray in that
Masjid.

Accordingly, one realizes that most of the Muslims who go for
'Umrah and Hajj try their best to visit that Masjid and pray in it.
Of course they first visit the Masjid of the Prophet, and
immediately they try to visit Masjid Qubaa' to get the blessings of
'Umrah. One observes that Masjid Qubaa' is full of Muslims
throughout the whole year. We pray to Allah (swt) to bless the
whole Muslims. We also pray to Allah (swt) to give a golden
opportunity to all the Muslims to perform 'Umrah and Hajj. We
pray for them to visit Masjid of the Prophet as well as Masjid
Qubaa'. Ameen.

Chapter (24)   **Masjid Of The Prophet**

I. Introduction

Masjid of the Prophet in the City of Madina is one of the three Masajid that one should try to visit and pray in them. It was reported that the Prophet (pbuh) said:

رُوَى الجَمَاعَةُ اَنَّ النّبِيَّ صَلَّى اللهُ عَلَيهِ وَسَلَّمَ قَالَ :

«لاَ تُشَدُّ الرِّحَالُ إِلاَّ إِلَى ثَلاَثَةِ مَسَاجِدَ: المَسْجِدُ الحَرَامِ،

وَمَسْجِدِيْ هَذَا، وَالمَسْجِدُ الأَقْصَى. »

ـ رواه البخاري ـ

Journeys should not be undertaken except to three mosques: The Sacred Mosque (in Makkah); this, my Mosque (in Madina), and Al-Aqsa Mosque. Bukhari

This Masjid was also built by the Prophet and his companions in the first year after migration. It was built after building Masjid Qubaa'. It should be mentioned here that praying in the Masjid of the Prophet is far better than praying in any other masjid in the world except that of Ka'bah in Makkah. It was reported by Abdullah Ibn 'Umar Ibn Al-Khattab ® that the Prophet (pbuh) said:

عن ابن عـمـر رضى الله عنهـمـا أن النبي ﷺ قال : « صلاة فى مسـجدي
هذا أفضل من ألف صلاة فيما سواه إلا المسـجد الحرام » . (١)

Praying in My Masjid is better than (1000) Salat to be offered anywhere else except Al-Masjid Al-Haram (Ka'bah in Makkah).

235

It should be stated here that the Masjid of the Prophet consisted of the prayer area, the Pulpit (Mimbar), and Al-Rawdah. He made sure that his house was wall-to-wall with the Masjid. He had a door that opens into the Masjid, and another door in the Northside that opens to meet Ahl-Assuffah. He made sure that Muslims should live next to the Masjid, and they should come to the Masjid and pray with him the five daily prayers, as well as Salat Jumu'ah. And indeed the Muslims did live next to the Masjid.

II. Visitation

Muslims all over the world yearn to visit Masjid of the Prophet (pbuh). They love to pray there as much as possible, and they love to live in the City of Madina so that they will be close to his Masjid. Most Muslims who go for 'Umrah and/or Hajj prefer to go to the City of Madina and stay there at least eight days so that they will be able to pray forty (40) Salat (5 x 8 = 40) in the Masjid of the Prophet. In so doing, they hope to gain the Blessings of Allah in many ways. It was Anas Ibn Malik ® who reported that the Prophet said:

وروى الإمام أحمد عـن أنـس بـن مـالك ﷺ أن النـبي ﷺ قـال : "مـن صلـى في مسجدي أربعين صلاة لاتفوته صلاة كتبت له بـراءة مـن النـار ونجـاة مـن العـذاب وبرئ من النفاق"(٢).

Whoever prays in my Masjid forty (40) Salat without missing any one of them, he will be saved from Hell fire, from penalty and from hypocrisy.

A similar Hadith narrated by Anas ® that the Messenger of Allah (swt) said:

وقد روى الترمذي عن أنس ﷺ قال قال رسول الله ﷺ : "مــن صلـى لله أربعين يوما في جماعة يدرك التكبيرة الأولى فيها كتبت له براءتان : براءة من النــار وبـراءة من النفاق"(٤). حديث حسن(٥).

Whoever prays for the love of Allah forty (40) days in a Jama'ah before the Iqamah starts (in the Masjid of the Prophet), he will be saved form two things: Safety from Hell fire, and safety from hypocrisy.

To visit the Masjid of the Prophet, the following is a partial list of things to be done:

1. Have Wudoo' (Ablution) before entering.
2. One has to pray two (2) Rak'at inside the Masjid, and preferably in the Rawdah. That place is between the Pulpit (Mimbar) of the Prophet and his house. It was reported by Abdullah Ibn Zeyd ® that the Prophet said:

٣٥٥ ـ عن عبدالله بن زيد أن رسول الله ﷺ قال: «وما بين بيتي ومنبري روضة من رياض الجنة»(٣٦).

أخرجاه.

A piece of Paradise is in between my pulpit and my house.

To reemphasize the idea of praying two Rak'at, it was reported by Abu Qatada Al-Salmy that the Prophet (pbuh) said:

237

ويستحب للقادم أن يصلي ركعتين تحية للمسجد في الروضة
الشريفة أو في أي ناحية من نواحي المسجد لما روى الشيخان عن أبي قتادة
السلمي أن رسـول الله ﷺ قـال : « إذا دخل أحدكم المسجد فليركع
ركعتين قبل أن يجلس » . (٢)

Whenever a person enters Al-Masjid, let him pray two Rak'at before he sits down.

3. After that, one may go forward and reach the house of the Prophet which is now his grave along with the two companions: Abu Bakr ® and 'Umar ®. The Muslim is to stand in front of that house facing it. He is to give greetings to all of the three. It was reported by Abdullah Ibn Dinar ® the following:

السلام على رسول الله ﷺ وصاحبيه :

يأتي الزائر الحجرة الشريفة ويقف مستقبلاً المواجهة الشريفة
ويصلي ويسلم على رسول الله ﷺ وصاحبيه أبي بكر وعمر رضي الله
عنهما لما روي عن عبدالله بن دينار أنه قال : « رأيت عبدالله بن عمر
يقف على قبر النبي ﷺ فيصلي على النبي ﷺ وعلى أبي بكر
وعمر » . (٣)

He saw Abdullah Ibn 'Umar used to stand in front of the graves and make salat (Du'a') on the Prophet, Abu Bakr and 'Umar.

4. Moreover, it was confirmed that a Muslim is to give greetings to all the three. It was reported by Abu Hurairah ® that the Prophet (pbuh) said:

238

قال ابن تيمية : واتفق الأئمة على أنه يسلم عليه عند زيارته ﷺ وعلى صاحبيه لما روي عن أبي هريرة رضي الله عنه أن رسول الله ﷺ قال : «ما من أحد يسلم علي إلا رد الله علي روحي حتى أرد عليـه السلام» .

Any person who says Salam unto me, Allah will bring the soul back to me till I answer him/her with Salam.

5. Giving Salam to the Prophet. Allah (swt) and His Angels gave Blessings unto the Prophet. Therefore, Allah (swt) instructed the faithful believers to give Salam to the Prophet. The Salam of the believers is a blessing to those who say Salam unto the Prophet. In Surah Al-Ahzab (The Confederates) Allah (swt) says the following:

إِنَّ ٱللَّهَ وَمَلَٰٓئِكَتَهُۥ يُصَلُّونَ عَلَى ٱلنَّبِيِّ يَٰٓأَيُّهَا ٱلَّذِينَ ءَامَنُوا۟ صَلُّوا۟ عَلَيْهِ وَسَلِّمُوا۟ تَسْلِيمًا ٥٦

God and His Angels send blessings on the Prophet: O you that believe! Send your blessings on him, and salute him, with all respect (33:56).

It was reported that the best greeting is to say:

وفي ضوء هذه الآية الشريفة قال ابن تيمية : "وإذا قال في سلامه السلام عليك يا رسول الله ، يا نبي الله ، يا خيرة الله من خلقه ، يا أكرم الخلق على ربه ، يا إمام المتقين ، فهذا كله من صفاته بأبي هو وأمي ﷺ ، وكذلك إذا صلى عليه مع السلام عليه فهذا مما أمر الله به" (٣) .

Peace on you O Messenger of Allah! O Prophet of Allah! O who is the best creation that Allah has created! O who is the most generous person that Allah created! O who is the Imam of the faithful! These are among your qualities! You are better than any father and mother.

III. Final Remarks

The most important Masajid in the world are Ka'bah in Makkah, Masjid of the Prophet in Madina, and Al-Masjid Al-Aqsa in Jerusalem. The best places to be visited are, therefore, Makkah, Madina and Jerusalem. To pray there is far better than praying anywhere else. Muslims who love the Prophet yearn to go there and be close to his grave, and pray in his Masjid. The Masjid of the Prophet has a special spiritual touch to the hearts of the Muslims before visiting, and much more after being there.

One feels the spiritual touch while he is there. A person recognizes that the Final Prophet and Final Messenger of Allah is there. His companions are also buried there with him, especially Abu Bakr ® and 'Umar ®. His other good companions and his wives are buried in Jannatul Baqee'. Battle of Uhud is there, and many negotiations took place in his Masjid with Christians, Jews and others. Ambassadors of the Prophet went from his Masjid to different parts of the world inviting kings, emperors, cardinals, bishops, leaders of different tribes and so on. We pray for Muslims to be given the golden opportunity to visit the Masjid of the Prophet and pray there. Ameen.

Chapter (25)   Masjid Of Two Qibla

I.   General Information

It is called Masjid of Two Qibla because the Prophet (pbuh) used to pray towards Jerusalem for about 16-17 months. While the Prophet was praying Zuhr in that Masjid, he received revelation ordering him to turn his face towards Ka'bah. The instruction came to him after he finished (2) two Raka'at. He and his companions, men and women turned towards Ka'bah. The men went to the place of women, while the women went to the place of the men. . For that reason it was called Masjid of Two Qible. The Prophet used to yearn from the bottom of his heart to be instructed by Allah to turn his face towards Ka'bah. The order finally came to him as seen in Surah Al-Baqarah (The Cow). Allah says the following:

قَدْ نَرَىٰ تَقَلُّبَ وَجْهِكَ فِى ٱلسَّمَآءِ

فَلَنُوَلِّيَنَّكَ قِبْلَةً تَرْضَىٰهَا فَوَلِّ وَجْهَكَ شَطْرَ ٱلْمَسْجِدِ

ٱلْحَرَامِ وَحَيْثُ مَا كُنتُمْ فَوَلُّوا۟ وُجُوهَكُمْ شَطْرَهُۥ وَإِنَّ ٱلَّذِينَ

أُوتُوا۟ ٱلْكِتَٰبَ لَيَعْلَمُونَ أَنَّهُ ٱلْحَقُّ مِن رَّبِّهِمْ وَمَا ٱللَّهُ بِغَٰفِلٍ

عَمَّا يَعْمَلُونَ ﴿١٤٤﴾

We see the turning of your face for guidance to the heavens: now shall We turn you to a Qibla that shall please you. Turn then your faces in the direction of the Sacred Mosque: Wherever you are, turn your faces in that direction. The people of the Book know well that that is the truth from their Lord, nor is Allah unmindful of what they do. (2:144)

One companion was praying with the Prophet and he went to his community and wanted to pray `Asr with them. He told them about the new direction towards Ka'bah. They believed him, and all of them prayed `Asr towards Ka'bah.

The Prophet came back to his Masjid in Madina, and prayed `Asr for the first time towards Ka'bah. However, the local Muslims of the Masjid Qubaa' were informed about the change of direction at Fajr time of the second day. They immediately directed their faces towards Ka'bah. The following is the summary of what has been mentioned above:

فتبين أن أمر التحويل نزل على النبي ﷺ في مسجد بني سلمة أثناء صــلاة الظهر، فتحول إلى الكعبة، ولذا سمي هذا المسجد بمسجد القبلتين، ثم صلى العصر في مسجده ﷺ متجهاً إلى الكعبة الشريفة وهي أول صلاة كاملة صلاها إلى الكعبة بعد نزول أمر التحويل، ومن جهة أخرى خرج رجل ممن صلى الظهر مع النبي ﷺ في مسجد بني سلمة ومر على بني حارثة وهم يصلون العصر فأخبرهم بالتحويل، فتوجهوا إلى الكعبة، أما أهل قباء فبلغهم الخبر أثناء صلاة الفجر فتحولوا إلى الكعبة.

II. Reactions

A. Negative Aspects

The only negative aspects came from Bani Israel at that time. They started making commotion and Fitna. Allah (swt) exposed their dirty tricks by saying in Surah Al-Baqarah (The Cow) the following:

242

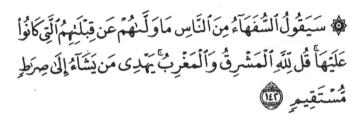

The fools among the people will say: "what has turned them from the Qibla to which they were used?" Say to Allah belongs both East and West: He guided whom He will to a way that is straight. (2:142)

As an encouragement to the Prophet and his Companions, Allah (swt) wanted the Muslims to be the best witnesses. He ordered them to be moderate in their life and religious commitment. Moderation is a sign of success in this world and in the hereafter. Allah told the Muslims in Surah Al-Baqarah (The Cow) the following:

وَكَذَٰلِكَ جَعَلْنَٰكُمْ أُمَّةً وَسَطًا لِّتَكُونُوا۟
شُهَدَآءَ عَلَى ٱلنَّاسِ وَيَكُونَ ٱلرَّسُولُ عَلَيْكُمْ شَهِيدًا وَمَا
جَعَلْنَا ٱلْقِبْلَةَ ٱلَّتِي كُنتَ عَلَيْهَآ إِلَّا لِنَعْلَمَ مَن يَتَّبِعُ ٱلرَّسُولَ
مِمَّن يَنقَلِبُ عَلَىٰ عَقِبَيْهِ وَإِن كَانَتْ لَكَبِيرَةً إِلَّا عَلَى ٱلَّذِينَ
هَدَى ٱللَّهُ وَمَا كَانَ ٱللَّهُ لِيُضِيعَ إِيمَٰنَكُمْ إِنَّ ٱللَّهَ بِٱلنَّاسِ
لَرَءُوفٌ رَّحِيمٌ ﴿١٤٣﴾

Thus have We made of you an Ummat justly balanced that you might be witnesses over the nations, and the Messenger a witness over yourselves; and We appointed the Qibla to which you used, only to test those

*who followed the Messenger from those who would turn
on their heels from the faith. Indeed it was a change
momentous, except to those guided by Allah. And never
would Allah make your faith of no effect. For Allah is to
all people most surely full of Kindness, Most Merciful.
(2:143)*

Finally Allah gave the final moral encouragement to His
Prophet and to all the Muslims. None should worry much about
Bani Israel, as they will never follow the Prophet. In this regard
Allah (swt) says in Surah Al-Baqarah (the Cow) the following:

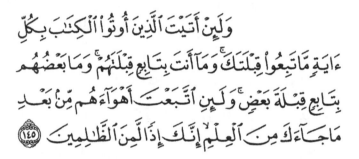

*Even if you were to bring to the people of the Book
all the signs together, they would not follow your Qibla;
are you going to follow their Qibla; nor indeed will they
follow each other's Qibla. If you after the knowledge
had reached you were to follow their vain desires, then
you were indeed in the wrong. (2:145)*

B.   Positive Aspects

The positive aspects of this incident were that all the Muslims believed the Prophet. No one made a single commotion or Fitna. Moreover, the early Muslims of Ansar and Mahajereen trusted each other and believed one another. The real success of those Muslims was that they trusted one another even if the Prophet were not with them. It was one person who prayed Zuhr with the Prophet and then he went to Bani Haritha who were from Al-Ansar. They were going to pray `Asr. He told them about the change of the direction of Qibla. They believed him and trusted him. They turned towards Ka'bah without making any commotion or disturbance. They never questioned his statement and his honesty. We hope that Muslims of today will reach that level of trusting one another, and work together for the love of Allah (swt). Ameen.

One has to mention here that the Muslims of Qubaa' listened to the advice of one Muslim about the change of the direction of Qibla on Fajr of the second day. They believed him, and immediately they prayed towards Ka'bah. Ma-sha-Allah! Early Muslims trusted one another. They obeyed the Prophet to the point that they never even argued with one another. They never waited till the Prophet comes by himself to approve what one of his companions mentioned on his behalf in his absence. We wish that the Muslims of today will reach that level of trust to one other. We should not suspect one another. If we trust one another then Allah will bless us and make us successful in this world and in the hereafter. Ameen.

245

III.   Final Remarks

Allah (swt) finally instructed the Prophet to pray towards Ka'bah from anywhere he may be. This is the really Truth from Allah. One may read the final revelation about changing the direction towards Ka'bah in Surah Al-Baqarah (The Cow):

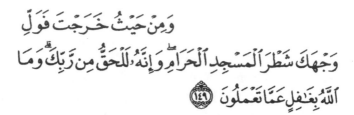

From when so ever you started forth, turn your face in the direction of the Sacred Mosque; that is indeed the truth from your lord. And Allah is not unmindful of what you do. (2:149)

Allah (swt) did not instruct only His Prophet, but He instructed every Muslim to pray towards Ka'bah from anywhere in the world. The following Ayah in Surah Al-Baqarah (The Cow) reflects the instructions:

وَمِنْ حَيْثُ خَرَجْتَ فَوَلِّ وَجْهَكَ
شَطْرَ ٱلْمَسْجِدِ ٱلْحَرَامِ وَحَيْثُ مَا كُنتُمْ فَوَلُّوا۟ وُجُوهَكُمْ
شَطْرَهُۥ لِئَلَّا يَكُونَ لِلنَّاسِ عَلَيْكُمْ حُجَّةٌ إِلَّا ٱلَّذِينَ ظَلَمُوا۟
مِنْهُمْ فَلَا تَخْشَوْهُمْ وَٱخْشَوْنِى وَلِأُتِمَّ نِعْمَتِى عَلَيْكُمْ وَلَعَلَّكُمْ
تَهْتَدُونَ ﴿١٥٠﴾

246

So from whensoever you started forth, turn your face in the direction of the Sacred Mosque; and wheresoever you are, turn your face there. That there be no ground of dispute against you among the people/ Except those of them that are bent on wickedness; so fear them not, but fear Me; and that I may complete My favors on you, and you may consent to be guided. (2:150)

Muslims should be grateful to Allah that they pray to Him facing Ka'bah. It is the First House of Worship on this planet Earth. No one nation or group of people can claim that Muslims are following them. We follow no body, but we follow the teachings of Allah in the Qur'an and as explained by His Prophet Muhammad. We are one Ummah of Muslims irrespective of color, nationality, language or position. Allah (swt) says in Surah Al-Anbiyaa' (The Prophets) the following:

Verily this Ummah of yours is a single Ummah and I am your Lord and Cherisher: therefore serve Me and no other. (21:92)

We hope and pray that we learn from our history a good number of lessons so that we will be able to live in peace, harmony, and happiness under the banner of La Ilaha Illa Allah. Ameen.

« غزوة بدر »

I. General Information

The City of Badr is about 150 km southwest of the City of Madina. It is a small city surrounded by a series of mountains and hills. There is also a spring of water. The mountains are of solid rocks covered partially with sand. The spring of water passes through the city as a creek. There is a small hill where the Prophet (pbuh) prayed to Allah (swt) to give him success in the Battle that took place there.

II. Historical Information

The people of Quraish were spoiling for a war with the Muslims. The Prophet in the first year of Hijra tried to consolidate the Muslim Community in Madina. Few skirmishes took place in the First Year of Hijra, but nothing of particular importance. During the second year of Hijra, Quraish decided to wage a war against the innocent Muslim community in Madina. They sent a large caravan with investments from people of Quraish in Makkah to Syria (Al-Sham). The profit will go to make a war against the Muslims. Most people in Makkah participated in the business investment. Abu Sufyan led the caravan.

Muslims recognized the decision of Quraish. Therefore, they decided to intercede the caravan. Abu Sufyan requested the Quraish to come and help him before they lose the business. The people of Quraish sent an army of more than one thousand well equipped with ammunition, foods, caravan, and expert archers to defeat Muhammad and his followers.

Muslims were not well equipped at all. Their number was about 319. They never thought that they would go into war. All what they were hoping was to stop the caravan so that the people of Quraish will not use the benefits of that business into a war. Allah (swt) reminded the Prophet that neither the Muslims nor the Prophet were interested into going to war, but Allah decides whatever He wants for the benefit of those who want to spread His Message. In Surah Al-Anfal (The Spoils of war/booties), Allah (swt) says the following:

وَإِذْ يَعِدُكُمُ ٱللَّهُ إِحْدَى ٱلطَّآئِفَتَيْنِ أَنَّهَا لَكُمْ وَتَوَدُّونَ أَنَّ غَيْرَ ذَاتِ ٱلشَّوْكَةِ تَكُونُ لَكُمْ وَيُرِيدُ ٱللَّهُ أَن يُحِقَّ ٱلْحَقَّ بِكَلِمَٰتِهِۦ وَيَقْطَعَ دَابِرَ ٱلْكَٰفِرِينَ ۝ لِيُحِقَّ ٱلْحَقَّ وَيُبْطِلَ ٱلْبَٰطِلَ وَلَوْ كَرِهَ ٱلْمُجْرِمُونَ ۝

Behold! Allah promised you one of the two parties, that it should be yours: you wished that the one unarmed should be yours, but Allah willed to establish the truth according to His words, and to cut off the roots of the Unbelievers; That He might establish Truth and prove Falsehood false, distasteful though it be to those in guilt. (8:7-8)

However, the Caravan escaped unharmed by changing its route. Abu Sufyan sent messages to the Quraish army to return, but Abu Jahal and other leaders of the army decided to continue moving to where the Prophet and his followers were. They camped at the City of Badr.

The Prophet was worried, he prayed with crying voice, requesting Allah to send His Help for victory. The Muslims were about 319, while the Quraish were 1000 and well equipped for

249

fighting. While the Prophet was praying, Allah revealed to him the following Ayat in the same Surah of Al-Anfal:

إِذْ تَسْتَغِيثُونَ رَبَّكُمْ فَاسْتَجَابَ لَكُمْ أَنِّي مُمِدُّكُم بِأَلْفٍ مِّنَ ٱلْمَلَـٰئِكَةِ مُرْدِفِينَ ۞ وَمَا جَعَلَهُ ٱللَّهُ إِلَّا بُشْرَىٰ وَلِتَطْمَئِنَّ بِهِ قُلُوبُكُمْ وَمَا ٱلنَّصْرُ إِلَّا مِنْ عِندِ ٱللَّهِ إِنَّ ٱللَّهَ عَزِيزٌ حَكِيمٌ ۞

Remember you implored the assistance of your Lord, and He answered to you: "I will assist you with a thousand angels, ranks on ranks," Allah made it but a message of hope, and an assurance to your hearts: in any case there is no help except from Allah: And Allah is Exalted in Power, Wise. (8:9-10)

Moreover, after sending Angels to fight with the Muslims, Allah gave them peace of mind and body. He made them to sleep and then He showered them with some rain for cleansing and for solid walking on the desert. Allah says the following in the same Surah:

إِذْ يُغَشِّيكُمُ ٱلنُّعَاسَ أَمَنَةً مِّنْهُ وَيُنَزِّلُ عَلَيْكُم مِّنَ ٱلسَّمَاءِ مَاءً لِّيُطَهِّرَكُم بِهِ وَيُذْهِبَ عَنكُمْ رِجْزَ ٱلشَّيْطَانِ وَلِيَرْبِطَ عَلَىٰ قُلُوبِكُمْ وَيُثَبِّتَ بِهِ ٱلْأَقْدَامَ ۞

250

Remember He covered you with drowsiness to give you calm as from Himself, and He caused rain to descend on you from heaven, to clean you therewith, to remove from you the stain of Satan, to strengthen your hearts, and to plant your feet firmly therewith. (8:11)

To give the Muslims more peace and good news in advance, He revealed to His Angels that they should help the Muslims in their fight. They should attack the enemies. Indeed they helped them. Allah (swt) says in this regard the following:

إِذْ يُوحِى رَبُّكَ إِلَى ٱلْمَلَٰٓئِكَةِ أَنِّى مَعَكُمْ فَثَبِّتُوا۟ ٱلَّذِينَ ءَامَنُوا۟ سَأُلْقِى فِى قُلُوبِ ٱلَّذِينَ كَفَرُوا۟ ٱلرُّعْبَ فَٱضْرِبُوا۟ فَوْقَ ٱلْأَعْنَاقِ وَٱضْرِبُوا۟ مِنْهُمْ كُلَّ بَنَانٍ ۝ ذَٰلِكَ بِأَنَّهُمْ شَآقُّوا۟ ٱللَّهَ وَرَسُولَهُۥ وَمَن يُشَاقِقِ ٱللَّهَ وَرَسُولَهُۥ فَإِنَّ ٱللَّهَ شَدِيدُ ٱلْعِقَابِ ۝ ذَٰلِكُمْ فَذُوقُوهُ وَأَنَّ لِلْكَٰفِرِينَ عَذَابَ ٱلنَّارِ ۝

Remember your Lord inspired the angels with the message: "I am with you: give firmness to the Believers: I will instill terror into the hearts of the Unbelievers: Smite you about their necks and smite all their fingertips off them." This because they contended against Allah and His Messenger: If any contend against Allah and His Messenger, Allah is strict in punishment. Thus will

251

it be said: "Taste you then of the punishment for those who reject is the chastisement of the Fire:" (8:12-14)

The Muslims won a decisive battle. Many of the leaders of Quraish were killed. Some of them were Abu Jahl, uncle of the Prophet; Umayyah Ibn Khalaf; Utbah Ibn Rabi'ah, etc...

III.   Reflections

1. Muslims never thought that they were going to war. For that reason they were small in number and not equipped for war.

2. Number is not a factor in war. Commitment for a noble cause is more important

3. Ammunition and war equipment are not the only factors for success. They may be a source of destruction of the superior army.

4. Those who really fight for a noble cause will receive the support from Allah. He sends them Angles in the shape of human beings to fight with them, and to give them moral support.

5. Victory is not for booties. But if there are booties, then it is left up to Allah to decide how to be distributed. In Surah Al-Anfal, Allah had advised the Prophet how to distribute the Spoils of war. He said the following:

وَٱعْلَمُوٓاْ أَنَّمَا غَنِمْتُم مِّن شَىْءٍ فَأَنَّ لِلَّهِ خُمُسَهُۥ وَلِلرَّسُولِ
وَلِذِى ٱلْقُرْبَىٰ وَٱلْيَتَـٰمَىٰ وَٱلْمَسَـٰكِينِ وَٱبْنِ ٱلسَّبِيلِ إِن
كُنتُمْ ءَامَنتُم بِٱللَّهِ وَمَآ أَنزَلْنَا عَلَىٰ عَبْدِنَا يَوْمَ ٱلْفُرْقَانِ
يَوْمَ ٱلْتَقَى ٱلْجَمْعَانِ ۗ وَٱللَّهُ عَلَىٰ كُلِّ شَىْءٍ قَدِيرٌ ﴿٤١﴾

And know that out of all the booty that you may
acquire in war, a fifth share is assigned to Allah, and to
the Messenger, and to near relatives, orphans, the
needy, and the wayfarer, if you do believe in Allah and
in the revelation We sent down to Our Servant on the
Day of Discrimination-- the Day of the meeting of the
two forces. For Allah has power over all things. (8:41)

IV.   Final Remarks

Muslims of today should go back and study Qur'an, Hadith,
Sirah of the Prophet, and other aspects of Islamic History. They
should benefit from the past so that they will be able to live in
peace and solidarity. They will be able to build a better future for
the Muslim Ummah. Nowadays, the whole Muslim world is in
trouble. Muslims have to wake up and come back to practice the
teachings of Allah in public as well as in privacy.

Muslims should unite under the Banner of La Ilaha Illa-Allah.
They should help one another. If they don't do that, then everyone
in the world is in trouble because of the disunity of the Muslims.
Allah reminded the Muslims about this factor by saying in the
same Surah the following:

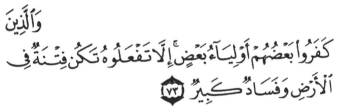

253

The unbelievers are protectors, one of another:
unless you do this. Protect each other, there would be
tumult and oppression on earth and great mischief.
(8:73)

We hope and pray that we benefit from our history, from Qur'an, from Hadith, from Sirah, and others, so as to build a better future for everyone. Ameen.

The name of the Prophet Muhammad
In mirror images,

جبل أحد

I.   General Information

It is a huge mountain on the East side of the City of Madina. It is about (3) three miles from the Masjid of the Prophet. It was called Uhud because it is a mountain by itself far from any other chain of mountains. To the north of this mountain, there is the grave of Prophet Haroon, the brother of Prophet Moosa. The mountain is (6) six kilometers long, and it has a series of up-and-down chains. Rain is collected in small swamp areas. At the top of the mountain there is a small room without roof. People used it to relax, and next to it is a spring of water.

II.   Significance

A. This particular mountain has its importance in history for many reasons. One of them is that the Battle of Uhud took place there in the third year of Hijra. At first, Muslims won the Battle but then they were defeated for a reason that will be explained later.

B. The other important facts about this Mountain are the Ahadith of the Prophet:

1. In one Hadith, the Prophet (pbuh) said:

قال رسـول الله صـلى الله عليـه وسلم « أحد جبل يحبنا ونحبه »⁽¹⁾،

Uhud is a mountain that likes us, and we too like him. (Bukhari)

2. Another Hadith the Prophet (pbuh) said:

وقال أيضا : « أحد جبل من جبال الجنة »،

255

Uhud is a mountain from the mountains of Paradise

3. The other Hadith, the Prophet (pbuh) said:

وسميت موقعة أحد المشهورة باسمه، وقال

فيه رسول الله صلى الله عليه وسلم : «إن جبل أحد هذا لعلى باب من أبواب

الجنة»^(٢) الحـديث،

This mountain of Uhud is indeed at one door of the doors of Paradise.

4. The Fourth Hadith, the Prophet (pbuh) said:

وقـال أيضـا: «اثبت أحـد فإنما عليك نبي وصديق

وشهيدان» الحديث.^(٣)

O Uhud be firm in your place! You have a Prophet, a Siddiq, and two (2) martyrs.

C. The other important fact about this place is the cemetery of the Martyrs who were killed in the battlefield and buried there. Hamzah, Uncle of the prophet, was killed there and buried after his body was mutilated by Hind, the wife of Abu Sufyan.

D. The battle of Uhud teaches the Muslims many lessons and the most important one is obedience. The instruction that was given to the archers was not to leave their positions till they are instructed to do so. But when they initially won, they abandoned their positions to collect the booties that gave the enemy chance to come back and win over the Muslim army.

E. Khalid ibn Al-Walid was still a Kafir. It was he who planned to attack the Prophet and his group, by coming around the archers' hillside.

256

F. The Prophet was injured too in that battle because of the disobedience of the Muslim archers who left their post in order to benefit from the booty.

G. Finally let us mention here that the defeated Quraish in the Battle of Badr waged another war against the Muslims. This was the Battle of Uhud. They were (3,000) three thousand while the Muslims were only (700) seven hundred. The army of Quraish were heavily armed while Muslims were not. Number is not the issue, the most important is obeying Allah (swt) and His Messenger. Ameen.

And He (Allah) has power over all things.
(Qur'an, 11:4)

Chapter (28)   Al-Khandaq

I. General Information

The word Khandaq means a Trench. In the fifth year of Migration of the Prophet to Yathrib, another war was waged against the Prophet and his followers. The Quraish along with Bani Israel at that time joined together to get rid of the Prophet. They planned a series of strategies to achieve their aims. They went to different tribes and promised to help them financially if they joined them to defeat the Prophet. They tried even to work with those who were weak in their faith and who were living in Madina to join them. They made sure that every tribe, every individual, and they themselves as Bani Israel and the people of Quraish will join together and fight the Prophet and conquer him and his Muslims. Therefore, they made a confederate. Although the Prophet had treaties with the Jews at that time, but they broke their agreements without telling him. The Qur'anic terminology of Confederates is Al-Ahzab. Allah revealed chapter (Surah) in the Qur'an under the title of Al-Ahzab. As far as the word of Al-Khandaq is: upon the recommendation of Salman Al-Farisi, the Prophet engaged in digging the Trench along with his companions. It took six days to make a trench around the city of Madina. It was deep enough and wide enough to stop the advance of the enemies into Madina. Moreover, Muslims stored stones on the inner side of the trench to be used against the invaders. The enemies were well equipped and their numbers exceeded 10,000. Some skirmishes took place at that time.

II. Qur'an and the Confederates

A. **Hypocrites:** Allah (swt) exposed the enemies and their plans against the Prophet and his companions. As far as the

Hypocrites in Madina are concerned, Allah Says about them in Surah Al-Ahzab (The Confederates) the following:

وَإِذْ يَقُولُ ٱلْمُنَٰفِقُونَ وَٱلَّذِينَ فِى قُلُوبِهِم مَّرَضٌ مَّا وَعَدَنَا ٱللَّهُ وَرَسُولُهُۥٓ إِلَّا غُرُورًا ۞ وَإِذْ قَالَت طَّآئِفَةٌ مِّنْهُمْ يَٰٓأَهْلَ يَثْرِبَ لَا مُقَامَ لَكُمْ فَٱرْجِعُوا۟ ۚ وَيَسْتَـْٔذِنُ فَرِيقٌ مِّنْهُمُ ٱلنَّبِىَّ يَقُولُونَ إِنَّ بُيُوتَنَا عَوْرَةٌ وَمَا هِىَ بِعَوْرَةٍ ۖ إِن يُرِيدُونَ إِلَّا فِرَارًا ۞ وَلَوْ دُخِلَتْ عَلَيْهِم مِّنْ أَقْطَارِهَا ثُمَّ سُئِلُوا۟ ٱلْفِتْنَةَ لَأَتَوْهَا وَمَا تَلَبَّثُوا۟ بِهَآ إِلَّا يَسِيرًا ۞ وَلَقَدْ كَانُوا۟ عَٰهَدُوا۟ ٱللَّهَ مِن قَبْلُ لَا يُوَلُّونَ ٱلْأَدْبَٰرَ ۚ وَكَانَ عَهْدُ ٱللَّهِ مَسْـُٔولًا ۞ قُل لَّن يَنفَعَكُمُ ٱلْفِرَارُ إِن فَرَرْتُم مِّنَ ٱلْمَوْتِ أَوِ ٱلْقَتْلِ وَإِذًا لَّا تُمَتَّعُونَ إِلَّا قَلِيلًا ۞

And behold! The Hypocrites and those in whose hearts is a disease say: "Allah and His Messenger promised us nothing but delusions!" Behold! A party among them said: "You men of Yathrib! You cannot stand the attack! Therefore go back!" And a band of them ask for leave of the Prophet saying, "Truly our houses are bare and exposed: they intended nothing but to run away. And if an entry had been effected to them from the sides of the city and they had been incited to sedition, they would certainly have brought it to pass, with none but a brief of delay! And yet they had already covenanted with Allah not to turn their backs, and a covenant with Allah must surely be answered for. Say: "Running away will not profit you if you are running away from death or slaughter; and even if you do escape, no more than a brief respite will you be allowed to enjoy!" (33:12-16)

B. **Believers:** Moreover, Allah had blessed the faithful believers by reminding them how He made them to win the Battle without going into it. In Surah Al-Ahzab (the confederates) Allah says the following:

يَٰٓأَيُّهَا ٱلَّذِينَ ءَامَنُوا ٱذْكُرُوا نِعْمَةَ ٱللَّهِ عَلَيْكُمْ إِذْ جَآءَتْكُمْ جُنُودٌ فَأَرْسَلْنَا عَلَيْهِمْ رِيحًا وَجُنُودًا لَّمْ تَرَوْهَا ۚ وَكَانَ ٱللَّهُ بِمَا تَعْمَلُونَ بَصِيرًا ۞ إِذْ جَآءُوكُم مِّن فَوْقِكُمْ وَمِنْ أَسْفَلَ مِنكُمْ وَإِذْ زَاغَتِ ٱلْأَبْصَٰرُ وَبَلَغَتِ ٱلْقُلُوبُ ٱلْحَنَاجِرَ وَتَظُنُّونَ بِٱللَّهِ ٱلظُّنُونَا۠ ۞ هُنَالِكَ ٱبْتُلِيَ ٱلْمُؤْمِنُونَ وَزُلْزِلُوا زِلْزَالًا شَدِيدًا ۞

O you who believe! Remember the Grace of Allah, bestowed on you, when there came down on you hosts to overwhelm you: but We sent against them a hurricane and forces that you saw not: but Allah sees clearly all that you do. Behold! They came on you from above you

*and from below you, and behold, the eyes swerved and
the hearts gaped up to the throats, and you imagined
various vain thoughts about Allah! In that situation
were the believers tried: they were shaken as by
tremendous shaking. (33:9-11)*

C. Rewards of Believers: Allah made the Muslims to succeed
and to take over the wealth, the properties and the lands of the
enemies. In the same Surah, of Al-Ahzab, Allah (swt) says the
following:

وَأَوْرَثَكُمْ أَرْضَهُمْ

وَدِيَـٰرَهُمْ وَأَمْوَٰلَهُمْ وَأَرْضًا لَّمْ تَطَـُٔوهَا وَكَانَ ٱللَّهُ عَلَىٰ كُلِّ

شَىْءٍ قَدِيرًا ٢٧

*And He made you heirs of their lands, their houses,
and their goods, and of a land, which you had not
frequented before. And Allah has power of all things.
(33:27)*

D. Hypocrites Again: Allah exposed them more and more by
saying in the same Surah, the following:

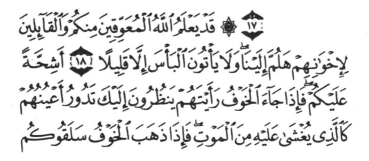

261

بِأَلْسِنَةٍ حِدَادٍ أَشِحَّةً عَلَى ٱلْخَيْرِ أُوْلَٰٓئِكَ لَمْ يُؤْمِنُوا۟ فَأَحْبَطَ ٱللَّهُ أَعْمَٰلَهُمْ وَكَانَ ذَٰلِكَ عَلَى ٱللَّهِ يَسِيرًا ۝ يَحْسَبُونَ ٱلْأَحْزَابَ لَمْ يَذْهَبُوا۟ وَإِن يَأْتِ ٱلْأَحْزَابُ يَوَدُّوا۟ لَوْ أَنَّهُم بَادُونَ فِي ٱلْأَعْرَابِ يَسْـَٔلُونَ عَنْ أَنۢبَآئِكُمْ وَلَوْ كَانُوا۟ فِيكُم مَّا قَٰتَلُوٓا۟ إِلَّا قَلِيلًا ۝

Verily Allah knows those among you who keep back men and those who say to their brethren, "Come along to us", but come not to fight except for just a little while, covetous over you. Then when fear comes, you will see them looking to us, their eyes revolving, like one who faints from death: but when fear is past they will smite you with sharp tongues, covetous of goods. Such men have no faith, and so Allah has made their deeds of none effect and that is easy for Allah. They think that the Confederates have not withdrawn; and if the confederates should come again, they would wish they were in the deserts wandering among the Bedouins, and seeking news about you from a safe distance and if they were in your midst, they would fight but little. (33: 18-20)

E. **Believers' Appreciation:** As far as the faithful believers are concerned, Allah had blessed them more and more. They were grateful to Allah for all what He has done for them. In the same Surah, Allah (swt) says the following:

وَلَمَّا رَءَا الْمُؤْمِنُونَ الْأَحْزَابَ قَالُوا هَٰذَا مَا وَعَدَنَا اللَّهُ وَرَسُولُهُ وَصَدَقَ اللَّهُ وَرَسُولُهُ وَمَا زَادَهُمْ إِلَّا إِيمَانًا وَتَسْلِيمًا ۝ مِّنَ الْمُؤْمِنِينَ رِجَالٌ صَدَقُوا مَا عَاهَدُوا اللَّهَ عَلَيْهِ فَمِنْهُم مَّن قَضَىٰ نَحْبَهُ وَمِنْهُم مَّن يَنتَظِرُ وَمَا بَدَّلُوا تَبْدِيلًا ۝ لِّيَجْزِيَ اللَّهُ الصَّادِقِينَ بِصِدْقِهِمْ وَيُعَذِّبَ الْمُنَافِقِينَ إِن شَاءَ أَوْ يَتُوبَ عَلَيْهِمْ إِنَّ اللَّهَ كَانَ غَفُورًا رَّحِيمًا ۝ وَرَدَّ اللَّهُ الَّذِينَ كَفَرُوا بِغَيْظِهِمْ لَمْ يَنَالُوا خَيْرًا وَكَفَى اللَّهُ الْمُؤْمِنِينَ الْقِتَالَ وَكَانَ اللَّهُ قَوِيًّا عَزِيزًا ۝

When the believers saw the Confederate forces, they said: "this is what Allah and His Messenger promised us, and Allah and His Messenger told us what was true." And it only added to their faith and their zeal in obedience. Among the believers are men who have been true to their covenant with Allah: of them some have died and some still wait: But they have never changed their determination in the least: That Allah may reward the men of truth for their truth, and punish the Hypocrites if that be His Will or turn to them in Mercy: For Allah is Oft-Forgiving, Most Merciful. And Allah turned back the Unbelievers for all their fury: no advantage did they gain; and enough is Allah for the Believers in their fight. And Allah is full of Strength, Exalted in might. (33:22-25)

263

III. Final Remarks

The Battle of Khandaq took place in Madina, the City of the Prophet. Most Muslims who try to visit the Masjid of the Prophet go and visit a series of historical places. Some of them are:

1. Masjid Qubaa'
2. Masjid of two Qibla
3. Jannatul Baqee'
4. Battle of Uhud at Mt. Uhud
5. Battle of Khandaq
6. Well of 'Uthman
7. Other Masajid

The new institutions that Muslims do visit also are:

1. The Islamic University of Madina
2. King Fahd complex for printing of the Holy Qur'an

While visiting all these places a Muslim will be more attached to go back and visit them again and again. Majority of Muslims prefer to live there the rest of their life, and to be buried there. In reality, Muslims will never understand Islam, Qur'an, Hadith, Sunnah and Fiqh unless they go to the Holy Land and visit the places as well as other such as:

1. The City of Badr
2. The City of Al-Ta'if
3. The City of Tabook
4. The City of Hunain
5. Other Cities such as Najd, Riyadh, Dammam, etc...

All what we hope and pray that Muslims will wake up and assume their responsibilities by protecting the Holy Land in case of a danger. Jerusalem is part of the Holy Land that Allah blessed, and He blessed all the lands around it. Muslims are obliged to free the Holy Land from any foreign occupations. We hope and pray that they will assume their responsibility as soon as possible, and before it is too late. Ameen.

The Most Beautiful Names of Allah

I.　Introduction

Before the migration of the Prophet to Madina, Abu Aamer, a man of Alkhazraj tribe, adopted Christianity. He later became a priest and was proud of himself with that title. After the Prophet migrated to Madina and was victorious against the Pagans of Makkah in the Battle of Badr, the priest was jealous of the Prophet and his followers. He became a rival to the Prophet in privacy and in public.

He went back to Makkah to entice the people there to come and defeat the Prophet and his companions. Indeed he was successful in recruiting them to get rid of the Muslims in Madina. The Battle of Uhud took place. It was that priest, Abu Aamer, who dug a trench in the area of the Battle of Uhud. The Prophet fell in the trench. He injured himself and his face. He broke his right arm and his head was injured too. The priest came to the Ansar of Madina requesting them to support him against the Prophet. They were honest and refused to listen to him.

It was reported that the Prophet invited him long before this incident to accept Islam. Moreover the Prophet read and recited Qur'an to him, but he refused to accept Islam. He insisted to defeat the Prophet internally and externally. Accordingly, he went to king Hercules, of the Romans requesting him to support him. He requested a huge army to come over to defeat the Prophet and the faithful believers. He was given hospitality by the king.

III.　Building Masjid Diraar

While he was there, he sent messages to some hypocrites of Al-Ansar telling them that he is bringing a huge army from the

Romans to get rid of the Prophet and the Muslims. In order to be successful, he asked them to make a place in Qubaa' for him so when he comes it will be his headquarters.

The best idea for them was to build another so-called Masjid with good fortresses from every corner. They indeed built a Masjid. Then the hypocrites informed the Prophet that they built such a Masjid because the number of the Muslims had increased. This Masjid would be used for the poor and homeless. It could easily be used as a shelter for travelers, and as a safe place from rain. They requested the Prophet to come and pray in it as a source of blessing and as a Masjid that was approved by the Prophet.

III. Exposing the Hypocrites

The Prophet was on his way to the Battle of Tabook. He informed them that he would be happy to do so after he comes back from the battlefield. After coming back from the Battle of Tabook, and just before arriving to the City of Madina, Allah (swt) revealed to the Prophet not to go there, and not to pray. Allah informed the Prophet that those people were hypocrites. They built it as a headquarters to fight the Muslims and to get rid of the Prophet as well. It was a shock to the Prophet that such a group of hypocrites were planning to destroy Islam and to kill Muslims and the Prophet too. The revelation that came to the Prophet in Surah Al-Tawbah goes as follows:

وَٱلَّذِينَ ٱتَّخَذُواْ مَسْجِدًا ضِرَارًا وَكُفْرًا وَتَفْرِيقًا بَيْنَ ٱلْمُؤْمِنِينَ وَإِرْصَادًا لِّمَنْ حَارَبَ ٱللَّهَ وَرَسُولَهُۥ مِن قَبْلُ وَلَيَحْلِفُنَّ إِنْ أَرَدْنَآ إِلَّا ٱلْحُسْنَىٰ وَٱللَّهُ يَشْهَدُ إِنَّهُمْ لَكَٰذِبُونَ

﴿١٠٧﴾

267

And there are those who put up a mosque by way of mischief and infidelity to disunite the Believers-and in preparation for one who warred against Allah and His Messenger aforetime. They will indeed swear that their intention is nothing but good; but Allah does declare that they are certainly liars. (9:107)

Then Allah continued His revelation to the Prophet by instructing him not to go to that Masjid and not to pray in it at all. In the same Surah, Allah (swt) says the following:

$$\text{لَا تَقُمْ فِيهِ أَبَدًا لَّمَسْجِدٌ أُسِّسَ عَلَى التَّقْوَىٰ مِنْ أَوَّلِ}$$
$$\text{يَوْمٍ أَحَقُّ أَن تَقُومَ فِيهِ فِيهِ رِجَالٌ يُحِبُّونَ أَن يَتَطَهَّرُواْ}$$
$$\text{وَٱللَّهُ يُحِبُّ ٱلْمُطَّهِّرِينَ ۝}$$

Never you stand forth therein. There is a mosque whose foundation was laid from the first day on piety; it is more worthy of you standing forth for prayer therein. In it are men who love to be purified; and Allah loves those who make themselves pure. (9:108)

The Prophet was reminded that His Own Masjid in Madina is the best Masjid after Ka'bah in the Book of Allah. Second in rank is Masjid Qubaa' in the suburb of Madina. However Masjid Diraar was a place for the hypocrites. Then the revelation from Allah (swt) continued by comparing it with the Masjid of the Prophet which was built on Deity and Righteousness. The other Masjid

Diraar was built on false hopes. They will definitely go to Hell. In the same Surah Allah (swt) says the following:

أَفَمَنْ أَسَّسَ بُنْيَـٰنَهُ
عَلَىٰ تَقْوَىٰ مِنَ اللَّهِ وَرِضْوَٰنٍ خَيْرٌ أَم مَّنْ أَسَّسَ بُنْيَـٰنَهُ
عَلَىٰ شَفَا جُرُفٍ هَارٍ فَٱنْهَارَ بِهِۦ فِى نَارِ جَهَنَّمَ وَٱللَّهُ لَا يَهْدِى
ٱلْقَوْمَ ٱلظَّـٰلِمِينَ ١٠٩

Which then is best? -He that lays his foundation on piety to Allah and his good pleasure? -Or he that lays his foundation on an undermined sand-cliff ready to crumble to pieces? And it does crumble to pieces with him, into the fire of Hell. And Allah guides not people that do wrong. (9:109)

IV. Demolishing Masjid Diraar

The Prophet instructed his companions to go to Masjid Diraar and demolish it by burning it. They went there and destroyed it as they were told. The hypocrites dispersed. The place that was built by the hypocrites was lost. They did recognize from day one that they built it not as a Masjid but as a headquarters for the enemies of Islam from within the Muslim Community. They wanted to act as spies, as FBI and CIA against the Prophet and the Muslims from within the Muslim Community. Allah (swt) revealed what was in their hearts by saying:

لَا يَزَالُ بُنْيَـٰنُهُمُ ٱلَّذِى بَنَوْاْ رِيبَةً
فِى قُلُوبِهِمْ إِلَّا أَن تَقَطَّعَ قُلُوبُهُمْ وَٱللَّهُ عَلِيمٌ حَكِيمٌ ١١٠

269

The foundation of those who so build is never free
from suspicion and shakiness in their hearts, until their
hearts are cut to pieces and Allah is All Knowing, Wise.
(9:110)

After demolishing the place and burning it, the Prophet
requested the Muslims to dump garbage and dead animals on that
place as a lesson for all those who would like to divide the Muslim
Ummah from within the community.

V.   Final Remarks

Qur'an speaks so many times against hypocrisy and
hypocrites. It was easy for the Prophet to know who were
hypocrites, because Allah (swt) used to inform him through
revelation. Allah cursed all hypocrites till the Day of Judgment.
More so, Allah (swt) revealed a Surah in the Qur'an, the title of
which is the Hypocrites (Al-Munafiqoon). Even Surah Al-Tawbah
chapter nine (9) speaks against the hypocrites.

It seems that in every society there are some individuals who
act and behave as hypocrites. There is no reason for anyone to be a
hypocrite. Those who practice hypocrisy are sick, dishonest, and
trouble makers. They should be penalized in one way or the other
as soon as possible. Otherwise, tragedies may take place in the
society. Hypocrisy is not a biological need of any human being;
and it is not even in animals. One has to be honest and sincere in
his private and public life. For those who practice honesty and
sincerity in their life will live in peace and harmony. For those who
practice hypocrisy will definitely live in misery and psychological
sufferings. Finally, they will be trapped sooner or later. Definitely,

they will be taken to jail and be penalized in one way or the other. The end of their life on this planet earth would be miserable, while in the Hereafter they definitely will go and live in Hell with all the torture and persecution in the fire.

Unfortunately, there are still some people in every society who act and behave as hypocrites with double standards. Therefore, one has to be careful as not to take it easy. One should not be naïve, but should be smart, and clever in his private and public life. We pray to Allah to protect us from such people in our Muslim societies. Ameen.

And He (Allah) has power over all things.
(Qur'an, 11:4)

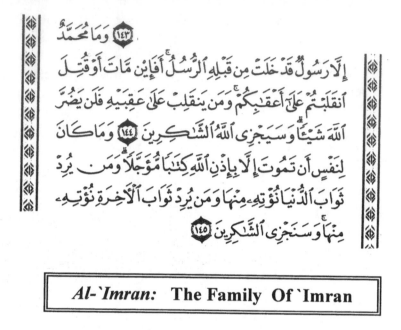

Al-'Imran: The Family Of 'Imran

Muhammad is no more than a Messenger: many were the Messengers that passed away before him. If he died or were slain will you then turn back on his heels? If any did turn back on his heels, not the least harm will he do to Allah; but Allah (on the other hand) will swiftly reward those who (serve him) with gratitude. Nor can a soul die except by Allah's leave, the term being fixed as by writing. If any do desire a reward in this life, We shall give it to him; and if any do desire a reward in the Hereafter, We shall give it to him. And swiftly shall We reward those that (serve us with) gratitude. (3:144-145)

I. General

The life history (Sirah) of Prophet Muhammad (pbuh) has been well documented by Muslims and non-Muslims. His private and public life are known to all those who wish to study his personality. The early Companions (Sahabah) were keen enough to write down and memorize every aspect of his life.

As far as the death of the Prophet (pbuh) is concerned, the Sahabah, Muhammad's (pbuh) relatives, and his close family have recorded by day-to-day and hour-to-hour his last sickness and the process of death that he had to go through.

By reading what has been recorded, one cannot control his emotions, his love, and his attachment to the Prophet (pbuh). At the same time, one has to ask himself about the dreadful period of life that every person has to go through (Sakatul Mawt) during the process of death. Since the Prophet (pbuh) himself had a hard time with a difficult process of sickness, sweat, unconsciousness, tiredness, and exhaustion, we should ask about what is going to happen to us at the time of death.

In this chapter, the author has selected a few narrations about the death of the Prophet (pbuh). The reader is requested to take a deep breath before reading this section. Try to read it slowly and reflect on what is going to happen to YOU at the time of death. In so doing, you will make sure to prepare yourself for the eventual death which is assured by Allah (swt) to come to each and every creature on this planet.

II. Prophet's Message During Illness

Hadrat Ibn Mas'ud said:

We entered the room of 'Aisha ® to meet the Holy Prophet (pbuh) at the time of his death. He stared at us and began to shed tears and said:

Welcome to you, may Allah (swt) grant you long life. May He give you refuge. May He help you. I give you my last instructions to fear Allah (swt). I give you my last advice as a warner of Allah (swt). Don't show pride over the dwellers of towns and cities and over Allah (swt). Death is near, I shall have to return to Allah (swt), to Sidratul Muntaha (farthest lote tree), to my resting place in Paradise, to the full Fountain. Take my words to your people and to those people who enter your religion after me. Salaam and Allah's mercy on my behalf.

It has been reported that the Prophet (pbuh) asked Jibreel:

Who will remain after me for my people?

Give good news to my friend that I will not give punishment to his people. Give him further good news that on the Resurrection Day he will rise first from the grave and he will be your leader. Paradise will be unlawful for the followers of other people till his people do enter it.

The Prophet (pbuh) said:

Then my eyes became cool.

Hadrat 'Aisha ® said:

The Messenger of God (pbuh) said to them during his illness: "Wash me with seven cups from seven waterskins." We did that. He became cool as a result and prayed with the people and prayed for the martyrs of Uhud. He gave instructions regarding the Ansars and said:

O Immigrant (Muhajireen), your number is increasing, but the number of Ansars will not increase and it will remain what is today. The Ansars are my own people and I took refuge with them. Honor their religious people and forgive their faults.

Thereafter he said:

One servant was asked to choose either of two things: this world or what is near Allah (swt). He chose what is near Allah (swt).

At this, Hadrat Abu Bakr ® began to weep as he applied it to the case of the Prophet (pbuh). The Prophet (pbuh) said:

O Abu Bakr, close these doors (pathways) towards the mosque for your people, but shut not the door of Abu Bakr as I know not of any companion better than Abu Bakr.

275

Hadrat 'Aisha said:

The Prophet (pbuh) expired leaning against the place between my breast and throat. Allah (swt) united my saliva and his at the time of death. My brother, Abdur Rahman, entered my room with a toothpick (siwak). The Prophet (pbuh) looked at it and my brother understood that he would be pleased to get it. I asked him: "Shall I take the toothpick for you?" He nodded his head and I took it from Abdur Rahman and put it in his mouth. When it seemed hard to him, I said to him: "I am making it soft for you." When he nodded with his head, I made it soft for him. There was a water pot in front of him. He put his hand in it and said: "There is no deity but Allah (swt), and there are surely death pangs." Then he put his hand in its right place and said: "To the Highest Companion.

Sa'eed Ibn Abdullah reported:

When the Ansars found the Prophet (pbuh) a little better, they informed him of the condition of their minds, so also Al-Fadl and Ali ®. The Prophet (pbuh) stretched out his hands and said: "Hold my hands." They held them and he said: "What are you talking about?"

They said: "We fear your death." The wives and their husbands began to raise cries at his condition. The Prophet (pbuh) leaned against the shoulders of Hadrat Al-Fadl and Ali and came to the mosque. His head was tied up with a piece of cloth. He stepped very slowly and sat upon the pulpit and the people advanced towards him. He prayed to Allah (swt) and said to the people:

I heard that you fear my death. It seems that you do not love death. Do you deny the death of your Prophet? Did I not tell you about my death? Did I not inform you about your death also? Did Prophets (peace and blessings of Allah (swt) be upon them) before me live forever? Look I shall meet with my Lord and you will also meet with Him.

I gave you instructions to treat well the first Muhajireen. Allah (swt) says:

By oath of time, people are surely in loss except those who believed and do good.

Everything is done according to the order of Allah (swt). When there is delay in any affair, let it not encourage you to hasten it, as Allah (swt) does not hasten at the hastiness of anybody. He who cheats Allah will be cheated by Him. Will you create disorder in the world? Will you cut off the ties of your relationship?

I am leaving instructions to you that you shall accord good treatment to the Ansars as they gave you refuge adopted iman before you. Treat them well. Did they not make you co-sharer in crop? Did they not give you shelter in their houses? Did they not put your needs above their needs at the time of your needs? Behold, if anybody is given power over two persons, he shall do good to them and forgive their faults. Behold, do not give superiority to yourselves over them. Behold, I am watching over you and you will meet me. Behold, the Fountain which has been promised to you is my fountain. That is wider than the distance between Basra in Syria and San'aa' in Yemen. The fountain of Kauthar flows therein. Its water is whiter than milk, softer than butter, and sweeter than honey. He who drinks therefrom will

277

never get thirsty. Its stones are emeralds and jewels and its foundation is of camphor. He who will be deprived of it tomorrow will be deprived of all good. Behold, he who loves to live with me there on the Resurrection Day should control his tongue except what is necessary.

Hadrat Abbas said:

O Prophet of Allah! Leave instructions about the Quraish. He said: "I leave instructions about the Quraish in this affair; The people will follow the Quraish. The virtuous will follow their virtuous and the sinners will follow their sinners. O Quraish, deal good with the people. O people, sin changes fortune and bad conduct corrupts character. When the people are good, the leaders are also good. Allah (swt) says:

Thus do I place some oppressors over others on account of what they did.

Abu Bakr ® said:

O Prophet of Allah, this death is a kind of welcome to the mercy that is with Allah (swt).

The Prophet (pbuh) said:

To Allah (swt), the farthest lote tree, to the paradise of Ma'wa the highest Paradise, to the full fountain, to the Highest Friend and to eternal happiness.

Abu Bakr ® said:

O Prophet of Allah, Who will wash you?

The Prophet (pbuh) said:

The close relations of my family and the closest of them.

Abu Bakr ® then asked:

With what kafan will you be shrouded?

He responded:

With this garment of mine which I am wearing, with the gown of Yemen and with the white cloth of Egypt.

Then Abu Bakr ® asked:

How should we pray your Janaza?

We then wept, and he wept too. Then he said:

Stop, may Allah (swt) forgive you and may He grant you good from your Prophet. When you will wash me fully and clothe me with the kafan (the shroud) and place me on bier in my room which will be the top portion of my grave, then go away from me for sometime because the first who will recite Du`aa' on me, will be the Almighty and His angels. Then He will order the angels to pray for me. He who will come first to pray Janaza on me among the Creation of Allah (swt) will be Jibreel, then Michael, then Israfeel, then the Angel of Death with his numerous hordes and then all the angels. Then you will pray in batches. Don't inflict trouble on me by raising wailings and cries. One of you will be

279

Imam, then the near ones of my family and then the boys will stand.

Abu Bakr asked:

Who will put you into your grave?

He answered:

The nearest ones of my family with many angels whom you will not see but who will see you. Now rise and go away from me. Convey my message to the people after me on my behalf.

(After awhile:) The Prophet (pbuh) said:

O Muhammad, surely your Lord is anxious to meet with you. By Allah (swt), the Angel of Death never sought permission of anybody to take his life and will never seek such permission. Allah (swt) will protect your honor and he is eager to meet you.

The Prophet (pbuh) then said:

Let the Angel of Death come and go away from here till he (Jibreel) comes.

Then the Prophet (pbuh) called his wives and said to his daughter Fatima ®:

Come close to me.

Fatima ® came close to him and he whispered again something to her. Then she raised her head and began to smile.

We wondered at her weeping and smiling and asked her the reason. Fatima ® said:

He informed me that he will expire shortly. I began to cry at that. Then he said: "I pray to Allah (swt) that you will be the first who will meet me and will be with me." I smiled at this.

When Hadrat Fatima ® took her two sons close to the Prophet (pbuh), he showed affection and fondness for them.

Then the Angel of Death came and saluted the Prophet (pbuh) and sought permission of the Prophet (pbuh) to take his life, to which he responded and gave permission. The Angel of Death said to him:

O Muhammad, what do you say to me?

The Prophet (pbuh) said:

Yes, take me to my Lord.

He said:

Yes, your Lord is eager today to meet you. Your Lord never hesitated in any other case than in your case. He never prohibited me to take the life of anybody without His permission, except in your case. Your death is in front of you.

Then the Angel of Death left the room.

281

III. Visit Of Angel Of Death

'Aisha ® said:

On the first part of the day of his death, he looked somewhat better and the people left him, returned to their respective houses and joined in their personal affairs. The Prophet (pbuh) remained alone with his wives. We remained then in hope and joy. Thereafter the Prophet (pbuh) said: "Leave me. An angel seeks to meet me." Everybody went out of the house except I. His head reclined on my lap, he sat up straight, and I also went to a corner of the house. The angel talked with him secretly for a long time. Then the Prophet (pbuh) called me and placed his head again on my lap.

He said to his wives: "Enter the house." I said: "Is he not perhaps Jibril." The Prophet said: "O 'Aisha, he is the Angel of Death. He came to me and said:

Allah (swt) sent me to you and advised me not to come to you without your permission. If you don't permit me, I will return; and if you give me permission, I will enter. Allah (swt) ordered me not to take your life until you give me permission. Now what is your permission?

I said: "Tarry a little, let Jibreel come in." This is the time of the coming of Jibreel.

'Aisha ® said:

Thereafter there appeared to us such an affair which was beyond our control. It seemed that we raised a hue and cry and struck our hands and feet. The people of Ahl-Al Bayt were all struck with awe and were silent. Nobody saw such an affair before. Then Jibreel descended and saluted the Prophet (pbuh). I felt his advent. The people of the house went out. He (Jibreel) said:

The Almighty One tender His Salaam to you and inquires about your health although He knows it. He has intended to make your honour and prestige perfect and wishes to establish it among your followers.

The Prophet (pbuh) said: " I am in anxiety." He said: "Give good news as Allah (swt) intends to take you to the place which He has prepared for you."

Hadrat 'Aisha ® said:

Jibreel came and said:

O Messenger of Allah (swt), salaam to you. This is my last descent to the earth. Revelation has come to an end and the earth comes near. I have no more need of this earth except for you. Hereafter, I will stay in my own place.

'Aisha ® continued:

I then went close to the Prophet (pbuh) and placed his head upon my bosom. He fainted and fainted and perspiration come out profusely on his forehead. I began to remove the perspiration, the fragrance of which I smelt. When he came around, I said to him: "May my parents, my life and my family be dedicated to you, why do you perspire so much?" The Prophet (pbuh) said:

283

O 'Aisha, the life of a believer goes out with excessive perspiration and the life of a non-believer goes out of the two sides like that of a donkey.

At this time, we hastened to run and send for the members of our families. The first man who came to us was my brother. I then sent him for my father. Before anybody could come, the Prophet (pbuh) breathed his last breathe.

When he fainted, he recited: "To the Blessed Companionship on High." When he talked, he said: "Prayer, prayer, you will never be routed if you continue to pray." He left instruction for prayer up until the last moment of his life.

Hadrat 'Aisha ® said:

The Holy Prophet (pbuh) expired between sunrise and the sun's peak over the meridian. When he died, there were wails and bewailing everywhere. He was covered by the angels with cloth. Some did not believe his death, some lost their senses and became dumb-founded. Omar ® said that the Prophet (pbuh) had not died. He said:

O People, hold your tongue about saying that the Prophet (pbuh) died as he has not expired. By Allah (swt), let me not hear that the Prophet (pbuh) has died, otherwise I will cut off his head by this sword.

Ali ® was seated within the house. `Uthman ® did not talk with anybody, people just led him here and there. Abbas ® said: "By Allah (swt), the apostle of Allah (swt) has tasted death. Allah (swt) said:

Certainly you will die and they will also die.
Thereafter, you will be quarrelling before your Lord on
the Day of Resurrection. (39:30-31)

IV. Reactions Of The Family Of The Prophet (Pbuh).

Abu Bakr ® received the news of the death while he was away
to Banu Haris bin Khazraj. He hurriedly came and went straight to
the dead body of the Prophet (pbuh) and began to kiss his cheeks
and said:

O Messenger of Allah (swt), may my parents be dedicated to
you. Allah (swt) will not give you the taste of death twice. By Allah
(swt), the Messenger of Allah has died.

Then he came out and addressed the people:

O people, he who worships Muhammad (pbuh) should know
that he has expired, and he who worships the Lord of Muhammad
(pbuh) should know that He is ever living and can not die. Allah
(swt) says:

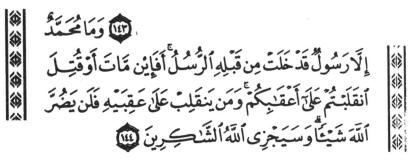

Muhammad is nothing but an apostle. Before him there passed many apostles. If he then dies or is killed, will you turn on your backs? (3:144)

On hearing this verse of the Qur'an, the people were in such a condition as they had never heard this verse before.

Ibn Omar ® reported:

When Abu Bakr ® entered the room of the Prophet (pbuh), he began to recite the Du`a' and Hamd and the inhabitants of the house raised such a hue and cry that those who were praying outside heard it. Whenever he said something, the noise increased. Someone stood by the door and on his advice the noise stopped. He said loudly:

O Ahl Al-Bayt, salam to you all. Everybody will die and everybody has got an agent in the affairs of Allah (swt), every desire has an object of hope and every fear has got a salvation. Rely on Allah (swt).

On hearing this, the dwellers of the house could not understand whose voice it was. They then stopped crying and weeping. Soon they came within the house and began to weep and cry again. This time an unknown voice said:

O Ahl Al-Bayt, remember Allah (swt) and glorify Him under all circumstances, you will then become sincere worshippers. There is consolation of Allah (swt) in each danger and there is an agent in every desired object. Remember Allah (swt) in your mind. Obey his commands and put them in execution.

Hadrat Abu Bakr said:

They (the speaker) are Al-Khidr and Al-Yasa'. They were present at the Janaza of the Prophet.

V. The Speech Of Abu Bakr ®

Qa'qaa' Ibn Amr ® recorded the full address of Abu Bakr ®. He said:

Abu Bakr addressed the people who began to shed tears at his address. After praising Allah (swt), he said:

I bear witness that there is no deity but God Who is One. He has shown His deity as truth; He has helped His servant and He has routed the allied enemies. All praise is due to Allah (swt). He is One. I bear witness that Muhammad is His servant and Messenger and that he is the last of the apostles. I bear witness that the Qur'an remains as it was revealed, the religion is as it came, and Hadith as it was spoken. Allah (swt) is open truth.

O Allah! Muhammad is Your servant and Messenger, Your Prophet, Your friend, Your hope, and Your chosen servant. Shower blessings on him, such blessings which You have not sent to anyone from among Your creatures.

O Allah! Give Your blessings, Your pardon, Your mercy, to the last of Your Messenger the leader of Your religious peoples and the guide to all good.

O Allah! Bring his honour near, honour his place and take him to the abode of praise. The sages of past and present ages will envy him. Give us the benefit of his praised abode, make him our representative in this world and the next. Give him honour and Paradise and make him our means. Send blessings on Muhammad and his family and send blessings on Ibrahim and his family. Surely You are praised and glorified.

O people! He who worships Muhammad (pbuh) shall know that Muhammad (pbuh) is dead. He who worships Allah (swt), shall know that Allah (swt) is ever-living and cannot die. Allah (swt) has chosen for His Prophet for what is near Him and has not chosen for him what is near you. He has taken his life in order to give him reward. He has left to you His Book and His Sunnah. He who holds fast to these things is a true believer and he who differentiates between these two things does not believe.

O Believers! Stand on justice. Don't allow the Devil to misguide you after the death of your Prophet (pbuh), and turn you from your religion. You can baffle his efforts if you meet him with good deeds. Don't look at him or else he will rule over you and will throw you into danger.

Ibn Abbas said:

When Abu Bakr finished his address, he said:

O Omar! You informed me that you are saying that the Messenger of Allah (swt) has not expired. Don't you see that the Prophet (pbuh) said such and such on such a day? Allah (swt) said in His Book:

You will die and they will also die.

Omar replied:

By Allah (swt), it seemed to me that I never heard before about the revelation of this verse in the Holy Book. The Book remains as it was revealed. Hadith remains as it was uttered. Allah (swt) is ever-living and will not die. We are for Allah (swt) and to Allah (swt) is our return. Blessings on His Prophet and we hope to see him near Allah (Swt).

Thereafter, Omar sat near Hadrat Abu Bakr.

VI. Washing And Kafan

'Aisha ® said:

When the people assembled for the washing of the body of the Prophet (pbuh), they said: "By Allah (swt), we don't know how to wash the Prophet (pbuh). Shall we uncover his wearing cloth as we do in other cases or shall we wash him within his wearing cloth?" I responded: "Allah (swt) has sent on them slumber and there was nobody among them who did not place his head over his bosom and sleep." Then a man (whom nobody knows) said: "Wash him within his wearing cloth." Then they got up from slumber and did so and the Prophet (pbuh) was washed within his wearing apparel. After this, they clothed him with kafan cloth (shroud). Ali ® said:

We began to take off his wearing apparel in order to wash him when it was proclaimed to us: "Don't take off the cloth of the Prophet (pbuh)." We washed him and turned him from one side to another. His side automatically turned to another side without our efforts. Thus we finished his washing.

This is, in short, the story of his death. There was no cloth of his which was not buried with him. Hadrat Abu Ja'far said: The bed sheet of the Prophet (pbuh) was spread in the grave and on it was placed the body of the Prophet (pbuh). There is a great lesson and an ideal in the death of the Holy Prophet (pbuh).

I seek the forgiveness of Allah.

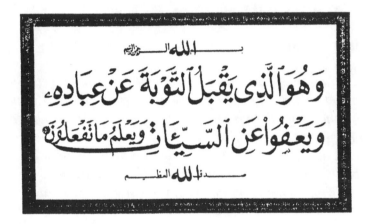

He is the One that accepts repentance from His Servants and forgives sins: and He knows all that you do. (42:25)

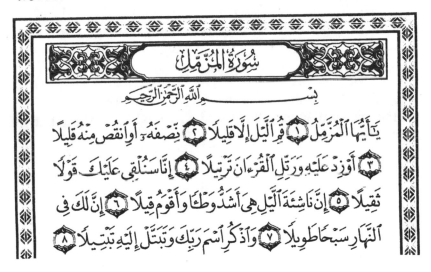

O you folded in garments! Stand (to prayer) by night, but not all night, half of it, or a little less, or a little more; and recite the Qur'an in slow measured rhythmic tones. Soon shall We send down to you a weighty Word. Truly the rising by night is a time when impression is more keen and speech more certain. True, there is for you by day prolonged occupation with ordinary duties: But keep in remembrance the name of your Lord, and devote yourself to Him wholeheartedly. (73:1-8)

Chronology of Prophet Muhammad

A.D.

570- Birth of Prophet Muhammad (pbuh) at Makkah in Arabia; His father, Abdullah bin Abdul Muttalib, belonging to the highly respected clan of Hashim, died a few months before Muhammad was born. His mother, Amina took care of her son.

575- Prophet Muhmmad's mother Amina died in Madina. His caring paternal grandfather, Abdul Muttalib, brought him up in Makkah.

578- Prophet Muhammad grandfather, Abdul Muttalib, died. He came under the care of his kindhearted uncle Abu Talib and his wife Fatima. They had twelve children and they accepted Muhammad as a fostered child.

582– Uncle Abu Talib took his young dutiful nephew on a trading mission to Syria where, at Bostra, a well known Christian monk, Bahira, discerned in the young Muhammad, the signs of God's Prophethood.

595- Well versed in commerce, Muhammad led a trading mission to Syria on behalf of a noble widow of Makkah, Khadijah. It was a very profitable, and Khadijah was highly impressed by his honesty, integry of character and his good manners. They were married; he was 25, she was 40.

605- Muhammad's honesty became a byword in Makkah and the Makkans honored him with the title of "Al-Ameen" (Trustee of the Trusted One). He showed remarkable tact in amicably settling a tribal row over the installation of the celestial Black Stone in the renovated Holy Ka'bah in Makkah.

610- In the cave of Hiraa' near Makkah, Prophet Muhammad often went for meditation. Angel Gabriel visited him and told him that he was chosen to be God's Prophet and he conveyed to him the word of God. Thus began his Prophetic Mission and the Revelation of the Holy Qur'an to him.

613- In a sermon at Mount Safa, Prophet Muhammad publicly preached the Word of God, urged the Makkans to give up the wordhip of idols, to join the fold of Islam and to worship the One and only One God. This alarmed Makkah's pagan rulers and they started presecuting Prophet Muhammad (pbuh) and his Muslim followers.

615- Due to persecution, Prophet Muhammad (pbuh) gave permission to a group of Muslims in Makkah to immigrate to the Christian-ruled Abyssinia, where the noble Negus gave them asylum. In desperation, Makkah's pagan rulers issued an edict imposing social and economic boycott of the Prophet along with his followers for three (3) years in Shu'ab Makkah.

620- The death of his dear uncle, Abu Talib, and of his beloved wife, Khadijah, in the same year was a double tragedy for the Prophet.

621- The Prophet's journey of (Israa' and Mi'raaj) to Jerusalem and to Heavens gave him fresh inspiration and the courage of heart to continue his Prophetic Mission in the service of God.

622- With divine consent, Prophet Muhammad, along with a band of Muslim followers, immigrated to Madina on the invitation of its wise elders who acknolwedeged him as the Prophet of God. He built a Mosque in the suburb of the City of Madina called Qubaa'.

293

Then he moved to the hub of the city and built his Mosque which is still in the same place. This was also the beginning of the Hijra Calendar. The First Islamic State was established by him in Madina.

623- Muslims were instructed by the Prophet to turn towards the Ka'bah in Makkah during their Prayer instead of Jeruslaem (Baitul Maqdis) as was the practice. The Prophet gave the Covenant of Madina to govern the relations between the Islamic State and its inhabitants, between the State and its non-Muslim citizens and the State.

624- The Battle of Badr in which the Prophet of Islam and his Muslim followers defeated the enemy forces from pagans of Makkah.

625- The Battle of Uhud in which the Makkan troops inflicted some losses on Madina's Muslim defenders who fought back bravely and forced the enemy to retreat to Makkah.

627- The Battle of the Trenches, in which a line of trenches dug by Madina's Muslim defenders under the Prophet's leadership, forced a large enemy force from Makkah to retreat.

628- Prophet Muhammad signed the Peace Treaty of Hudaibya with Makkah's emissaries under which Muslims were, interalia, allowed to go to Ka'bah for the Annual Pilgrimage in restricted numbers. Muslims won the battle of Khaybar in the same year. Prophet Muhammad wrote to the heads of many States to enter the fold of Islam.

630- Liberation of the pagan-ruled Makkah by the Muslims under Prophet Muhammad's command; amnesty and magnanimity to the defeated Makkans; smashing of the 360 idols in the Ka'bah by the Prophet and his companions. Triumph of Islam: Military encounters at Mu'tah, Hunain, Taa-if and Tabuk in defence of Islam and the Islamic State of Madina.

631- First large Muslim group from Madina went to Makkah for Hajj pilgrimage at the Ka'bah and its vicinities.

632- Prophet Muhammad's last Hajj pilgrimage at the Ka'bah in Makkah. Then to Mina, Arafat, Muzdalifa, Mina and back to Makkah. He requested the Muslims to practice what he was practicing. He had about 124,000 Muslims where they were following him and practicing the ritiuals of 'Umra and Hajj. He delivered his historic sermon at Mount Arafat on the outskirts of Makkah.

632– The demise of Prophet Muhammad at the age of 63; burial in Madina in his own house wall-to-wall to his Masjid. The commencement of the Caliphate of his close companion, Abu Bakr, as the spiritual and temporal head of the Islamic State.

مِنْ أمثالِ الرَّسُولِ

١٤٩٥ - عن جابرٍ رضي الله عنه قال : قال رسول الله صلى الله عليه وسلم :

« مَثَلِي وَمَثَلُكُمْ كَمَثَلِ رَجُلٍ أَوْقَدَ نَاراً ، فَجَعَلَ الْجَنَادِبُ وَالْفَرَاشُ يَقَعْنَ فِيهَا وَهُوَ يَذُبُّهُنَّ عَنْهَا (٤) وَأَنَا آخذٌ بِحُجَزِكُمْ عَنِ النَّارِ ، وَأَنْتُمْ تَفَلَّتُونَ مِنْ يَدِيَ » رواه مسلم .

« الْجَنَادِبُ » : نَحْوُ الْجَرَادِ وَالْفَرَاشِ ، هَذَا هُوَ الْمَعْرُوفُ الَّذِي يَقَعُ فِي النَّارِ . « وَالْحُجَزُ » : جَمْعُ حُجْزَةٍ ، وَهِيَ مَعْقِدُ الإِزَارِ وَالسَّرَاوِيل .

1495
Jabir (may Allah be pleased with him) related: "The Messenger of Allah (pbuh) said: 'My parable and yours is like a man who lit a fire, after which insects [such as grasshoppers and butterflies] were falling in it while he [the man] was preventing them from falling in it; [the prophet continued by saying] and I hold on to you by your belts but you slip away from my hand.'"
(Reported by Muslim)

١٤٩٦ - وعن النُّعْمَانِ بَشِيرٍ رضي الله عنهما قال : قال رسول الله صلى الله عليه وسلم : « مَثَلُ الْمُؤْمِنِينَ فِي تَوَادِّهِمْ وَتَرَاحُمِهِمْ وَتَعَاطُفِهِمْ ، مَثَلُ الْجَسَدِ إِذَا اشْتَكَى مِنْهُ عُضْوٌ تَدَاعَى لَهُ سَائِرُ الْجَسَدِ بِالسَّهَرِ وَالْحُمَّى » متفقٌ عليه (٥) .

1496
An-Nu'man Basheer (may Allah be pleased with him) related: "The Messenger of Allah (pbuh) said: 'the parable of believers in their [ways of expressing] their amicability, mercy, and affection

toward each others is like a body, if an organ is afflicted, the entire rest of the body rushes [to its rescue] all night long and with fever. (Agreed upon)

١٤٩٧ ـ وعن أبي موسى الأشعري رضيَ اللهُ عنهُ قالَ : قالَ رسولُ اللهِ صلى اللهُ عليهِ وسلّمَ : « مَثَلُ المؤمن الَّذي يَقْرَأُ القرآنَ ،ثلُ الأُتْرُجَّةِ : ريحُها طَيِّبٌ وطَعمُها طَيِّبٌ ، ومثلُ المؤمن الَّذي لايَقَرأُ القرآنَ كَثَلِ التَّمرَةِ : لاريح لها وطعمها حُلْوٌ ، ومَثَلُ المُنَافقِ الذي يَقْرَأُ القرآنَ كَثَلِ الرَّيحانَةِ : رِيحها طَيِّبٌ وطَعْمُها مُرٌّ ، ومَثَلُ المُنَافقِ الذي لايَقْرَأُ القرآنَ كَثَلِ الحَنْظَلَةِ : لَيْسَ لها ريحٌ وطَعمُها مُرٌّ » متفقٌ عليه .

1497

Abu Musa Al-Ash'ari related: "The Messenger of Allah (pbuh) said: 'The example of the believer who recites the Qur'an is like that of a citron which tastes good and smells good. And the believer who does not recite the Qur'an is like a date which has no smell but tastes good. And the example of a hypocrite [dissolute wicked person] who recites the Qur'an is like sweet basil, it smells good but tastes bitter. And the example of a hypocrite [dissolute wicked person] who does not recite the Qur'an is like the colocynth which smells bad and tastes bitter. (Agreed upon)

١٤٩٨ ـ وعن ابن عُمَرَ رَضيَ اللهُ عنهمَا أنَّ رسولَ اللهِ صلَّى اللهُ عليهِ وسلّمَ قال : « إنَّمَا مَثَلُ صَاحِبِ القُرْآنِ (١) كَمَثَلِ الإبلِ المُعَقَّلَةِ (٢) ، إنْ عَاهَدَ عَلَيْها ، أمْسَكَهَا ، وَإنْ أطْلَقَها ، ذَهَبَتْ » متفقٌ عليه .

297

1498

Ibn Umar related: "the Messenger of Allah (pbuh) said: 'The example of the person who knows the Qur'an by heart is like the owner of camels that are tied [to a post]. If he keeps them tied, he will control them, but if he releases them, they will run away."
(Agreed upon)

١٥٠٠ – وعن أبي موسى الأشعري رضيَ اللهُ عنه أن النَّبي صلى الله عليه وسلم قال : « إِنَّمَا مَثَلُ الْجَلِيسِ الصَّالِحِ وَجَلِيسِ السُّوءِ : كَحَامِلِ الْمِسْكِ ، وَنَافِخِ الْكِيرِ (١) ، فَحَامِلُ الْمِسْكِ ، إِمَّا أنْ يُحْذِيَكَ ، وَإِمَّا أنْ تَبْتَاعَ مِنْهُ (٢) وَإِمَّا أنْ تَجِدَ مِنْهُ رِيحاً طَيِّبَةً ، وَنَافِخُ الْكِيرِ ، إِمَّا أنْ يُحْرِقَ ثِيَابَكَ ، وَإِمَّا أنْ تَجِدَ مِنْهُ رِيحاً مُنْتِنَةً » متفق عليه .

(يُحْذِيكَ) : يُعْطِيكَ .

1500

Abu Musa al-Ash'ari (may Allah be pleased with him) related that the Prophet (pbuh) said: "The example of a good pious companion and an evil one is that of a person carrying musk and another blowing a [blacksmith's] bellow. The one who is carrying musk will either give you some perfume as a present, or you will buy some from him, or you will get a good smell from him, but the one who is blowing the bellow will either burn your clothes or you will get a bad smell from him."   (Agreed upon)

١٥٠١ ـ عن النعْمان بن بَشير رضي الله عنهما عن النبي صلى اللهُ عليه وسلم قال :

« مَثَلُ القائم في حُدود الله ، والواقع فيها .. كَمَثَلِ قومٍ اسْتَهَمُوا على سَفينةٍ ، فَصَارَ بَعْضُهُمْ أعلاها وبَعْضُهُمْ أسْفَلَهَا ، وكانَ الذين في أسْفَلِها إذا اسْتَقَوْا من الماء مَرُّوا على مَنْ فَوْقَهُمْ فَقَالُوا : لو أنَّا خَرَقْنَا في نَصِيبنا خَرْقاً ولم نُؤْذِ مَنْ فَوْقَنَا، فإنْ تَرَكُوهُمْ وما أرَادُوا هَلَكُوا جَميعاً ، وإنْ أخَذُوا على أيْديهم نَجَوْا ونجَوْا جَميعاً » رواهُ البخاري .

« القائمُ في حُدود الله تعالى » مَعْناهُ : المُنْكِرُ لها ، القائمُ في دفْعِها وإزالتِها،والمُرادُ بالحُدُودِ : ما نهى اللهُ عنْهُ . « اسْتَهَمُوا » : اقْتَرَعُوا .

1501
An-Nu'man bin Bashir (may Allah be pleased with both of them) related that the Prophet (pbuh) said: "The example of the person abiding by Allah's order and restrictions in comparison to the one who violates them is like the example of a group of people who drew lots for their seats in a boat. Some of them got seats in the upper part while the others in the lower part. When the latter needed water, they had to go up to bring water (and that troubled the others), so they said, 'Let us make a hole in our share of the ship (and get water) saving those who are above us from troubling them. So, if the people in the upper part left the others to do what they had suggested, all the people of the ship would be destroyed, but if they prevented them, both parties would be safe."
(Reported by Bukhari)

١٥٠٢ - وعن أبي هريرة رضي الله عنه أنه سمع رسول الله صلى الله عليه وسلم يَقُول : « مَثَلُ البَخيلِ والمُنْفِقِ ، كَمَثَلِ رَجُلَيْنِ عَلَيْهِمَا جُنَّتَانِ مِن حَديدٍ مِن ثُدِيَّهِمَا إلى تَرَاقِيهِمَا (٣) ، فَأَمَّا المُنْفِقُ ، فَلا يُنْفِقُ إلاَّ سَبَغَتْ ، أَوْ وَفَرَتْ على جِلدِهِ حتى تُخْفِيَ بَنَانَهُ ، وتَعْفُوَ أَثَرَهُ . وَأَمَّا البَخيلُ ، فَلا يُريدُ أَنْ يُنْفِقَ شيئاً إلاَّ لَزِقَتْ كُلُّ حَلْقَةٍ مَكَانَهَا،فَهُوَ يُوَسِّعُهَا فَلا تَتَّسِعُ » متفق" عليه (١) .

وَ « الجُنَّةُ » الدِّرْعُ ؛ وَمَعْنَاهُ : أَنَّ المُنْفِقَ كُلَّمَا أَنْفَقَ سَبَغَتْ ، وطَالَتْ حتى تَجُرَّ وَرَاءَهُ ، وتُخْفِي رِجْلَيْهِ وأَثَرَ مَشْيِهِ وخُطُوَاتِهِ (٢) .

1502
Abu Huraira (may Allah be pleased with him) relates that he heard the Prophet (pbuh) saying: "The example of an alms-giver and a miser is like the example of two persons who have two iron cloaks on them from their breasts to their collar bones. When the alms-giver wants to give in charity, the cloak becomes capacious till it covers his whole body to such an extent that it hides his fingertips and covers his footprints (obliterates his tracks). But when the miser wants to spend, it (the iron cloak) sticks and every ring gets stuck to its place. So, he [keeps] trying to widen it, but it [keeps] preventing] him from become wide. (Agreed Upon)

١٥٠٥ - وَعَنْ جَابِرٍ رَضِيَ الله عَنْهُ قَالَ : قَالَ رَسُولُ الله صَلَّى الله عَلَيْهِ وَسَلَّمَ : « مَثَلُ الصَّلَوَاتِ الخَمْسِ كَمَثَلِ نَهْرٍ جَارٍ غَمْرٍ عَلَى بَابِ أَحَدِكُمْ يَغْتَسِلُ مِنْهُ كُلَّ يَوْمٍ خَمْسَ مَرَّاتٍ » رواه مسلم .

« الغَمْرُ » بفتح الغين المعجمة : الكثيرُ .

300

1505

Jabir narrated: the Messenger of Allah (pbuh) said: "The similitude of the five prayers is like an overflowing river passing by the gate of one of you. He bathes from it five times a daily. (No filthiness can remain on him.) (Reported by Muslim)

١٥٠٦ ـ وعَنْ أَبِي حَمْزَةَ أَنَسٍ بن مَالِكٍ الأَنْصَارِيِّ خَادِمِ رسول الله صلى الله عليه وسلم، رضي الله عنه قال : قال رسول الله صلى الله عليه وسلم :« اللهُ أَفْرَحُ بِتَوْبَةِ عَبْدِهِ مِنْ أَحَدِكُمْ سَقَطَ عَلَى بَعِيرِهِ وقد أَضَلَّهُ في أرضٍ فَلاةٍ » متفقٌ عليه .

1506

Abu Hamza Anas bin Malik, the servant of Prophet Muhammad (pbuh) related that: "Allah's Apostle said, 'Allah is more pleased with the repentance of His slave than anyone of you would be pleased with finding his camel which he had lost in an abandoned land." (Agreed Upon)

If Allah helps you, none can overcome you: (3:160)

Chapter (33)　　　Comprehensive Statements

١٥٦١ – عَنْ أَبِي عَمْرٍو ، وقيل : أبي عَمْرَةَ سُفْيَانَ بنِ عبدِ اللهِ رضي
الله عنه قال : قُلْتُ : يَارسُولَ اللهِ قُلْ لِي في الإِسْلامِ قَوْلاً لا أَسْأَلُ عَنْه
أَحَداً غَيْرَكَ . قال : « قُلْ : آمَنْتُ باللهِ : ثُمَّ اسْتَقِمْ » رواه مسلم .

1561

Abi Amrou (also pronounced Abi Amra) Sufyan bin Abdullah
(may Allah be pleased with him narrated: *I said: O Messenger of
Allah, tell me a proclamation in Islam that I don't ask anyone
other than you about. [The prophet] said: Say, I believed in Allah,
then become righteous.* (Reported by Muslim)

١٥٦٢ – وَعَنْ أَبِي مَالِكٍ الحَارِثِ بنِ عَاصِمٍ الأَشْعَرِيِّ رضي الله عنه قال :
قَالَ رسولُ اللهِ صلى الله عليه وسلم : « الطُّهُورُ شَطْرُ الإِيمَانِ (١) ، وَالحَمْدُ للهِ
تَمْلأُ المِيزَانَ ، وَسُبْحَانَ اللهِ وَالحَمْدُ للهِ تَمْلآنِ – أَوْ تَمْلأُ – مَا بَيْنَ
السَّمَوَاتِ وَالأَرْضِ ، وَالصَّلاةُ نُورٌ ، وَالصَّدَقَةُ بُرْهَانٌ (٢) ، وَالصَّبْرُ ضِيَاءٌ ،
وَالقُرْآنُ حُجَّةٌ لَكَ أَوْ عَلَيْكَ . كُلُّ النَّاسِ يَغْدُو (٣) ، فَبَائِعٌ نَفْسَهُ
فَمُعْتِقُهَا ، أَوْ مُوبِقُهَا » رواه مسلم .

1562

Abi Malik al-Hareth Bin Assem al-Ash'ari (may Allah be pleased
with him) narrated: *The Messenger of Allah (pbuh) said:
Cleanliness is half of faith; and al-Hamdu Lillah (Praise be to
Allah) fills the scale; and Subhan Allah (Glory be to Allah) and al-
Hamdu Lillah (Praise be to Allah) fill up what is between the
heavens and the earth; and prayer is a light; and charity is proof
(of one's faith); and endurance is a brightness; and the Qur'an is a
proof on your favor or against you. All people go out early in the*

*morning [for errands] and sell their souls, some of them set it free
(i.e., preserve it from hell) or [others] destroy it.*
(Reported by Muslim)

١٥٦٣ ، - وعن أبي صَفْوَانَ بن عبد الله بُشْرٍ الأَسْلَـــمِيّ ، رضي
الله عنه ، قال : قال رسول الله صلى الله عليه وسلم : « خَيْرُ النَّاسِ مَنْ طَالَ
عُمُرُه وَحَسُنَ عَمَلُه » رواه الترمذي ، وقال : حديثٌ حسنٌ .

1563
Abi Safwan Bin Abdullah Busr al-Aslami (may Allah be pleased
with him) narrated: *The Messenger of Allah (pbuh) said: the best
[person] among people is the one who lives long and whose
actions [behavior] are righteous.*
(Reported by Tirmithi) Hadith classified as Hasan (sound)

١٥٦٤ - طُوبَى لِمَنْ شَغَلَهُمْ عَيْبُهُمْ عَنْ عُيُوبِ النَّـــاسِ .
(الديلمي)

1564
*Blessed are those who are occupied with [or who worry about]
their own shortfalls instead of the shortfalls of [other] people.*
(Reported By Ad-Daylami)

١٥٦٥ - الْمُسْتَشَارُ مُؤْتَمَنٌ .   (الشهاب والسنن الأربعة)

1565
*The [person] who is consulted is entrusted [with
confidentiality]* (Ash-shahab and the four collectors of Hadith)

١٥٦٦ - اَلْمَجَالِسُ بِالْأَمَانَةِ . (أبو داود)

1566

Assemblies (i.e., when people meet and share information or discuss issues) are entrusted [confidential]. (Reported by Abu Dawood)

١٥٦٧ - اَلدَّالُّ عَلَى الْخَيْرِ كَفَاعِلِهِ . (البخاري)

1567

The [person] who guides to good will be rewarded equally [to the person who performs it]. (Reported by Bukhari)

١٥٦٨ - اَلْهَمُّ نِصْفُ الْهَرَمِ ، وَقِلَّةُ الْعِيَالِ أَحَدُ الْيَسَارَيْنِ . (الشهاب)

1568

Anxiety (i.e. being worry) is half of old age, and limited family member is one of the two easy [aspects of life]. (Reported by Ash-Shahab)

١٥٦٩ - شَرُّ الْعَمَى عَمَى الْقَلْبِ . (الشهاب)

1569

The worst [type] of blindness is the blindness of the heart. (Reported by Ash-Shahab)

١٥٧٠ - أَشْقَى الْأَشْقِيَاءِ مَنِ اجْتَمَعَ عَلَيْهِ فَقْرُ الدُّنْيَا وَعَذَابُ الْآخِرَةِ . (الطبراني والشهاب)

1570

The most unfortunate [individual] of all unfortunate people is the one who ends up with both poverty in the earthly world and hellfire in the afterlife. (Reported by At-Tabarani and Ash-Shahab)

١٥٧١ ـ رَأْسُ الْحِكْمَةِ مَخَافَةُ اللهِ . وَخَيْرُ مَا وَقَرَ فِي الْقَلْبِ
الْيَقِينُ . الإِرْتِيَابُ مِنَ الْكُفْرِ . الشَّبَابُ شُعْبَةٌ مِنَ الْجُنُونِ . السَّعِيدُ
مَنْ وُعِـــظَ بِغَيْرِهِ ، وَالشَّقِيُّ مَنْ شَقِيَ فِي بَطْنِ أُمِّهِ . كُلُّ مَا هُوَ
آتٍ قَرِيبٌ .
(البيهقي)

1571

The ultimate (i.e. most important part of) wisdom is fearing Allah (swt), and the best settlement in the heart is certitude in Allah (swt) (i.e. absolute conviction of His existence). Skepticism (i.e. suspicion and doubt about Allah (swt), is an aspect of disbelief (Kufr). Youth (young people) is a branch of madness (i.e., foolishness, insanity). The joyful [person] is the one who learns (or gets admonished) from others, and the unfortunate [person] is the one who was unfortunate in his mother's womb. Everything that is yet to happen will shortly arrive. (Reported by Al-Bayhaqi)

١٥٧٢ ـ مَا خَابَ مَنِ اسْتَخَارَ وَلَا نَدِمَ مَنِ اسْتَشَارَ وَلَا عَالَ مَنِ
اقْتَصَدَ .
(الطبراني)

1572

He who asks Allah for what is good (Istikhara) will never be deceived, and he who consults will never be remorseful, and he who economizes (i.e. manages money wisely and saves) will never be poor. (Reported by A-Tabarani)

١٥٧٣ ـ الْاقْتِصَادُ في النَّفَقَةِ نِصْفُ الْمَعِيشَةِ ، وَالتَّوَدُّدُ إلى النَّاسِ نِصْفُ الْعَقْلِ ، وَحُسْنُ السُّؤَالِ نِصْفُ الْعِلْمِ . (الطبراني)

1573

Being economical (i.e. managing money wisely and being thrifty) in expenditures is half of sustenance (i.e. subsistence and livelihood), being cordial (i.e. amicable and warmhearted) to people is half of the mind (i.e. reasonable and intellectual), and asking question (i.e. making query) in a proper manner is half of knowledge. (Reported by At-Tabarani)

١٥٧٤ ـ صَنَائِعُ الْمَعْرُوفِ تَقِي مَصَارِعَ السُّوءِ ، وَالصَّدَقَةُ خِفِيّاً تُطْفِيءُ غَضَبَ الرَّبِّ ، وَصِلَةُ الرَّحِمِ زِيَادَةٌ في الْعُمُرِ ، وَكُلُّ مَعْرُوفٍ صَدَقَةٌ ، وَأَهْلُ الْمَعْرُوفِ في الدُّنْيَا هُمْ أَهْلُ الْمَعْرُوفِ في الآخِرَةِ ، وَأَهْلُ الْمُنْكَرِ في الدُّنْيَــا هُمْ أَهْلُ الْمُنْكَرِ في الآخِرَةِ ، وَأَوَّلُ مَنْ يَدْخُلُ الْجَنَّةَ أَهْلُ الْمَعْرُوفِ . (الطبراني)

1574

The actions of virtuous deeds shield (i.e. protect) against the demise of evil deeds; giving charity in secret (as opposed to in public) extinguishes (the heat from) the wrath of the Lord; rekindling family relationships lengthens [ones] age; every kind act is a charity and the kind people in this world are the kind people in the Hereafter, [similarly], the people of abominable deeds in this world are the people of abominable deeds in the Hereafter, and the first [group of people] who will enter paradise are the kind people. (Reported by At-Tabarani)

١٥٧٥ ـ لَا فَقْرَ أَشَدُّ مِنَ الْجَهْلِ ، وَلَا مَالَ أَعْوَدُ مِنَ الْعَقْلِ ،
وَلَا وَحْدَةَ أَوْحَشُ مِنَ الْعُجْبِ ، وَلَا اسْتِظْهَارَ أَوْثَقُ مِنَ الْمَشَاوَرَةِ ،
وَلَا عَقْلَ كَالتَّدْبِيرِ ، وَلَا حَسَبَ كَحُسْنِ الْخُلُقِ ، وَلَا وَرَعَ كَالْكَفِّ ،
وَلَا عِبَادَةَ كَالتَّفَكُّرِ ، وَلَا إِيَانَ كَالْحَيَاءِ وَالصَّبْرِ .
(ابن ماجه والطبراني)

1575
Ignorance is the worst kind of poverty; intellect is the most valuable wealth; arrogance is the most alienating (i.e. inhumane) loneliness; consultation is the most solid act of seeking assistance; organization (i.e. planning and devising) is the best intellect; good mannerism is the best nobleness (i.e. honor); refraining (i.e. abstention) is the best devoutness (i.e. piety and God-fearingness); reflection is the best act of worship; and modesty and patience are the best act of belief. (Reported by Ibn Majah and At-Tabarani)

١٥٧٦ ـ الْحِكْمَةُ ضَالَّةُ الْمُؤْمِنِ يَأْخُذُها مِمَّنْ سَمِعَهَا وَلَا يُبَالِي مِنْ
أَيِّ وِعَاءٍ خَرَجَتْ .
(ابن حبان)

1576
Wisdom is the believer's aim; he takes it from whomever he hears it from and he does not care from where it came out from. (Reported by Ibn Habban)

١٥٧٧ _ شَرَفُ الدُّنْيَا الْغِنَى ، وَشَرَفُ الآخِرَةِ التَّقْوَى · وَأَنْتُمْ
مِنْ ذَكَرٍ وَأُنْثَى شَرَفُكُمْ غِنَاكُمْ وَكَرَمُكُمْ تَقْوَاكُمْ ، وَأَحْسَابُكُمْ
أَخْلَاقُكُمْ ، وَأَنْسَابُكُمْ أَعْمَالُكُمْ · (الديلمي)

1577

Wealth is the honor of this world but piety is the honor of the hereafter. [Indeed for] all of you, whether male or female, your wealth is your honor; your piety is your graciousness; your good manners are your nobility; and your actions are your lineage (i.e. ancestry). (Reported by Ad-Daylimi)

١٥٧٨ _ مَا رَأَيْتُ مِثْلَ الْجَنَّةِ نَامَ طَالِبُهَا ، ولا مِثْلَ النَّـــارِ
نَامَ هَارِبُهَـــا · (الطبراني والترمذي)

1578

I have never seen someone sleeping [if his aim is] to seek paradise or escapes from hell. (Reported by At-Tabarani and At-Tirmithi)

١٥٧٩ _ يَهْرَمُ ابْنُ آدَمَ وَيَشِبُّ فِيهِ اثْنَتَانِ : الْحِرْصُ عَلَى الْمَالِ ،
وَالْحِرْصُ عَلَى الْعُمْرِ · (مصابيح السنة)

1579

The son of Adam ages (i.e. grows old and matures) yet two aspects increase (i.e. rise) in him: worrying about wealth and being concerned about aging. (Masabeeh as-Sunnah)

١٥٨٠ - اِتقِ المَحَارِمَ تَكُنْ أَعْبَدَ النَّاسِ ، وَارْضَ بِمَا قَسَمَ اللهُ لَكَ تَكُنْ أَغْنَى النَّاسِ ، وَأَحْسِنْ إلى جارِكَ تَكُنْ مُؤمِناً ، وَأَحِبَّ لِلنَّاسِ مَا تُحِبُّ لِنَفْسِكَ تَكُنْ مُسْلِماً ، وَلَا تُكْثِرِ الضَّحِكَ فَإِنَّ كَثْرَةَ الضَّحِكِ تُمِيتُ القَلْبَ . (أحمد والترمذي)

• • •

1580

Be wary of forbidden deeds, [you become] the most pious [individual] of [all] people; be content with what Allah has decreed for you, [it will make you] the richest [individual] of [all] people; be good to your neighbor, [you turn into] a believer; wish for others what you wish for you yourself, you become a Muslim; and don't be excessive in your laughter, excess laughter kills (i.e. destroys) the heart. (Reported by Ahmad and at-Tirmithi)

O Allah
Allahumma Ameen

O Allah! Expand my knowledge and make it easy for me!

Chapter (34)	Prophecies

١٦٣٦ - إذا اقْتَرَبَ الزَّمَانُ كَثُرَ لُبْسُ الطَّيَالِسَةِ وَكَثُرَتِ التِّجَارَةُ وَكَثُرَ المَالُ وَعُظِّمَ رَبُّ المَالِ وَكَثُرَتِ الفَاحِشَةُ وَكَانَتْ إمْرَةُ الصِّبْيَانِ وَكَثُرَ النِّسَاءُ وَجَارَ السُّلْطَانُ وَطُفِّفَ في المِكْيَـــالِ وَالمِيزَانِ . يُرَبِّى الرَّجُلُ جِرْوَ كَلْبٍ خَيْرٌ لَـهُ مِنْ أَنْ يُرَبِّيَ وَلَدَاً . وَلا يُوَقَّرُ كَبِيْرٌ وَلا يُرحَمُ صَغِيْرٌ . وَيَكْثُرُ أَوْلادُ الزِّنا حَتَّى أَنَّ الرَّجُلَ لَيَغْشَى المَرأة عَلى قَارِعَةِ الطَّرِيقِ فَيَقُولُ أَمْثَلُهُمْ في ذلكَ الزَّمانِ : لَوِ اعْتَزَلْتُمْ عَنِ الطَّرِيقِ ، يَلْبِسُونَ جُلُودَ الضَّأْنِ عَلى قُلُوبِ الذِّئَابِ أَمْثَلُهُمْ في ذَلكَ الزَّمانِ المُدَاهِنُ .

(الطبراني)

1636

"When the end of time approaches, long cloaks [for men, also known as pallium] will be trendy, trade will be prevalent, wealth will augment, the rich [person] will be glorified, abomination will be common, authority will be [given] to the youth, obliviousness will increase, the leader will deviate [from righteousness], and measures and scales will be altered [inaccurate to mislead consumers and maximize profits]. The individual will be raised that [taking care of] a puppy is more beneficial to him than raising a child. The elderly will not be respected and the youth receive compassion. Children from out of wedlock will be numerous, and [it won't be uncommon for] a man to have sexual intercourse with a woman in the middle of the street. Then, during this period of time, the pious [people] will say [to the men who have intercourse *on the street]: why don't you seclude [yourselves] away from the street, but they will still wear leather from sheep over hearts of wolves, the best among them during that period of time would be the today."* (Reported by at-Tabarani)

١٦٣٧ - سَيَأْتِيْ عَلَى النَّاسِ زَمَانٌ لَا يُنَالُ المُلْكُ فِيهِ إِلَّا بِالْقَتْلِ وَالتَّجَبُّرِ ، وَلَا الْغِنَى إِلَّا بِالْغَصْبِ وَالْبُخْلِ ، وَلَا الْمَحَبَّةُ إِلَّا بِاسْتِخْرَاجِ الدِّينِ وَاتِّبَاعِ الْهَوَى . فَمَنْ أَدْرَكَ ذَلِكَ الزَّمَانَ فَصَبَرَ عَلَى الْفَقْرِ وَهُوَ يَقْدِرُ عَلَى الْغِنَى وَصَبَرَ عَلَى الْبِغْضَةِ وَهُوَ يَقْدِرُ عَلَى الْمَحَبَّةِ وَصَبَرَ عَلَى الذُّلِّ وَهُوَ يَقْـــدِرُ عَلَى الْعِزِّ آتَاهُ اللهُ ثَوَابَ خَمْسِينَ صِدِّيقاً مِّمَّنْ صَدَّقَ بِيْ . (الطحاوي)

1637

"There will come a time upon people when property [or wealth] is not obtained without killing [others] and oppressing [them], richness [is not achieved] without compulsion and niggardliness, affection [is not expressed] without drifting away from religion and following ones' own desires. So, whoever witnesses [lives to experience] that time yet stays patient [in times of] poverty while he is able to get wealthy, and remains patient against hate while he is able to be affectionate, and endures humiliation when he is able to be honored, Allah will bestow upon him a reward equivalent to that of fifty companions from among those who believed in me [Prophet Muhammad]." (At-Tahawi)

311

١٦٤٠ ـ يَأْتِي عَلَى النَّاسِ زَمَانٌ هِمَّتُهُمْ بُطُونُهُمْ ، وَشَرَفُهُمْ مَتَاعُهُمْ وَقِبْلَتُهُمْ نِسَاؤُهُمْ ، وَدِينُهُمْ دَرَاهِمُهُمْ وَدَنَانِيرُهُمْ ، أُولَئِكَ شَرُّ الْخَلْقِ لَا خَلَاقَ لَهُمْ عِنْدَ اللهِ . (الديلمي)

1640

"There will come a time upon people when [filling up] their stomachs [becomes] their endeavor [in life], their leisure is [the measure for] their dignity, their women turn into their Qibla [as a focus in life], and their moneys are their religion. These [people] are the most evil of creatures, they will not be worthy of anything in the site of Allah." [Reported by Ad-Daylami]

١٦٤١ ـ لَيَأْتِيَنَّ عَلَى النَّاسِ زَمَانٌ لَا يَبْقَى أَحَدٌ إِلاَّ أَكَلَ الرِّبَا فَإِنْ لَمْ يَأْكُلْهُ أَصَابَهُ مِنْ بُخَارِهِ (أَوْ غُبَارِهِ) . (أبو داوود)

1641

"There will surely come a time upon people when no one will be spared from dealing with usury [such as interest and other forms of Riba prohibited in Islam], and even if [an individual] doesn't [directly] transacts with usury, it [usury] will affect him from its steam [i.e. it will indirectly have an impact on everyone's life]." (Reported by Abu Dawoud)

١٦٤٢ ـ إِنَّ بَيْنَ يَدَيِ السَّاعَةِ فِتَناً كَأَنَّهَا قِطَعُ اللَّيْلِ الْمُظْلِمِ ، يُصْبِحُ الرَّجُلُ مُؤْمِناً وَيُمْسِي كَافِراً ، وَيُمْسِى مُؤْمِناً وَيُصْبِحُ كَافِراً يَبِيعُ دِينَهُ بِعَرَضٍ مِنَ الدُّنْيَا . (أبو داود)

312

1642

"There will be afflictions in the midst of the end of time which are similar to the segments of those pitch dark nights, an individual will wake up [i.e. starts his day] as a believer and will return in the evening [i.e. ends his day] as a Kafir [unbeliever], and [in other times] he will start his evening as a believer but will wake up [in the morning] as a Kafir [unbeliever]. He will sell his religion for vanities [or non-essential] of the world." (Reported by Abu Dawood)

١٦٤٣ ـ تَكُونُ فِتْنَةُ النَّائِمِ فِيهَا خَيْرٌ مِنَ الْيَقْظَانِ ، وَالْيَقْظَانُ فِيهَا خَيْرٌ مِنَ الْقَائِمِ ، وَالْقَائِمُ فِيهَـــا خَيْرٌ مِنَ السَّاعِي ، فَمَنْ وَجَدَ مَلْجَأً أَوْ مَعَاذاً فَلْيَسْتَعِذْ بِهِ . (احمـد)

1643

"The affliction of a sleeping person will be better than [that of] a person who is awake, the affliction of a person who is awake will be better than [that of] a person who is getting up [or rising to start his day], and the affliction of a person who is getting up [or rising to start his day] will be better than [that of] a person who is seeking provisions. So whoever [amongst you is able to] find a shelter or a refuge [from evilness], let him seek that refuge." (Reported by Ahmad)

١٦٤٤ ـ الْفِتْنَةُ نَائِمَةٌ لَعَنَ اللهُ مَنْ أَيْقَظَهَا . (الرافعي)

1644

"Allah will curse [the person] who will revive an affliction that is sleeping [i.e. that people are not aware of or are not practicing]." (Reported by Ar-Rafi'ee)

١٦٤٥ - نَهَى ﷺ عَنْ بَيْعِ السِّلَاحِ فِي الْفِتَنِ · (الطبراني)

• • •

1645
"The Prophet (pbuh) prohibited the sale of weapons during afflictions." (At-Tabarani)

١٦٤٧ - وَعَنْهُ رَضِيَ اللهُ عَنْهُ قَالَ : قَالَ رَسُولُ اللهِ صَلَّى اللهُ عَلَيْهِ وَسَلَّمَ : « لَا تَقُومُ السَّاعَةُ حَتَّى يَحْسِرَ (٢) الْفُرَاتُ عَنْ جَبَلٍ مِنْ ذَهَبٍ يُقْتَتَلُ عَلَيْهِ ، فَيُقْتَلُ مِنْ كُلِّ مَائَةٍ تِسْعَةٌ وَتِسْعُونَ ، فَيَقُولُ كُلُّ رَجُلٍ مِنْهُمْ : لَعَلِّي أَنْ أَكُونَ أَنَا أَنْجُو » .

وَفِي رِوَايَةٍ : « يُوشِكُ أَنْ يَحْسِرَ الْفُرَاتُ عَنْ كَنْزٍ مِنْ ذَهَبٍ ، فَمَنْ حَضَرَهُ فَلَا يَأْخُذْ مِنْهُ شَيْئاً » متفقٌ عليه .

1647
Abu Huraira (may Allah be pleased with him) narrated: "The Messenger of Allah (pbuh) said: "the [final] hour will not rise until the Euphrates river becomes exposed [dries up] over a mountain of gold [i.e. it could be gold or black gold as in oil] that will be fought over. Amongst every hundred individuals, ninety nine will be killed, then, every person will say: 'I wish I would be the one who is saved'" In another narration: "The Euphrates river will be on the verge of drying up over a treasure of gold, whoever witnesses this time, let him not take [benefit] anything from it [from its proceeds]." (Agreed upon)

١٦٤٨ - وعن أبي هريرة رضي الله عنه أن رسول الله ﷺ قال : « لا تقوم الساعة حتى تخرجَ نارٌ من أرض الحجاز تضيء أعناق الإبل ببصرى » . . « مسلم » .

1648

Abu Huraira (may Allah be pleased with him) narrated: "The Messenger of Allah (pbuh) said: "the [final] hour will not rise until a fire emerges from the land of Hijaz, it [the light] will light up the necks of the camels in Basra." (Reported by Muslim)

١٦٤٩ - لا تَقُومُ السَّاعَةُ حَتَّى يَتَبَاهى النَّاسُ بِالمَسَاجِدِ .
(أبو داود)

1649

"The [final] hour will not rise until people start bragging about their masjids." (Reported by Abu Dawood)

١٦٥٠ - لا تَقُومُ السَّاعَةُ حَتَّى يَتَطَاوَلَ النَّاسُ بِالْبُنْيَانِ .
(البخاري)

1650

"The [final] hour will not rise until people start bragging about their buildings [structures]." (Reported by Bukhari)

١٦٥١ - لا تَقُومُ السَّاعَةُ حَتَّى يَتَقَارَبَ الزَّمَانُ فَتَكُونَ السَّنَةُ كَالشَّهْرِ ، وَالشَّهْرُ كَالْجُمُعَةِ ، وَتَكُونَ الْجُمُعَةُ كَالْيَوْمِ ، وَيَكُونَ الْيَوْمُ كَالسَّاعَةِ وَتَكُونَ السَّاعَةُ كَالضَّرْمَةِ بِالنَّارِ . (الترمذي)

315

1651

"The [final] hour will not rise until time span shortens [i.e., time goes fast]: the year becomes like a month, the month like a week, the week like a day, the day like an hour, and the hour like the flare of the fire." (Reported by Tirmithi)

١٦٥٣ ــ لاَتَقُومُ السَّاعَةُ حَتَّى يَكْثُرَ الْهَرْجُ ، قَالُوا : وَمَا

الْهَرْجُ يَا رَسُولَ اللهِ قَالَ : الْقَتْلُ ، الْقَتْلُ . (احمد)

1653

"The [final] hour will not rise until commotion [al-Harj] becomes common. [The companions] asked: 'what is al-Harj O messenger of Allah'? He said: 'Killing, Killing'" (Reported by Ahmad)

١٦٥٤ ــ لاَ تَقُومُ السَّاعَةُ حَتَّى يَقْتُلَ الرَّجُلُ جَارَهُ وَأَخَاهُ وَأَبَاهُ . (البخاري)

1654

"The [final] hour will not rise until the man kills his own neighbor, brother, and father." (Reported by Bukhari)

١٦٥٤ّ ــ لاَ تَقُومُ السَّاعَةُ حَتَّى يَمُرَّ الرَّجُلُ بِقَبْرِ الرَّجُلِ فَيَقُولُ : يَا لَيْتَنِي مَكَانَهُ . (البخاري)

316

1654

"The [final] hour will not rise until [the time] when a man would be passing by another person's gravesite and he would say: 'I wish I was in his place'" (Reported by Bukhari)

١٦٥٥ ـ لَا تَقُومُ السَّاعَةُ حَتَّى تَطْلُعَ الشَّمْسُ مِنْ مَغْرِبِهَا ، فَإِذَا طَلَعَتْ مِنْ مَغْرِبِهَا آمَنَ النَّاسُ كُلُّهُمْ أَجْمَعُونَ ، فَيَوْمَئِذٍ لَا يَنْفَعُ نَفْسًا

1655

"The [final] hour will not rise until the sun rises from the west; and when it does rise from the west, all people will attain faith. On that day [when this happens], a person's faith will no longer be of any benefit to its [own] soul unless the soul had attained faith prior to that day, or it had earned good (by deeds of righteousness) through its Faith." (Reported by Bukhari and Muslim)

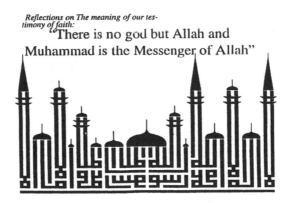

Reflections on The meaning of our testimony of faith:
"There is no god but Allah and Muhammad is the Messenger of Allah"

وَإِذَا يَـٰٓأَيُّهَا ٱلرَّسُولُ

لَا يَحْزُنكَ ٱلَّذِينَ يُسَـٰرِعُونَ فِى ٱلْكُفْرِ مِنَ ٱلَّذِينَ

قَالُوٓاْ ءَامَنَّا بِأَفْوَٰهِهِمْ وَلَمْ تُؤْمِن قُلُوبُهُمْ وَمِنَ ٱلَّذِينَ

هَادُواْ سَمَّـٰعُونَ لِلْكَذِبِ سَمَّـٰعُونَ لِقَوْمٍ

ءَاخَرِينَ لَمْ يَأْتُوكَ يُحَرِّفُونَ ٱلْكَلِمَ مِنۢ بَعْدِ مَوَاضِعِهِۦ

يَقُولُونَ إِنْ أُوتِيتُمْ هَـٰذَا فَخُذُوهُ وَإِن لَّمْ تُؤْتَوْهُ فَٱحْذَرُواْ

وَمَن يُرِدِ ٱللَّهُ فِتْنَتَهُۥ فَلَن تَمْلِكَ لَهُۥ مِنَ ٱللَّهِ شَيْـًٔا

أُوْلَـٰٓئِكَ ٱلَّذِينَ لَمْ يُرِدِ ٱللَّهُ أَن يُطَهِّرَ قُلُوبَهُمْ لَهُمْ فِى

ٱلدُّنْيَا خِزْىٌ وَلَهُمْ فِى ٱلْأَخِرَةِ عَذَابٌ عَظِيمٌ ٤١

Al-Ma`ida: **The Table Spread**

O Messenger! Let not those grieve you, who race each other into Unbelief: (whether it be) among those who say "We believe" with their lips but whose hearts have no faith or it be among the Jews- men who will listen to any lie, -will listen even to others, who have never so much as come to you. They change the words from their (right) places they say, "if you are given this, take it but if not, beware!" If any one's trial is intended by Allah, you have no authority in the least for him against Allah. For such-it is not Allah's will to purify their hearts. For them there is disgrace in this world, and in the Hereafter a heavy punishment. (5:41)

It is much easy to study the life history (Sirah) of the previous prophets and messengers, as well as their missions. However, to study the life history of Prophet Muhammad (pbuh) is much more interesting. One cannot complete the Sirah of the Prophet (pbuh) in one book, because he's the Summation, Culmination and Purification of all the previous prophets and messengers. Each prophet came to one group of people, for one time, and with one single mission. Prophet Muhammad (pbuh) came to te whole people of the world till the Day of Judgment. His Message did include a series of systems such as: Religious, Social, Cultural, Economical, Political, and many more system. It also included history of previous prophets and nations from the birth of Adam and Eve. It has information about Life, Death and Life After. The Message has information about the unseen creatures such as Angels and Jinns (Satans). The Messgae does include Science, Arts, Astronomy, Medicine, Navigations and so on.

Therefore, the personality charater, behavior, attitude and manners have been presented by Allah (swt) in the best way to the whole world. People may try their best to imitate and mimic his personality privately and publicly. Nothing was hidden. In order to do so, one has to study all these subjects through knowledgeable scholars on a daily basis for a number of years to recognize the Prophet. Then one will do his best to mimic the Prophet's Personlaity, and to practice what was revealed to him, namely the Qur'an. This means that one has to study the Qur'an, Hadith, Sirah, and Jurisprudence (Shari'ah).

Moreover, one has to try to practice the teachings of Islam on a daily basis so as to enjoy life with peace and happiness. No one should judge the religion of Islam and the personality of the Prophet, through the behaviors of people, and mainly Muslims. It

319

should be the other way around; one has to judge people through the teachings of their religion.

Muslims of today are about 1.9 billion all over the world, out of which (10) million are in the USA. They are found in every county, and they are grouped together as one nation. They may speak different laguages, but they have the same Qur'an in Arabic and they all practice the same religious obligations such as the Daily prayers (Salat), and the Friday Congregation Prayer because Friday is a Holy Day. They fast during the month of Ramadan, they pay Zakat, and perform Pilgrimage (Hajj) to Makkah, in the Arabian Penninsula.

Muslims throughout history have contributed quite a bit to Modern Civilization, and to the Industrial Revolution of Europe. Muslims were pioneers in science, technology, navigation, arts, astronomy, medicine, mathematics, algebra, logarithm, chemistry, biology, etc. Even now in the 20th and 21st century, Muslims have contributed to the success of American and Western Civilizations. All of these came from Prophet Muhammad (pbuh), who inspired millions of people to accept Islam. They do try to mimic his personality character and his teachings.

Finally, one would like to say here that one book is not enough to explain about Prophet Muhammad (pbuh). We hope and pray that Allah (swt) will give us a chance to live longer so as to write more books about the Final Prophet, and the Final Messenger of Allah to the whole world. Ameen.

Addendum A

LIST OF COMPANIONS OF PROPHET MUHAMMAD

English/Transliteration	Attribute	Arabic
1. Muss'ab Ibn Umair	First Ambassador of Islam	مصعب بن عمير
2. Salman The Persian	The Researcher for the Truth	سلمان الفارسي
3. Abu Tharr Al-Ghaffari	Leader of Opposition and Enemy of Monopoly	أبو ذرّ الغفاري
4. Bilal Ibn Rabah	The Mockerer of the Horrors	بلال بن رباح
5. Abdullah Ibn Omar	The Steadfaster, The Repenter	عبدالله بن عمر
6. Sa'ad Ibn Abi Waqqas	The Lion in His Teeth	سعد بن أبي وقاص
7. Suhaib Ibn Sinan	Abu Yahya Won the Trade	صهيب بن سنان
8. Mu'az Ibn Jabal	The Most Knowledgeable of the Lawful and the Unlawful	معاذ بن جبل
9. Al-Miqdad Ibn 'Amir	The first Knight in Islam	المقداد بن عمرو
10. Sa'id Ibn 'Aamer	Greatness Beneath the Rags	سعيد بن عامر
11. Hamzah Ibn Abdul Mattalib	Lion of God and the Master of Martyrs	حمزة بن عبد المطلب

321

List of Companions of Prophet Muhammad (cont.)

English/ Transliteration	Attribute	Arabic
12. Abdullah Ibn Mas'oud	The First Reciter of the Qur'an	عبدالله بن مسعود
13. Huthaifah Ibn Al-Yaman	Enemy of Hypocrisy and Friend of Openness	حذيفة بن اليمان
14. 'Ammar Ibn Yasir	A Man from Paradise	عمار بن ياسر
15. 'Ubadah Ibn As-Samit	A Leader in the Party of Allah	عبادة بن الصامت
16. Khabbab Ibn Al-Arath	A Teacher in Sacrifice	خبّاب بن الأرث
17. Abu Ubaidah Ibn Al-Jarrah	A Trust Worthy of this Ummah	أبو عبيدة بن الجرّاح
18. Othman Ibn Maz'oun	A Monk, Life is his Monastery	عثمان بن مظعون
19. Zaid Ibn Harithah	One of the Dearest to the Prophet	زيد بن حارثة
20. Ja'far Ibn Abi Talib	He is Similar to my Appearance and Manners	جعفر بن أبي طالب
21. Abdullah Ibn Rawaha	Oh My Soul! If You Are Not Killed You Will Die	عبدالله بن رواحة

List of Companions of Prophet Muhammad (cont.)

English/ Transliteration	Attribute	Arabic
22. Khalid Ibn Al-Waleed	Does Not Sleep and Does Not Allow Others to Sleep	خالد بن الوليد
23. Quais Ibn Saad Ibn 'Ubadah	Most Cunning Arab Except for Islam	قيس بن سعد بن عبادة
24. 'Umayr Ibn Wahab	Satan of the Ignorant Era, and Angelic in Islam	عمير بن وهب
25. Abu Al-Dardaa'	What a Wise Person He Was!	أبو الدرداء
26. Zaid Ibn Al-Khattab	Falcon During the Battle of Yamamah	زيد بن الخطاب
27. Talha Ibn Oubai-dullah	Falcon During the Battle of Uhud	طلحة بن عبيد الله
28. Al-Zubeir Ibn Al-Awwam	Disciple of the Prophet	الزبير بن العوّام
29. Khubaib Ibn Adiyy	A Hero Above the Cross	خنيب بن عديّ
30. Umair Ibn Sa'ad	Unique of His Own	عمير بن سعد
31. Zaid Ibn Thabit	Collector of the Qur'an	زيد بن ثابت

List of Companions of Prophet Muhammad (cont.)

English/ Transliteration	Attribute	Arabic
32. Khalid Ibn Saeed	One of the Early Martyrs (Fidais)	خالد بن سعيد
33. Abu Ayyub Al-Ansari	Go Forth, Lightly or Heavily	أبو أيوب الأنصاري
34. Al-Abbas Ibn Abdel Muttalib	Offering of Water in Two Sacred Mosques	العباس بن عبد المطلب
35. Abu Hurairah	Memory of the Revelation Era	أبو هريرة
36. Al-Baraa' Ibn Maalik	Allah and Paradise	البراء بن مالك
37. Utbah Ibn Ghazwan	Tomorrow You will See the Emirs After Me!	عتبة بن غزوان
38. Thabit Ibn Qais	Spokesman for the Messenger of Allah	ثابت بن قيس
39. Usaid Ibn Khudair	Hero of the Day of Al-Saqeefah	اسيد بن حضير
40. Abdur Rahman Ibn 'Aouf	O Father of Muhammad! What Makes you Cry?	عبد الرحمن بن عوف
41. Abu Jaabir: Abdullah Ibn 'Amr Ibn Hiraam	The Shadower for Angels	ابو جابر . عبدالله بن عمرو بن حرام

324

List of Companions of Prophet Muhammad (cont.)

English/ Transliteration	Attribute	Arabic
42. Amr Ibn Al-Jamooh	Limping in the Paradise	عمرو بن الجموح
43. Habib Ibn Zaid	Tale of Martyrdom and Love	حبيب بن زيد
44. Ubayy Ibn Kaab	Congratulations for Your Knowledge O! Aba Mundhir	أبيّ بن كعب
45. Sa'ad Ibn Mua'az	Glad Tidings for you Aba Amr!	سعد بن معاذ
46. Saad Ibn 'Ubadah	Carrying the Flag of Ansar	سعد بن عبادة
47. Usamah Ibn Zaid	The Most Beloved One, The son of the Most Beloved	أسامة بن زيد
48. Abdur Rahman Ibn Abu Bakr	Hero till the End	عبد الرحمن بن أبي بكر
49. Abdullah Ibn Amr Ibn Al-Aass	Obedient and Penitent to Allah	عبدالله بن عمرو بن العاص
50. Abu Sufyan Ibn Al-Harith	From Darkness to Light	أبو سفيان بن الحارث
51. 'Imran Ibn Husayn	Similar to Angels	عمران بن حصين
52. Salamah Ibn Al Akwa	A Hero of the Battalions	سلَمة بن الأكوع

List of Companions of Prophet Muhammad (cont.)

English/ Transliteration	Attribute	Arabic
53. Abdullah Ibn Al-Zubayr	What a Man and a Martyr!	عبدالله بن الزبير
54. Abdullah Ibn Al-Abbas	The Knowledge-able of This Nation	عبدالله بن العبّاس
55. Abbad Ibn Bishr	He Has Light from Allah	عبّاد بن بشر
56. Suhail Ibn 'Amr	From Freedom of Slavery to Mar-tyrdom	سهيل بن عمرو
57. Abu Moosa Al-Ash'ari	Sincerity and Let There Be What-ever Comes	أبو موسى الأشعري
58. Al-Toufail Ibn 'Amr Al-Dowsy	The Natural Wis-dom	الطفيـل بن عمرو الدوسي
59. 'Amr Ibn Al-Aass	The Liberator of Egypt from the Romans	عمرو بن العاص
60. Salem, the Adopted Son of Ali Huthaifah	Indeed he is a Good Carrier of the Qur'an	سالم ، مولى أبي حذيفة

326

Addendum B

Family Tree Of Prophet Muhammad

Salasilah Nabi/Rasul

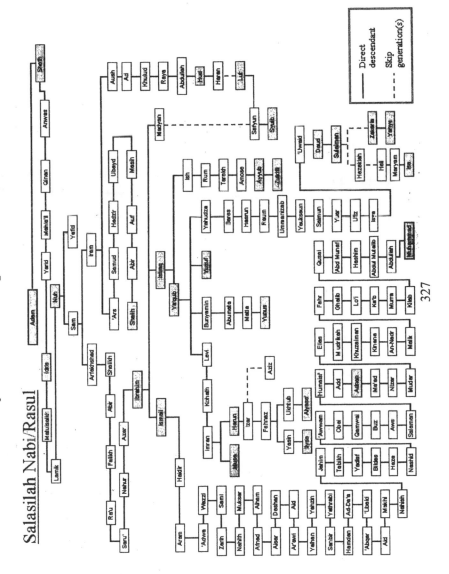

Direct descendant

Skip generation(s)

Addendum C

LIST OF NOBLE LADIES IN ISLAM

English	Arabic

1. Master of the Mothers: Aminah Bint Wahab, mother of Prophet Muhammad

• سَــيِّدة الأمهـات
آمنـــة بـنت وهـب
أم الرسـول (صلى)

2. The Ideal Wife: Khadijah Bint Khuwailid, wife of the Prophet

• الزوجَــة المثـلى
خديجـة بـنت خويـلد
زوجـة الرسـول (صلى)

3. Fatimah the Luminous: Daughter of Prophet and wife of Ali

• فاطمة الزهـــراء
بنت الرسول (صلى) وزوجة
علـي كرم الله وجهه

4. The Wife, the Teacher: 'Aisha, the Mother of the Believers

• الزوجـة المعـلمة
عائشـة أم المؤمنـين

5. The Guardian of the Qur'an: Hafsah, daughter of Umar bin Khattab; wife of the Prophet

• حارسـة القـرآن
حفصة بنت عـمر
بن الخطاب، زوجة الرسول (صلى)

6. The Valiant (bravest, most courageous mother): Asma' (the one with two girths of belts), daughter of Abu Bakr

• الأم الشجـاعء
ذات النطاقـين
أسـماء بنت أبـي بكر

7. The First Immigrant Lady: Hind, daughter of Abi Umayyah Umm (mother of) Salamah; wife of Prophet

• المهـاجـرة الأولـى
هنـد بنت أبـي أميـة
أم سـلمة
زوجة الرسـول (صلى)

8. The Redeemer of her Husband: Zainab, daughter of Prophet Muhammad

• فاديـة زوجها
زينب بنت محمد (صلى)

328

List of Noble Ladies in Islam (Cont.)

English	Arabic
9, The One with two Immigra- tions: Ruquayyah, daughter of Prophet Muhammad; wife of Usman bin Affan	ذات الهجرتين رقية بنت محمد(ص) زوجة عثمان بن عفان
10. The Righteous Advisor: Khowla, daughter of Tha'ala- ba, The Resentful (vengeant), the Repentant	الصالحة الناصحة خولة بنت ثعلبة - قد سمع الله قول التى تجادلك فى ـ زوجها وتشتكى الى الله' زوجة اوس بن الصمت الناقمة التائبة
11. Hind, daughter of 'Utbah, son of Rabee'a The Eater of the Livers	هند بنت عتبة بن ربيعة آكلة الأكباد
12. The Mother of the martyrs: Khansa;' wife of Abi Sufiyan, the poet Tamadir, daughter of 'Amr, the son of Al-Sha- reed Al-Salamiyah Al-Madariyah	أم الشهداء الخنساء زوجة أبى سفيان، الشاعرة تماضر بنت عمرو بن الشريد السلمية المضرية
13. Th Everlasting Remem- brance: Zubaidah, slave girl of Al-'Aziz. She is white like froth, indeed she is Zubaidah.	خالدة الذكر زبيدة أمة العزيز هى كالزبد بيضاء .. بل هى زبيدة ،زوجة هارون الرشيد
14. The Worshipper, the Ascetic Rabi'ah Al-Adawiya. Mother of Al-Khair, daughter of Ismail died 135 A.H. at 80 years of age.	العابدة الزاهدة رابعة العدوية أم الخير بنت اسماعيل توفيت عام ١٣٥هـ عن ٨٠ عاماً

329

List of Noble Ladies in Islam (Cont.)

English	Arabic
15. The Veiled Knight: Khawlah, daughter of Azwar; fought against the Romans during Khalid's generalship	● الفــارس الملثـم خولة بنت الأزور حاربت ضد الرومان اثناء قيادة خالد
16. The Judicious Ruler: Queen of Saba' Belqees	● الحاكمة الحازمة ملكة سبأ بـلقيس

Addendum D

LIST OF THE MOTHERS OF THE BELIEVERS	
English	**Arabic**
1. Khadijah Bint Khuwaylid	خديجة بنت خويلد
2. Aysha Bint Abi Bakr	عائشة بنت ابي بكر
3. Zaynab Bint Jahsh	زينب بنت جحش
4. Mariya (the Copt)	مارية القبطية
5. Maymoonah	ميمونة
6. Umm Salamah	ام سلمة
7. Zaynab Bint Khuzaymah	زينب بنت خزيمة
8. Hafsah Bint 'Umar	حفصة بنت عمر
9. Sawdah Bint Zam'ah	سودة بنت زمعة
10. Juwayraiyah Bint Al-Harith	جويرية بنت الحارث
11. Safiyah Bint Hayiy Ibn Al-Akhtab	صفية بنت حيي بن الاخطب

WRITERS OF THE REVELATION OF THE QUR'AN

Name (Transliteration)	Arabic
1. Abu Bakr	ابو بكر الصديق
2. 'Umar	عمر ابن الخطاب
3. 'Uthman	عثمان بن عفان
4. 'Ali	علي بن ابي طالب
5. Mu'awiyah	معاوية
6. Zayd Ibn Thabit	زيد ابن ثابت
7. Ubay Ibn Ka'ab	ابيّ ابن كعب
8. Khalid Ibn Al-Walid	خالد بن الوليد
9. Thabit Ibn Qais	ثابت ابن قيس

There is no God but Allah, Muhammad is the Messenger of Allah

Addendum F

WRITERS OF THE PROPHET

Name (Transliteration)	Arabic
1. Aban Ibn Saeed Ibn Al-'Aass, Al-Umawi	أبان بن سعيد بن العاص الاموي
2. Ubay Ibn Ka'ab, Al-Ansari; the first Ansari from Madina who started writing for the Prophet	أبي بن كعب الانصاري (أول من كتب له من الانصار)
3. Al-Arqam Ibn Abi Al-Arqam, Al-Zahri	الأرقم بن أبي الارقم الزهري
4. Buraidah Ibn Al-Husayb, al-Asslami	بريدة بن الحصيب الاسلمي
5. Abu Bakr Al-Siddiq	أبو بكر الصديق
6. Thabit Ibn Qayss Ibn Shammass, Al-Khazragi	ثابت بن قيس بن شماس الخزرجي
7. Juhaym Ibn Al-Salt, Al-Mutlabi	جهيم بن الصلت المطلبي
8. Haatib Ibn 'Amr, Al-'Aamiri	حاطب بن عمرو العامري
9. Al-Hussayn Ibn Nameer, Al-Ansari	الحصين بن نمير الانصاري
10. Hanthalah Ibn Al-Rabee,' Al-Assadi	حنظلة بن الربيع الاسدي
11. Huwaytib Ibn Abd Al-Uzzaa, Al-Qurashi	حويطب بن عبد العزى القرشي

WRITERS OF THE PROPHET (Cont.)

Name (Transliteration)	Arabic
12. Khalid Ibn Zayd, Al-Ansari	خالد بن زيد الانصاري .
13. Khalid Ibn Saeed Ibn Al-'Aass, Al-Umawi	خالد بن سعيد بن العاص الاموي
14. Khalid Ibn Al-Waleed	خالد بن الوليد .
15. Al-Zubayr Ibn Al-'Awaam	الزبير بن العوام .
16. Zayd Ibn Thabit, Al-Ansari	زيد بن ثابت الانصاري .
17. Saeed Ibn Saeed Ibn Al-'Aass, Al-Umawi	سعيد بن سعيد بن العاص الاموي
18. Sakhr Ibn Harb (Abu Sufiyan) Al-Umawi	صخر بن حرب (أبو سفيان) الاموي .
19. Abu Salamah, Al-Khazragi	ابو سلمة الخزرجي .
20. Sharhabeel Ibn Hassanah, Al-Kindy	شرحبيل بن حسنة الكندي
21. Talha Ibn Abi Sufyan	طلحة بن ابي سفيان .
22. 'Uthman Ibn 'Affaan	عثمان بن عفان .
23. 'Aamir Ibn Faheer Al-Tamimi	عامر بن فهير التميمي .
24. Abdullah Ibn Al-Arqam, Al-Zahri	عبد الله بن الارقم الزهري .
25. Abdullah Ibn Rawaha, Al-Ansari, Al-Khazragi	عبد الله بن رواحة الانصاري الخزرجي
26. Abdullah Ibn Zayd Al-Damari	عبد الله بن زيد الضمري .

WRITERS OF THE PROPHET (Cont.)

Name (Transliteration)	Arabic
27. Abdullah Ibn Sa'ad Ibn Abi Sarh, Al-'Aamiri	عبد الله بن سعد بن أبي سرح العامري .
28. Abdullah Ibn Abdil Assad, Al-Makhzoomi	عبد الله بن عبد الاسد المخزومي .
29. Abdullah Ibn Abdillah Ibn Abi Al-Ansari, Al-Khazragi	عبد الله بن عبد الله بن ابي الانصاري الخزرجي .
30. Al-'Alaa' Ibn Al-Hadrami	العلاء بن الحضرمي .
31. Al-'Alaa' Ibn 'Uqbah	العلاء بن عقبة .
32. 'Ali Ibn Abi Talib	علي بن أبي طالب .
33. 'Umar Ibn Al-Khattab	عمر بن الخطاب .
34. 'Amr Ibn Al-'Aass	عمرو بن العاص .
35. Muhammad Ibn Masslama Al-Awssi	محمد بن مسلمة الاوسي
36. Mu'awiyah Ibn Abi Sufiyan	معاوية بن أبي سفيان .
37. Mu'aiqeeb Ibn Abi Fatimah Al-Dawssi	معيقيب بن أبي فاطمة الدوسي
38. Al-Mugheerah Ibn Shu'ba	المغيرة بن شعبة .
39. Al-Nizaal Ibn Subrah	النزال بن سبرة .
40. Yazeed Ibn Abi Sufiyan	يزيد بن أبي سفيان

335

Addendum G

LIST OF THE MEMORIZERS OF THE QUR'AN

Name (Transliteration)	Arabic
1. Abdullah Ibn Masood	عبد الله ابن مسعود
2. Mu'az Ibn Jabal	معاذ ابن جبل
3. Zayd Ibn Thabit	زيد ابن ثابت
4. Huthayfa	حذيفة
5. Abu Musa Al-Ash-'Ari	ابو موسى الاشعرى
6. Abu Hurayrah	ابو هريرة
7. Abu Dardaa'	ابو الدرداء
8. Abdullah Ibn Abbas	عبد الله ابن عباس
9. Abdullah Ibn 'Amr Ibn Al-'Aas	عبد الله ابن عمرو ابن العاص
10. Abdullah Ibn Umar	عبد الله ابن عمر
11. Abdullah Ibn Al-Zubayr	عبد الله ابن الزبير
12. Talha Ibn Al-Zubayr	طلحة ابن الزبير
13. Ubadah Ibn Al-Samit	عبادة ابن الصامت
14. Sa'ad Ibn Abi Waqqass	سعد بن ابي وقاص
15. Abdullah Ibn Al-Saaib	عبد الله ابن السائب
16. Fudalah Ibn 'Ubaid	فضالة ابن عبيد

LIST OF THE MEMORIZERS OF THE QUR'AN (Cont.)

Name (Transliteration)	Arabic
17. Sa'eed Ibn 'Ubaid	سعيد ابن عبيد
18. Musslamah Ibn Makhlid	مسلمة ابن مخلد
19. Ubayy Ibn Ka'ab	ابيّ ابن كعب
20. Majma' Ibn Jariyah	مجمع بن جارية
21. Abu Zayd Ibn Al-Sakan	ابو زيد ابن السكن
22. Salem Ibn Ma'qal	سالم ابن معقل
23. A'iysha, wife of the Prophet	عائشة زوجة الرسول
24. Hafsa, daughter of Abu Bakr	حفصة ، بنت عمر
25. Umm Salamah, Hind Bint Abi Umaya	ام سلمة ، هند بنت ابي امية

337

Narrators Of Hadiths

LIST OF MEN NARRATORS

Name (Transliteration)	Arabic
1. Abu Hurairah	ابو هريرة
2. Abdullah Ibn Umar	عبد الله بن عمر
3. Abdullah Ibn Abbas	عبد الله بن عباس
4. Abdullah Ibn Masood	عبد الله بن مسعود
5. Anas Ibn Malik	انس بن مالك
6. Abu Zarr Al-Ghaffari	ابو ذر الغفاري
7. Abu Sa'eed Al-Khudri	ابو سعيد الخدري
8. Abu Musa Al-Ash'ari	ابو موسى الاشعري
9. Abu Aiyub Al-Ansari	ابو ايوب الانصاري
10. Sa'd Ibn Abi Waqqass	سعد بن ابي وقاص
11. Abdullah Ibn 'Amr Ibn Al-'Aass	عبد الله بن عمرو بن العاص
12. Jabir Ibn Abdallah Al-Ansari	جابر بن عبد الله الانصاري
13. Usama Ibn Zaid	اسامة بن زيد

LIST OF MEN NARRATORS (Cont.)

Name (Transliteration)	Arabic
14. Abu Bakr Al-Siddiq	ابو بكر الصديق
15. 'Ali Ibn Abi Talib	علي بن ابي طالب
16. 'Umar Ibn Al-Khattab	عمر بن الخطاب
17. 'Uthman Ibn Affan	عثمان بن عفان
18. Abdel Rahman Ibn 'Awf	عبد الرحمن بن عوف
19. Abdullah Ibn Qais	عبد الله بن قيس
20. Abdullah Ibn Zubair	عبد الله بن الزبير
21. Abu Darda'	ابو الدرداء
22. 'Amir Ibn Sa'd Ibn Abi Waqqas	عامر بن سعد بن ابي وقاص
23. Bilal Ibn Rabah	بلال بن رباح
24. Hassaan Ibn Thabit	حسان بن ثابت
25. Huzaifah Ibn Al-Yaman	حذيفة بن اليمان
26. Jabir Ibn Abdullah	جابر بن عبد الله
27. Ja'far Ibn Abi Talib	جعفر بن ابي طالب
28. Khalid Ibn Al-Waleed	خالد بن الوليد
29. Ubada Ibn Al-Samit	عبادة بن الصامت
30. Abu Qatadah Al-Ansari	ابو قتادة الانصاري

LIST OF MEN NARRATORS (Cont.)

Name (Transliteration)	Arabic
31. Abu Mas'ood Al-Ansari Al-Badri	ابو مسعود الانصاري البدري
32. Al-Baraa' Ibn 'Aazib	البراء بن عازب
33. Jabir Ibn Samarah	جابر بن سَمُرة
34. Huzaifah Ibn Al-Yaman	حذيفة ابن اليمان
35. Zayd Ibn Al-Arqam	زيد بن الارقم
36. Salamah Ibn Al-Akwa'	سلمة بن الاكوع
37. Sahl Ibn Sa'd Al-Saa'idi	سهل بن سعد الساعدي
38. Ubadah Ibn Al-Samit	عبادة ابن الصامت
39. Abbas Ibn Abdel Muttalib	العباس بن عبد المطلب
40. Abdullah Ibn Jaafar Ibn Abi Talib	عبد الله بن جعفر بن ابي طالب
41. Abdullah Ibn Al-Zubayr Ibn Al-Awam	عبد الله بن الزبير بن العوام
42. 'Uqbah Ibn 'Amer Al-Juhani	عقبة بن عامر الجهني
43. Imran Ibn Husayn Al-Khuza'ee	عمران بن حصين الخزاعي
44. Ka'ab Ibn Malik Al-Ansari Al-Sulamiy	كعب بن مالك الانصاري السُلمي

LIST OF MEN NARRATORS (Cont.)

Name (Transliteration)	Arabic
45. Mu'az Ibn Jabal	معاذ بن جبل
46. Mu'awiyah Ibn Abi Sufiyan	معاوية بن ابي سفيان
47. Al-Maghirah Ibn Shu'bah	المغيرة بن شعة
48. Nu'man Ibn Basheer	النعمان بن بشير
49. Nafi' Ibn 'Utbah	نافع بن عتبة

LIST OF WOMEN NARRATORS

Name (Transliteration)	Arabic
1. Aiysha Bint Abu Bakr	عائشة بنت ابو بكر
2. Asma' Bint Abu Bakr	اسماء بنت ابي بكر
3. Umm Salamah: Hind Bint Abi Umayah	ام سلمة
4. Hafsah Bint 'Umar	حفصة بنت عمر
5. Maimoonah Bint Al-Harith	ميمونة
6. Hafsah Bint Abu Bakr	حفصة بنت ابو بكر
7. Juwairiyah Bint Al-Harith	جويرية بنت الحارث
8. Khadija Bint Khuwaylid	خديجة بنت خويلد

LIST OF WOMEN NARRATORS (Cont.)

Name (Transliteration)	Arabic
9. Umm Habibah Bint Abi Sufiyan	ام حبيبة بنت ابي سفيان
10. Umm Hani' Bint Abi Talib	ام هاني بنت ابي طالب
11. Umm 'Atiyah, Nusaybah, Bint Ka'ab	ام عطية ، نسيبة بنت كعب
12. Umm Qais Bint Mihsan	ام قيس بنت محصن
13. Fatimah Bint Prophet Muhammad	فاطمة الزهراء بنت محمد
14. Fatimah Bint Qais	فاطمة بنت قيس
15. Safiyah Bint Huyay Ibn Akhtab	صفية بنت حيي بن اخطب
16. Zaynab Bint Jahsh	زينب بنت جحش
17. Zaynab Bint Abi Salamah	زينب بنت ابي مسلمة المخزومية
18. Zaynab Al-Thaqafiyah	زينب الثقفية
19. Umm Shareek, Al-Aamiryah	امرأة عبد الله بن مسعود ام شريك العامرية
20. Umm Salamah, Hind Bint Abee Umayah	ام سلمة ، هند بنت ابي امية

Addendum I

Collectors Of Hadith

COLLECTORS OF HADITH

Hijra Years	50	100	150	200	250	300	350

	Name	Age	Life Span
1.	Imam Bukhari	62 years old	194-256
2.	Imam Muslim	57 years old	204-261
3.	Imam Abu Dawood	73 years old	202-275
4.	Imam Tarmazi	61 years old	209-270
5.	Imam Ibn Majah	66 years old	207-273
6.	Imam Nisa-ee	88 years old	215-303

SCHOOLS OF THOUGHT IMAMS

Hijra Years	50	100	150	200	250	300	Life Span	Age	Name
1.			<------------------> 80-150 H					70 years old	Imam Abu Hanifa
2.			<--------------------------> 93-179 H					86 years old	Imam Malik
3.				<-----------------> 150-204 H				54 years old	Imam Shafii
4.				<--------------------> 164-241 H				77 years old	Imam Ahmad

Addendum J

Ambassadors Of The Prophet

List of Ambassadors

1. Name: Haatib Ibn Abi Bala'tah
   Place: Egypt
   Leader: Muqawqass
   Qualification: Attended Battle of Badr, and the treaty of Hudaybiyah. He was a poet and a knight before Islam. He was received well by Al-Muqawqas.
   Results: A gift was sent to the Prophet.

2. Name: Duhiyah Ibn Khaleefah Alkalby
   Place: Rome
   Leader: Hercules
   Qualification: Attended many of the battles. He was considered as an early Muslim. He was very handsome and beautiful.
   Results: He was received well by the king.

3. Name: Saleet Ibn 'Amr, Al-'Aamiry
   Place: Yamamah
   Leader: Huwatha Ibn Ali
   Qualification: Attended Battle of Badr; early Muslim. He used to visit Yamaamah and he knew the king.
   Results: The king, Huwatha, accepted Islam and continued to be the leader.

4. Name: Shujaa' Ibn Wahab, Al-Asadi
   Place: Damascus
   Leader: Al-Harith Ibn Abi-Shamar, Al-Ghassani
   Qualification: He attended Battle of Badr. He was among those who accepted Islam very early. He migrated to Ethiopia.
   Results: The leader refused to receive him and did not treat him well.

5. Name: Abdullah Ibn Huthaafah, Al-Sahmi
   Place: Persia
   Leader: Abroweeze Ibn Hormoz
   Qualification: Attended Battle of Badr. He used to visit the King of Persia. He was a captive with the Romans during Umar's caliphate. Romans demanded that he should convert to Christianity, but refused. He was put on cross to be crucified, and was to be killed by putting him in boiling water as was done by one of his friends in front of his eyes.
   Results: He was treated bad; the king tore the letter of the Prophet that he brought with him. The King of Persia threatened to wage a war against the Prophet and the Muslims.

6. Name: Al-'Alaa' Ibn Al-Hadrami
   Place: Bahrain
   Leader: Al-Munthir Ibn Sari
   Qualification: A leading member of the Companions of the Prophet. He had some brothers among the non-Muslims in Makkah. One of his brother died as a non-Muslim. His du'a' was accepted and he was good sailor.
   Results: Al-Munthir accepted Islam and followed the Prophet.

7. Name: 'Amr Ibn Umaiyah, Al-Damri
   Place: Ethiopia
   Leader: Najashi
   Qualification: He became Muslim after the Battle of Uhud; he was very courageous.
   Results: Najashi, the King of Ethiopia, became Muslim. He sent his son with gifts to the Prophet.

8. Name: 'Amr Ibn Al-'Aass
   Place: Oman
   Leaders: Two brothers: Jeefar and Abd sons of Al-Jildy.
   Qualification: He became Muslim before the victory of Makkah. The Prophet used to treat him with kindness and recognized his qualities. He was one of the smartest person among the Arabs.
   Result: Both kings became Muslims.

جدول سفراء الرسول ومزاياهم

السفير	الجهة المرسل إليها وملكها	سابقته في الاسلام	ميزاته الاخرى	نتيجة سفارته
١ ـ حاطب بن أبي بلتعة	مصر ـ المقوقس	بدري ـ شهد الحديبية	كان أحد فرسان قريش وشعرائها في الجاهلية .	استقبال حسن وهدية للنبي
٢ ـ دحية بن خليفة الكلبي	الروم ـ هرقل	قديم الاسلام ـ شهد المشاهد	كان مضرب المثل في جمال الصورة .	استقبال حسن
٣ ـ سليط بن عمرو العامري	اليمامة ـ هوذة بن علي	قديم الاسلام ـ بدري	كان يختلف إلى اليمامة ويعرف ملكها أخوه سهيل ابن عمرو المفاوض باسم قريش في صلح الحديبية .	اشترط هوذة للاسلام اشراكه في الامر
٤ ـ شجاع بن وهب الاسدي	دمشق ـ الحارث بن أبي شمر الغساني	بدري ـ من السابقين الأولين	هاجر إلى الحبشة .	استقبال سيء ورفض
٥ ـ عبدالله بن حذافة السهمي	فارس ـ ابرويز بن هرمز	بدري ـ	كان يتردد كثيراً على ابرويز ابن هرمز ـ وأسره ملك الروم في إحدى الغزوات التي وجهه فيها عمر ، وعرض عليه التنصر وإشراكه في الملك فأبى فأمر به فصلب وأمر برميه بالسهام فلم يجزع ، وأمر بأن يلقى أمامه بأسير مسلم في قدر به ماء يغلي حتى أنه شاهد عظام الاسير تلوح من جسمه ، وأمر بالقائه ان لم يتنصر ، فبكى . فسئل عن بكائه فقال : تمنيت أن لي مائة نفس تلقى هكذا .. فخلي عنه .	تمزيق الرسالة وتهديد بالحرب
٦ ـ العلاء بن الحضرمي	البحرين ـ المنذر بن ساوى	من سادة الصحابة ، كان له عدة إخوة في صفوف المشركين واخوه أول قتيل منهم .	مجاب الدعوة ـ خاض البحر بكلمات قالها مشهورة	اسلم المنذر واجاب النبي بالطاعة .
٧ ـ عمرو بن أمية الضمري	الحبشة ـ الاصحم بن ابجر النجاشي	اسلم منصرف الناس من أحد . أول مشاهده بئر معونة ـ مشهور بالشجاعة	كان من مشاهير العرب جرأة ونجدة .	اسلم النجاشي واجاب النبي كتابة
٨ ـ عمرو بن العاص	عمان ـ جيفر وعبد ابني الجلندي	اسلم قبل الفتح ـ كان النبي صلى الله عليه وسلم يقربه ويدنيه لمعرفته وشجاعته	كان أحد دهاة العرب المعدودين للمعضلات وله فتوح مشهورة .	تودد من الاخوين الملكين انتهى باسلامهما

KNOWLEDGE

Islam emphasizes the importance of knowledge to all mankind. It is only through true knowledge that one can appreciate the Creator of the Universe namely Allah (swt). Muslims are ordained to seek knowledge from cradle to grave and as far as a person can to obtain it.

In as much as seeking knowledge is a must on every Muslim, dissemination of knowledge is also incumbent on Muslims to the members of the society. The methods of disseminating the information should be lawful, as well as the truth is to be released to everyone. Hiding or keeping the true knowledge away from those who seek it, is considered a sin.

The best investment for every human being is through: perpetual charity (Sadaqa Jariya), useful knowledge that people shall benefit or, and a loving child who shall make special prayers for his/her parents.

LEGALITY

The Foundation has been established and registered with the Secretary of the State of Illinois since January 8,1987 as a non-profit, charitable, educational, religious and /or scientific society within the meaning of section 501 (c) (3) of the Internal Revenue Code.

The Foundation has a tax-exempt status with the IRS, and donations are considered tax-deductible.

FINANCES

The finances of the FOUNDATION are mainly from donations and contributions in the form of cash, assets and wills.

INUMERENT OF INCOME

No part of the net earnings of the Corporation shall inure to the benefit of, or be distributed to, its members, directors, officers or other private persons except that the Corporation shall be authorized and empowered to pay reasonable compensation for services rendered.

PURPOSES

The purposes of the FOUNDATION are summarized as follows:

1. To promote Islamic Knowledge through education.
2. To create a better understanding of Islam among Muslims and non-Muslims through education and communication.
3. To publish books and other literature about Islam and its teachings
4. To disseminate Islamic Knowledge and education through TV, Radio, Video, and other means of mass communications.
5. To establish ecumenical among the religious people of America so that a better understanding will be created.

ACTIVITIES

The activities of the FOUNDATION shall include, but not be limited to the following:

1. Publishing literature pertaining to Islam.
2. Producing audio cassettes and audio-visual tapes on certain topics of Islam.
3. Giving lectures related to Islam as a religion, culture and civilization.
4. Cooperation with other societies, foundations and organizations whose aims and objectives are similar to the FOUNDATION.

KNOWLEDGE IN THE QUR'AN

The word knowledge ('ILM) is mentioned in the Qur'an more than 700 times in 87 different forms. Some of the pertinent Ayat are listed below.

1. The first Ayat revealed to Prophet Muhammad (pbuh) at Cave Hira' are in Surah Al-Alaq (The Clot) (96:1-5). They are related to knowledge of embryology through scientific investigation.

2. Allah honors all those who are knowledgeable. These people cannot be compared with the ignorant ones. See Surah Al-Zumar (The Troops) (39:28)

3. Only the knowledgeable people are those who do appreciate the creations of Allah (swt) . They are the ones who respect Him and worship Him with knowledge and humility. Please read Surah Fatir (The Creator) (35:28)

Knowledge is in the Hands of Allah and it is at His disposal. People are to seek the true knowledge from its source namely Allah. Read Surah Al-Mulk (The Sovereignty) (67:26).

4. People are to seek knowledge from Allah (swt) are to request Him to enrich them daily with 'ILM. Read Surah Taha (20:114).

KNOWLEDGE IN THE HADITH

Prophet Muhammad (pbuh) emphasized 'ILM tremendously and encouraged Muslims to seek knowledge in any part of the world. The following is a summary:

1. In one Hadith the Prophet says: "The Knowledgeable people ('Ulama) are the inheritors to the Prophets."

2. In another Hadith He encouraged Muslims to seek knowledge, saying: "Seeking knowledge is a must on every Muslim."

3. In another place, He demanded that knowledge is to be sought throughout lifetime, saying: "Seek knowledge from cradle to grave."

4. Knowledge is to be disseminated to all, and the best knowledge is that of the Qur'an, saying: "The best amongst you are the ones who learn Qur'an and teach it to others."

5. Knowledge is to be taught and to be carried on even after death. In His Hadith the Prophet said: "When a person dies, his deeds are over, except from three things; perpetual charity, a useful knowledge, or a good child who makes supplications for him."

The FOUNDATION will continue, with the help of Almighty God (Allah), to publish more useful literature.

With the generous help of the friends, The Foundation will be able to achieve its purposes, Insha'allah.

For More Information, Please Write To:

Foundation For Islamic Knowledge
P.O. Box 665 Lombard, Illinois 60148 U.S.A.
Phone: (630) 495-4817   Fax (630) 627-8894

email: ahmadsakr@yahoo.com

website: www.ahmadsakr.com

To those who do good there is good in this world
And the Home of the Hereafter is even better
and excellent indeed is the Home of the righteous.

Publications

I.   BOOKS ON HEALTH, FOOD AND NUTRITION:

1. Dietary Regulations & Food Habits of Muslims
2. Overeating and Behavior
3. Islam on Alcohol
4. Alcohol in Beverages, Drugs, Foods and Vitamins
5. Cheese
6. AFTO and FAO
* 7. Fasting in Islam
8. Food and Overpopulation
9. Honey: Food and a Medicine
* 10. Gelatin
11. Shortening in Foods
12. A Manual on Food Shortenings
13. Food Supplementation
14. World Health Organization for Muslim Nations
* 15. A Muslim Guide to Food Ingredients
16. Natural Therapeutics of Medicine in Islam (co-authored)
17. Islamic Dietary Laws & Practices (co-authored)
18. Food and Nutrition Manual (co-authored)
19. A Handbook of Muslim Foods
* 20. Understanding Halal Foods: Fallacies and Facts
21. Pork: Possible Reasons For Its Prohibition
* 22. Book of Healing

II.   BOOKS ABOUT FRIDAY KHUTAB:

* 1.   Book of Al-Khutab
* 2.   Islamic Orations
* 3.   Orations from the Pulpit
* 4.   Chronicle of Khutab
* 5.   Friday Khutab

* 6. Khutab Al-Masjid
* 7. Khutab From Mihrab
* 8. Farewell Khutbah of the Prophet – Its Universal Values
* 9. A Manual of Friday Khutab

III.   GENERAL SUBJECTS:

* 1. Islamic Fundamentalism (co-authored)
* 2. Prostration – Sujood (new edition)
  3. Guidelines of Employment by Muslim Communities (co-authored)
* 4. Understanding Islam and Muslims(Revised Edition)
* 5. Muslims and non-Muslims: Face to Face
* 6. The Golden Book of Islamic Lists
* 7. Al-Jinn
* 8. Islam and Muslims: Myth or Reality
* 9. Islamic Awareness
* 10. Life, Death and the Life After
* 11. Death and Dying
* 12. Family Values in Islam
* 13. Matrimonial Education in Islam (New Edition)
* 14. Social Services and Counseling
* 15. The Adolescent Life
* 16. A Course on Islamic Shari'ah
* 17. Da'wah Through Dialogue
* 18. Understanding the Qur'an
* 19. Themes of the Qur'an
* 20. Book of Knowledge
* 21. Reflections from a Flying Falcon
* 22. Feasts, Festivities and Holidays
* 23. Book of Hajj and Umrah
* 24. A Lifetime Journey

355

*   25.   Pillars of Islam
*   26.   Most Beautiful Names of Allah Vol. (1)
*   27.   Most Beautiful Names of Allah Vol. (2)
*   28.   Book of Inquiries Volume I
*   29.   Book of Inquiries Volume II
*   30.   About Prophet Muhammad

IV.   PAMPHLETS:

*   1.   Introducing Islam
*   2.   Non-Muslims Through Muslim History
*   3.   What Does Islam Say About ----
*   4.   Living Together

V.   DVD

*   1.   **Friday Khutbah**   By. Dr. Ahmad H. Sakr

*   2.   **Variety of Salat**   By. Dr. Ahmad H. Sakr
(The Obligatory and Recommended Islamic Prayers)

     *   These publications are available from:
Foundation for Islamic Knowledge

NEWSLETTER

The Foundation has a Newsletter called **Perspectives.** It is published bi-monthly, and distributed free. If you wish to have a copy of the Newsletter, please write to the address below.

<u>Virginia Office</u>
(Newsletter/Perspectives)
31 Towler Drive, Hampton, VA 23665

Books To Be Published

1. Book of Du `aa'
2. Book of Wisdom
3. Islamic Perspectives
4. Islamic Understanding
5. Islam vs. Muslims
6. Speakers Bureau Guide Book
7. Health, Hygiene and Nutrition
8. The Book of Targheeb
9. Scientific Reflections from the Qur'an
10. Biological Terms in the Qur'an
11. Educational Institutions in Islam
12. Writing An Islamic Will
13. Qur'an Commentary in Summary
14. Welcome to the World of Islam
15. Al-Insaan: The Human Being
16. Book of Pledges
17. Khutab of Sacred Ahadith
18. Book of Khutab: Halal and Haram Foods
19. Khutab of the Prophet

These and other books will not be published unless someone like you comes forward and extend a hand of help. You may sponsor any of the above books, or any number of copies of a particular book.

Your help in any capacity is greatly needed even to pay the previous debts to the printers.

The foundation is tax-exempt from the IRS and your donations are tax-deductible. The Employer Identification Number with the I.R.S. is **36-377-4566.**

For more information, or to send your donation, please contact:

Foundation for Islamic Knowledge

P.O. Box 665
Lombard, IL 60148
Phone: (630) 495-4817 / Fax: (630) 627-8894
email: ahmadsakr@yahoo.com
website: www.ahmadsakr.com

Al-Fatihah, or the Opening Chapter

1. In the name of Allah, Most Gracious, Most Merciful.
2. Praise be to Allah.
   The Cherisher and Sustainer of the Worlds:
3. Most Gracious, Most Merciful;
4. Master of the Day of Judgement.
5. You do we worship, and Your aid we seek.
6. Show us the straight way,
7. The way of those on whom You had bestowed Your Grace, those whose (portion) is not wrath.
   And who go not astray.

INDEX

A

Abu Lahab, 217
Abdul Muttalib, 34
Abu Talib, 34
Abundance. *See* Al-Kawthar
Al-Ahzab, 36, 164
  Hypocrites in, 259, 261
  Reward for believers, 261, 263
Al-Anbiyaa, 203
Al-Aqsa Masjid, 80
Al-A'raf, 84
Al-Fath, 211
Al-Hujurat, 50
Al-Kaafiroon, 223
Al-Ma'idah, 188
Al-Shifa' (Midwife of Muhammad), 33
Aminah (Mother of Muhammad), 33
An-Naas, 227
An-Nasr, 91
An-Nur, 111

B

Badr, 65
  Battle of, 249
  City of, 248
  Lessons learned from, 252
  Quraish in, 248
Bani Quraitha, 225
Barakah (Babysitter of Muhammad), 33
Besant, Annie, 89
Bonaparte, Napoleon, 88
Bucaille, Maurice, 90

C

Calyle, Thomas, 86
Catholics. *See* People of the Book
Christians. *See* People of the Book
Chronology of important events, 224-226
Commandments (Muhammad's)
  1st Commandment, 94-97
  2nd Commandment, 97-99
  3rd Commandment, 100-103
  4th Commandment, 103-104
  5th Commandment, 104-105
  6th Commandment, 105-106
  7th Commandment, 106-107
  8th Commandment, 107-108
  9th Commandment, 108
  10th Commandment, 109
  11th Commandment, 109-110
  12th Commandment, 110
Confederates. *See* Al-Ahzab, *See* Al-Ahzab
Custodians of the Ka'bah. *See* Quraish

D

Dawn. *See* Al-Falaq
Diraar (Masjid), 268
Divine Message (finality of), 31
Du'a
  After Azan, 168
  After Salat, 166
  Ayub (Job's), 180
  During sujood, 172-176
  Fajr prayer 165
  For distress, 167
  For forgiveness, 166
  For the deceased, 171

Ibrahim (Abraham's), 179
Issa (Jesus'), 184
Moosa (Mose's), 183
Muhammad's, 185-187
Nooh's (Noah), 178
Of the Prophets, 177
Yunus (Jonas'), 181
Zakariya's, 181-182

E

Encyclopedia Britannica, 85
Expansion. *See* Al-Inshirah

F

Flame. *See* Lahab

G

Ghandi, Mahatma, 86
Gibbon, Edward, 86-87

H

Haleemah
  Nursing mother of Muhammad, 33
Hamzah, 224
Hart, Michael, 87
Hiraa (Cave of), 211-212
Hurgronje, 87
Hypocrites, 267-268

I

Imran (Family of), 272
Inner Appartments. *See* Al-Hujurat
Islamic Civilization, 320
Islamic University of Madina, 264
Isra' and Mi'raj, 79-80

J

Jesus predicting coming of
  Muhammad, 25
Jews. *See* People of the Book

K

Ka'bah (reconstruction by Prophet
  Ibrahim), 24
Khandaq (Battle of), 258-265
Khaybar (Battle of), 225
King Fahd Qur'an Complex, 264

L

Lamartine, 85
Light. *See* An-Nur

M

Madinah
  Masjids in Madinah, 230-231
  Significance of, 228-230
Mankind. *See* An-Naas
Marriage Sermon, 169-170
Michener, James, 88
Montgomery, Watt, 89
Muhammad (Prophet)
  Abu Bakr speaks upon death of,
    287-289
  Arrival from long journey, 63
  Attributes of, 45
  Birth of, 6, 12-13
  Character of a living Qur'an, 55
  Chronology of his life, 292-295
  Coming of Muhammad. *See* Jesus
  Commandments, 94-110
  Final days, 274-281
  Finality of prophethood, 81
  Hadiths of, 296
  Human nature of, 25-26
  In Abrahamic prayer, 18

Books Available From the
Foundation for Islamic Knowledge

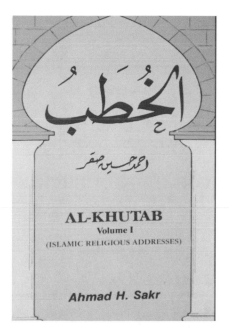

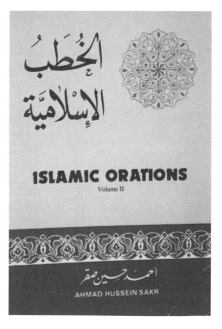

Books Available From the Foundation for Islamic Knowledge

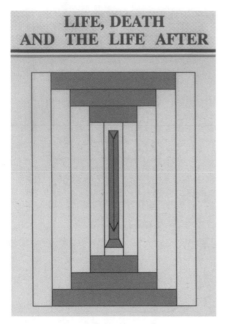

LIFE, DEATH AND THE LIFE AFTER

الخِــنْزيــر ..

PORK

POSSIBLE REASONS FOR ITS PROHIBITION

by

Ahmad H. Sakr
Professor of Biochemistry and Nutrition

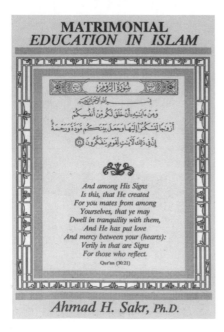

MATRIMONIAL EDUCATION IN ISLAM

And among His Signs
Is this, that He created
For you mates from among
Yourselves, that ye may
Dwell in tranquility with them,
And He has put love
And mercy between your (hearts):
Verily in that are Signs
For those who reflect.
Qur'an (30:21)

Ahmad H. Sakr, Ph.D.

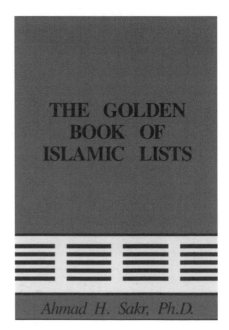

THE GOLDEN BOOK OF ISLAMIC LISTS

Ahmad H. Sakr, Ph.D.

Books Available From the
Foundation for Islamic Knowledge

Farewell Khutbah of The Prophet ﷺ

Its Universal Values

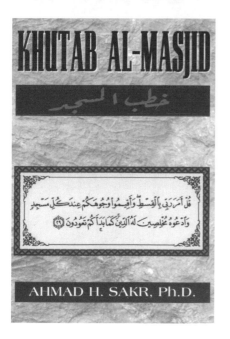

KHUTAB AL-MASJID

AHMAD H. SAKR, Ph.D.

A
Muslim Guide
to Food
Ingredients

AHMAD H. SAKR, Ph.D.
Professor of Nutritional Biochemistry

365

Books Available From the
Foundation for Islamic Knowledge

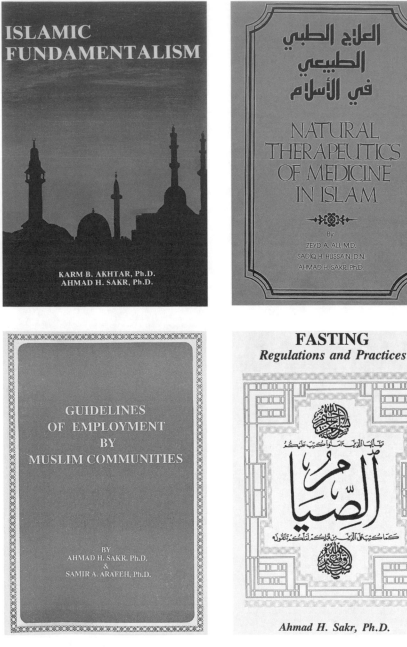

366

Books Available From the Foundation for Islamic Knowledge

367

Books Available From the
Foundation for Islamic Knowledge

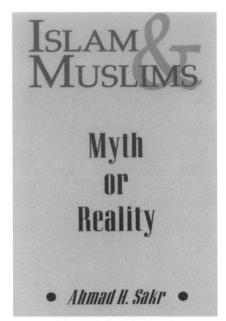

Books Available From the
Foundation for Islamic Knowledge

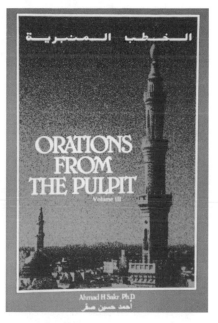

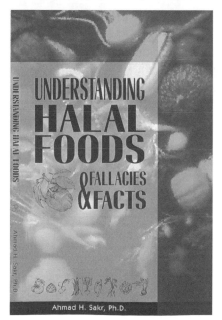

Books Available From the Foundation for Islamic Knowledge

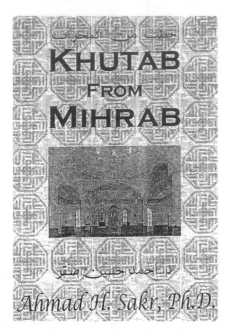

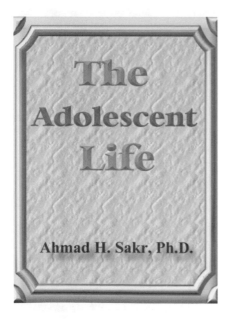

Books Available From the
Foundation for Islamic Knowledge

Books Available From the Foundation for Islamic Knowledge

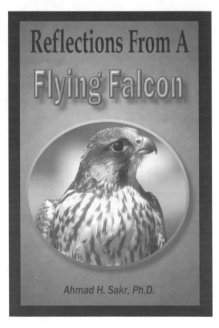

Books Available From the Foundation for Islamic Knowledge

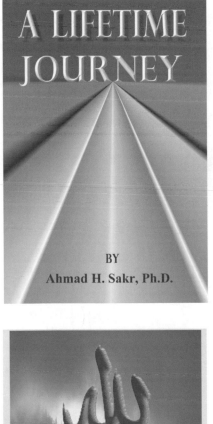

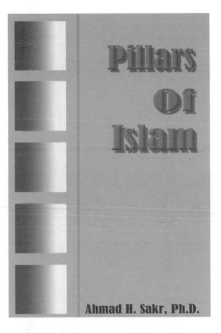

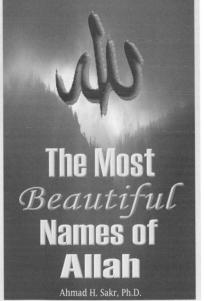

Books Available From the
Foundation for Islamic Knowledge

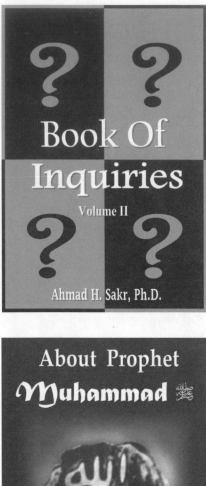